Essential

# French
## phrase book

PERIPLUS

Published in 2000 by Periplus Editions (HK) Ltd.

Library of Congress Catalog Card Number: 99-066981
ISBN: 962-593-801-X

Distributed by:

*North America, Latin America & Europe*
Tuttle Publishing
Airport Industrial Park
364 Innovation Drive
North Clarendon, VT 05759-9436
Tel: (802) 773 8930; Fax: (802) 773 6993

*Japan & Korea*
Tuttle Publishing
RK Building, 2nd Floor
2-13-10 Shimo-Meguro, Meguro-ku
Tokyo 153 0064
Tel: (03) 5437 0171; Fax: (03) 5437 0755

*Asia Pacific*
Berkeley Books Pte. Ltd.
130 Joo Seng Road, #06-01/03
Singapore 368357
Tel: (65) 6280 1330; Fax: (65) 6280 6290

*Indonesia*
PT Java Books Indonesia
Jl. Kelapa Gading Kirana
Blok A14/17, Jakarta 14240
Indonesia
Tel: 62 (21) 451 5351
Fax: 62 (21) 453 4987

First edition
07 06 05 04 03 02     10 9 8 7 6 5 4 3

Printed in Singapore

# Contents

Introduction 5

Pronunciation guide 6

### 1 Useful lists 7–16

**1.1** Today or tomorrow? 8
**1.2** Legal holidays 9
**1.3** What time is it? 9
**1.4** One, two, three ... 10
**1.5** The weather 12
**1.6** Here, there ... 13
**1.7** What does that sign say? 15
**1.8** Telephone alphabet 15
**1.9** Personal details 16

### 2 Courtesies 17–23

**2.1** Greetings 18
**2.2** How to ask a question 19
**2.3** How to reply 20
**2.4** Thank you 21
**2.5** Sorry 22
**2.6** What do you think? 22

### 3 Conversation 24–32

**3.1** I beg your pardon? 25
**3.2** Introductions 26
**3.3** Starting/ending a conversation 28
**3.4** Congratulations and condolences 28
**3.5** A chat about the weather 28
**3.6** Hobbies 29
**3.7** Being the host(ess) 29
**3.8** Invitations 29

**3.9** Paying a compliment 30
**3.10** Intimate comments/ questions 31
**3.11** Arrangements 32
**3.12** Saying good-bye 32

### 4 Eating out 33–42

**4.1** On arrival 34
**4.2** Ordering 35
**4.3** The bill 37
**4.4** Complaints 38
**4.5** Paying a compliment 39
**4.6** The menu 39
**4.7** Alphabetical list of drinks and dishes 39

### 5 On the road 43–56

**5.1** Asking for directions 44
**5.2** Customs 45
**5.3** Luggage 46
**5.4** Traffic signs 47
**5.5** The car 48
*The parts of a car* 50–51
**5.6** The gas station 48
**5.7** Breakdown and repairs 49
**5.8** The bicycle/moped 52
*The parts of a bicycle* 54–55
**5.9** Renting a vehicle 53
**5.10** Hitchhiking 56

### 6 Public transportation 57–64

**6.1** In general 58
**6.2** Questions to passengers 59

| | | |
|---|---|---|
| **6.3** | **T**ickets | 60 |
| **6.4** | **I**nformation | 61 |
| **6.5** | **A**irplanes | 63 |
| **6.6** | **T**rains | 63 |
| **6.7** | **T**axis | 63 |

**7** **O**vernight accommodation **65–73**

| | | |
|---|---|---|
| **7.1** | **G**eneral | 66 |
| **7.2** | **C**amping | 67 |
| | *Camping* | |
| | *equipment* | 68–69 |
| **7.3** | **H**otel/B&B/apartment/ | |
| | holiday rental | 70 |
| **7.4** | **C**omplaints | 72 |
| **7.5** | **D**eparture | 73 |

**8** **M**oney matters **74–76**

| | | |
|---|---|---|
| **8.1** | **B**anks | 75 |
| **8.2** | **S**ettling the bill | 76 |

**9** **M**ail and telephone **77–81**

| | | |
|---|---|---|
| **9.1** | **M**ail | 78 |
| **9.2** | **T**elephone | 79 |

**10** **S**hopping **82–90**

| | | |
|---|---|---|
| **10.1** | **S**hopping | |
| | conversations | 83 |
| **10.2** | **F**ood | 85 |
| **10.3** | **C**lothing and shoes | 86 |
| **10.4** | **P**hotographs and video | 87 |
| **10.5** | **A**t the hairdresser's | 89 |

**11** **A**t the Tourist Information Center **91–96**

| | | |
|---|---|---|
| **11.1** | **P**laces of interest | 92 |
| **11.2** | **G**oing out | 94 |
| **11.3** | **R**eserving tickets | 95 |

**12** **S**ports **97–100**

| | | |
|---|---|---|
| **12.1** | **S**porting questions | 98 |
| **12.2** | **B**y the waterfront | 98 |
| **12.3** | **I**n the snow | 99 |

**13** **S**ickness **101–107**

| | | |
|---|---|---|
| **13.1** | **C**all (get) the doctor | 102 |
| **13.2** | **P**atient's ailments | 102 |
| **13.3** | **T**he consultation | 103 |
| **13.4** | **M**edication and | |
| | prescriptions | 105 |
| **13.5** | **A**t the dentist's | 106 |

**14** **I**n trouble **108–113**

| | | |
|---|---|---|
| **14.1** | **A**sking for help | 109 |
| **14.2** | **L**oss | 110 |
| **14.3** | **A**ccidents | 110 |
| **14.4** | **T**heft | 111 |
| **14.5** | **M**issing person | 111 |
| **14.6** | **T**he police | 112 |

**15** **W**ord list **114–153**

| | |
|---|---|
| **B**asic grammar | 154 |

# Introduction

● **Welcome to the Periplus Essential Phrase Books series, covering the world's most popular languages and containing everything you'd expect from a comprehensive language series. They're concise, accessible, and easy to understand, and you'll find them indispensable on your trip abroad.**

Each guide is divided into 15 themed sections and starts with a pronunciation table that explains the phonetic pronunciation for all the words and phrases you'll need to know for your trip. At the back of the book is an extensive word list and grammar guide that will help you construct basic sentences in your chosen language.

Throughout the book you'll come across colored boxes with a 🔄 beside them. These are designed to help you if you can't understand what your listeners are saying to you. Hand the book over to them and encourage them to point to the appropriate answer to the question you are asking.

Other colored boxes in the book—this time without the symbol—give alphabetical listings of themed words with their English translations beside them.

For extra clarity, we have put all English words and phrases in **black**, foreign language terms in red, and their phonetic pronunciation in *italic*.

This phrase book covers all subjects you are likely to come across during the course of your visit, from reserving a room for the night to ordering food and drink at a restaurant and what to do if your car breaks down or you lose your traveler's checks and money. With over 2,000 commonly used words and essential phrases at your fingertips, you can rest assured that you will be able to get by in all situations, so let the Essential Phrase Book become your passport to a secure and enjoyable trip!

# Pronunciation guide

The pronunciation provided should be read as if it were English, bearing in mind the following main points:

## Vowels

| a, à or â | a in man | ah | table | tahbl |
|---|---|---|---|---|
| é | like a in make | ay | été | aytay |
| è, ê, e | like ai in air | eh | rêve | rehv |
| e | sometimes | uh | le, ne, je, me | luh, nuh, |
| | like u in fluff | | | jhuh, muh |
| i | like ee in seen | ee | si | see |
| ô | like o in foam | oa | hôtel | oatehl |
| o | like o in John | o | homme | om |
| | sometimes like ô | oa | arroser | ahroasay |
| u | between ee and ew | ew | tu | tew |

Combinations of letters which represent vowel sounds:

| ais, ait | the eh sound | eh | fait | feh |
|---|---|---|---|---|
| an | ohn as in John | ohn | janvier | jhohnvyay |
| au, eau | similar to ô | oa | beau | boa |
| ail | like i in side | ahy | travail | trahvahy |
| ei | similar to è | eh | Seine | sehn |
| eille | eh + y as in yes | ehy | bouteille | bootehy |
| eu | similar to e above | uh | feu | fuh |
| ez, er | similar to é | ay | louer | looay |
| iè | ye as in yes | yeh | siècle | syehkl |
| ié, ier, iez | y + the ay sound | yay | janvier | jhohnvyay |
| ille | ee + y as in yes | eey | famille | fameey |
| oi, oy | combines w + a | wah | moi | mwah |
| ou, oû | oo as in hoot | oo | vous | voo |
| ui | combines w and ee | wee | cuir | kweer |

## Consonants

| ch | like sh in shine | sh | chaud | shoa |
|---|---|---|---|---|
| ç | like s in some | s | garçon | gahrsawn |
| g | before e, i and y | | | |
| | like s in leisure | jh | nager | nahjhay |
| | before a, o and u | | | |
| | like g in got | g | gâteau | gahtoa |
| gn | like ny in canyon | ny | agneau | ahnyoa |
| h | silent | | | |
| j | like s in leisure | jh | jour | jhoor |
| qu | like k in kind | k | que | kuh |
| r | rolled at the back of the throat | | | |
| w | like v in vine | v | wagonlit | vahgawnlee |

## Nasal sounds

Nasal sounds are written in French by adding an n to a vowel or a combination of vowels pronounced as the English ng:

| an/am, en/em | a little like song | ohn | français, lentement | frohnseh, lohntmohn |
|---|---|---|---|---|
| in/im, ain, aim, ein | a little like bang | ahn | instant, faim | ahnstohn, fahn |
| on/om | a nasal form of awn | awn | non | nawn |
| un/um | a little like rung | uhn | un | uhn |
| ien | y + the ahn sound | yahn | bien | byahn |

# Useful lists

**1.1** Today or tomorrow? 8

**1.2** Legal holidays 9

**1.3** What time is it? 9

**1.4** One, two, three... 10

**1.5** The weather 12

**1.6** Here, there... 13

**1.7** What does that sign say? 15

**1.8** Telephone alphabet 15

**1.9** Personal details 16

# **U**seful lists

**Useful lists**

## **1 .1 T**oday or tomorrow?

| | |
|---|---|
| What day is it today? _____ | C'est quel jour aujourd'hui? |
| | *seh kehl jhoor oajhoordwee?* |
| Today's Monday_____ | Aujourd'hui c'est lundi |
| | *oajhoordwee seh luhndee* |
| – Tuesday _____ | Aujourd'hui c'est mardi |
| | *oajhoordwee seh mahrdee* |
| – Wednesday_____ | Aujourd'hui c'est mercredi |
| | *oajhoordwee seh mehrkruhdee* |
| – Thursday _____ | Aujourd'hui c'est jeudi |
| | *oajhoordwee seh jhuhdee* |
| – Friday_____ | Aujourd'hui c'est vendredi |
| | *oajhoordwee seh vohndruhdee* |
| – Saturday _____ | Aujourd'hui c'est samedi |
| | *oajhoordwee seh sahmdee* |
| – Sunday _____ | Aujourd'hui c'est dimanche |
| | *oajhoordwee seh deemohnsh* |
| in January _____ | en janvier |
| | *ohn jhohnvyay* |
| since February _____ | depuis février |
| | *duhpwee fayvryay* |
| in spring_____ | au printemps |
| | *oa prahntohn* |
| in summer_____ | en été; l'été |
| | *ohn naytay; laytay* |
| in autumn _____ | en automne |
| | *ohn noatonn* |
| in winter_____ | en hiver; l'hiver |
| | *ohn neevehr; leevehr* |
| 1999_____ | mille neuf cent quatre-vingt-dix-neuf |
| | *meel nuhf sohn kahtr vahn deez nuhf* |
| the twentieth century _____ | le vingtième siècle |
| | *luh vahntyehm syehkl* |
| What's the date today? ____ | Quelle est la date aujourd'hui? |
| | *kehl eh lah daht oajhoordwee?* |
| Today's the 24th_____ | Aujourd'hui on est le vingt-quatre |
| | *oajhoordwee awn neh luh vahnkahtr* |
| Monday 3 November _____ 1999 | lundi, le trois novembre 1999 |
| | *luhndee, luh trwah novohnbr meel nuhf sohn kahtr vahn deez nuhf* |
| in the morning _____ | le matin |
| | *luh mahtahn* |
| in the afternoon _____ | l'après-midi |
| | *lahpreh meedee* |
| in the evening _____ | le soir |
| | *luh swahr* |
| at night_____ | la nuit |
| | *lah nwee* |
| this morning_____ | ce matin |
| | *suh mahtahn* |
| this afternoon_____ | cet après-midi |
| | *seht ahpreh meedee* |

8

| this evening | ce soir |
| | *suh swahr* |
| tonight | ce soir |
| | *suh swahr* |
| last night | hier soir |
| | *yehr swahr* |
| this week | cette semaine |
| | *seht suhmehn* |
| next month | le mois prochain |
| | *luh mwah proshahn* |
| last year | l'année passée |
| | *lahnay pahsay* |
| next... | prochain/prochaine |
| | *proshahn/proshehn* |
| in...days/weeks/ months/years | dans...jours/semaines/mois/ans |
| | *dohn...jhoor/suhmehn/mwah/ohn* |
| ...weeks ago | il y a...semaines |
| | *eel ee ah...suhmehn* |
| day off | jour de congé |
| | *jhoor duh kawnjhay* |

## .2 Legal holidays

● **The most important** legal holidays in France are the following:

| January 1 | Le Jour de l'An (New Year's Day) |
| March/April | Pâques, (Easter) |
| | le lundi de Pâques (Easter Monday) |
| May 1 | La Fête du Travail (May Day; Labor Day) |
| May 8 | Le Jour de la Libération (Liberation Day) |
| May/June | L'Ascension; la Pentecôte (Ascension; Pentecost) |
| July 14 | La Fête Nationale (Bastille Day) |
| August 15 | L'Assomption (Assumption) |
| November 1 | La Toussaint (All Saints' Day) |
| November 11 | L'Armistice (Armistice Day) |
| December 25 | Noël (Christmas) |

Most shops, banks and government institutions are closed on these days. Banks close the afternoon before a holiday and some banks close on Mondays in the provinces. Good Friday and December 26 are not holidays.

## .3 What time is it?

| What time is it? | Quelle heure est-il? |
| | *kehl uhr eh teel?* |
| It's nine o'clock | Il est neuf heures |
| | *eel eh nuh vuhr* |
| – five past ten | Il est dix heures cinq |
| | *eel eh dee zuhr sahnk* |
| – a quarter past eleven | Il est onze heures et quart |
| | *eel eh tawnz uhr ay kahr* |
| – twenty past twelve | Il est douze heures vingt |
| | *eel eh dooz uhr vahn* |
| – half past one | Il est une heure et demie |
| | *eel eh tewn uhr ay duhmee* |
| – twenty–five to three | Il est trois heures moins vingt-cinq |
| | *eel eh trwah zuhr mwahn vahn sahnk* |

| | | |
|---|---|---|
| – a quarter to four _____ | Il est quatre heures moins le quart | |
| | *eel eh kahtr uhr mwahn luh kahr* | |
| – ten to five _____ | Il est cinq heures moins dix | |
| | *eel eh sahnk uhr mwahn dees* | |
| – twelve noon _____ | Il est midi | |
| | *eel eh meedee* | |
| – midnight _____ | Il est minuit | |
| | *eel eh meenwee* | |
| half an hour _____ | une demi-heure | |
| | *ewn duhmee uhr* | |
| What time? _____ | A quelle heure? | |
| | *ah kehl uhr?* | |
| What time can I come _____ round? | A quelle heure puis-je venir? | |
| | *ah kehl uhr pwee jhuh vuhneer?* | |
| At... _____ | A... | |
| | *ah...* | |
| After... _____ | Après... | |
| | *ahpreh...* | |
| Before... _____ | Avant... | |
| | *ahvohn...* | |
| Between...and... _____ | Entre...et... | |
| | *ohntr...ay...* | |
| From...to... _____ | De...à... | |
| | *duh...ah...* | |
| In...minutes _____ | Dans...minutes | |
| | *dohn...meenewt* | |
| – an hour _____ | Dans une heure | |
| | *dohn zewn uhr* | |
| – ...hours _____ | Dans...heures | |
| | *dohn...uhr* | |
| – a quarter of an hour _____ | Dans un quart d'heure | |
| | *dohn zuhn kahr duhr* | |
| – three quarters of _____ an hour | Dans trois quarts d'heure | |
| | *dohn trwah kahr duhr* | |
| early/late _____ | trop tôt/tard | |
| | *troa toa/tahr* | |
| on time _____ | à temps | |
| | *ah tohn* | |
| summertime _____ | l'heure d'été | |
| | *luhr daytay* | |
| wintertime _____ | l'heure d'hiver | |
| | *luhr deevehr* | |

## **1.4 O**ne, two, three...

| | | |
|---|---|---|
| 0 _____ | zéro | *zayroa* |
| 1 _____ | un | *uhn* |
| 2 _____ | deux | *duh* |
| 3 _____ | trois | *trwah* |
| 4 _____ | quatre | *kahtr* |
| 5 _____ | cinq | *sahnk* |
| 6 _____ | six | *sees* |
| 7 _____ | sept | *seht* |
| 8 _____ | huit | *weet* |
| 9 _____ | neuf | *nuhf* |
| 10 _____ | dix | *dees* |

| | | | |
|---|---|---|---|
| 11 | | onze | *awnz* |
| 12 | | douze | *dooz* |
| 13 | | treize | *trehz* |
| 14 | | quatorze | *kahtorz* |
| 15 | | quinze | *kahnz* |
| 16 | | seize | *sehz* |
| 17 | | dix-sept | *dee seht* |
| 18 | | dix-huit | *dee zweet* |
| 19 | | dix-neuf | *deez nuhf* |
| 20 | | vingt | *vahn* |
| 21 | | vingt et un | *vahn tay uhn* |
| 22 | | vingt-deux | *vahn duh* |
| | | | |
| 30 | | trente | *trohnt* |
| 31 | | trente et un | *trohn tay uhn* |
| 32 | | trente-deux | *trohnt duh* |
| | | | |
| 40 | | quarante | *kahrohnt* |
| 50 | | cinquante | *sahnkohnt* |
| 60 | | soixante | *swahssohnt* |
| 70 | | soixante-dix | *swahssohnt dees* |
| 80 | | quatre-vingts | *kahtr vahn* |
| 90 | | quatre-vingt-dix | *kahtr vahn dees* |
| 100 | | cent | *sohn* |
| 101 | | cent un | *sohn uhn* |
| 110 | | cent dix | *sohn dees* |
| 120 | | cent vingt | *sohn vahn* |
| 200 | | deux cents | *duh sohn* |
| 300 | | trois cents | *trwah sohn* |
| 400 | | quatre cents | *kahtr sohn* |
| 500 | | cinq cents | *sahnk sohn* |
| 600 | | six cents | *see sohn* |
| 700 | | sept cents | *seht sohn* |
| 800 | | huit cents | *wee sohn* |
| 900 | | neuf cents | *nuhf sohn* |
| 1,000 | | mille | *meel* |
| 1,100 | | mille cent | *meel sohn* |
| 2,000 | | deux mille | *duh meel* |
| 10,000 | | dix mille | *dee meel* |
| 100,000 | | cent mille | *sohn meel* |
| 1,000,000 | | un million | *uhn meelyawn* |
| | | | |
| 1st | | le premier | *luh pruhmyay* |
| 2nd | | le deuxième | *luh duhzyehm* |
| 3rd | | le troisième | *luh trwahzyehm* |
| 4th | | le quatrième | *luh kahtryehm* |
| 5th | | le cinquième | *luh sahnkyehm* |
| 6th | | le sixième | *luh seezyehm* |
| 7th | | le septième | *luh sehtyehm* |
| 8th | | le huitième | *luh weetyehm* |
| 9th | | le neuvième | *luh nuhvyehm* |
| 10th | | le dixième | *luh deezyehm* |
| 11th | | le onzième | *luh awnzyehm* |
| 12th | | le douzième | *luh doozyehm* |
| 13th | | le treizième | *luh trehzyehm* |
| 14th | | le quatorzième | *luh kahtorzyehm* |
| 15th | | le quinzième | *luh kahnzyehm* |

| | | |
|---|---|---|
| 16th _____ | le seizième | *luh sehzyehm* |
| 17th _____ | le dix-septième | *luh dee sehtyehm* |
| 18th _____ | le dix-huitième | *luh dee zweetyehm* |
| 19th _____ | le dix-neuvième | *luh deez nuhvyehm* |
| 20th _____ | le vingtième | *luh vahntyehm* |
| 21st _____ | le vingt et unième | *luh vahn tay-ewnyehm* |
| 22nd _____ | le vingt-deuxième | *luh vahn duhzyehm* |
| 30th _____ | le trentième | *luh trohntyehm* |
| 100th _____ | le centième | *luh sohntyehm* |
| 1,000th _____ | le millième | *luh meelyehm* |

| | | |
|---|---|---|
| once _____ | une fois | *ewn fwah* |
| twice _____ | deux fois | *duh fwah* |
| double _____ | le double | *luh doobl* |
| triple _____ | le triple | *luh treepl* |
| half _____ | la moitié | *lah mwahtyay* |
| a quarter _____ | un quart | *uhn kahr* |
| a third _____ | un tiers | *uhn tyehr* |

a couple, a few, some _____ quelques, un nombre de, quelques
*kehlkuh, uhn nawnbr duh, kehlkuh*

2 + 4 = 6 _____ deux plus quatre égalent six
*duh plews kahtr aygahl sees*

4 - 2 = 2 _____ quatre moins deux égalent deux
*kahtr mwahn duh aygahl duh*

2 x 4 = 8 _____ deux fois quatre égalent huit
*duh fwah kahtr aygahl weet*

4 ÷ 2 = 2 _____ quatre divisé par deux égalent deux
*kahtr deeveezay pahr duh aygahl duh*

odd/even _____ impair/pair
*ahnpehr/pehr*

total _____ (au) total
*(oa) totahl*

6 x 9 _____ six fois neuf
*see fwah nuhf*

##  .5 The weather

| | |
|---|---|
| Is the weather going to be good/bad? | Va-t-il faire beau/mauvais? *vah teel fehr boa/moaveh?* |
| Is it going to get colder/hotter? | Va-t-il faire plus froid/plus chaud? *vah teel fehr plew frwah/plew shoa?* |
| What temperature is it going to be? | Quelle température va-t-il faire? *Kehl tohnpayrahtewr vah teel fehr?* |
| Is it going to rain? | Va-t-il pleuvoir? *vah teel pluhvvwahr?* |
| Is there going to be a storm? | Va-t-il faire de la tempête? *vah teel fehr duh lah tohnpeht?* |
| Is it going to snow? | Va-t-il neiger? *vah teel nehjhay?* |
| Is it going to freeze? | Va-t-il geler? *vah teel jhuhlay?* |
| Is the thaw setting in? | Va-t-il dégeler? *vah teel dayjhuhlay?* |
| Is it going to be foggy? | Y aura-t-il du brouillard? *ee oarah teel dew brooy-yahr?* |

|  |  |  |
|---|---|---|
| Is there going to be a _____ thunderstorm? | Va-t-il faire de l'orage? | *vah teel fehr duh lorahjh?* |
| The weather's _____ changing | Le temps change | *luh tohn shohnjh* |
| It's cooling down _____ | Ça se rafraîchit | *sah suh rahfrehshee* |
| What's the weather _____ going to be like today/ tomorrow? | Quel temps va-t-il faire aujourd'hui/demain? | *kehl tohn vah teel fehr oajhoordwee/duhmahn?* |

|  |  |
|---|---|
| nuageux | cloudy |
| beau | fine |
| chaud | hot |
| ...degrés (au-dessous/au-dessus de zéro) | ...degrees (below/above zero) |
| couvert | overcast |
| le crachin | drizzle |
| doux | mild |
| ensoleillé | sunny |
| frais | chilly |
| froid | cold |
| humide | damp |
| pluvieux | raining |
| la canicule | scorching hot |
| la grêle | hail |
| la neige | snow |
| la pluie | rain |
| la vague de chaleur | heatwave |
| l'averse (f.) | shower |
| le brouillard | fog |
| le gel | ice |
| le vent | wind |
| le verglas | black ice |
| les nuages | clouds |
| les rafales de vent | squalls |
| l'ouragan (m.) | hurricane |
| lourd | muggy |
| l'orage (m.) | thunderstorm |
| orageux | stormy |
| pénétrant | bleak |
| ciel dégagé | clear |
| brumeux | misty |
| vent faible/modéré/fort | light/moderate/strong wind |
| venteux | windy |

## .6 Here, there...

### See also 5.1 Asking for directions

|  |  |  |
|---|---|---|
| here/there | ici/là | *eesee/lah* |
| somewhere/nowhere | quelque part/nulle part | *kehlkuh pahr/newl pahr* |
| everywhere | partout | *pahrtoo* |
| far away/nearby | loin/à côté | *lwahn/ah koatay* |
| right/left | la droite/la gauche | *lah drwaht/lah goash* |
| to the right/left of | à droite de/à gauche de | *ah drwaht duh/ah goash duh* |
| straight ahead | tout droit | *too drwah* |

**Useful lists**

| | | |
|---|---|---|
| via _____ | par | *pahr* |
| in _____ | dans | *dohn* |
| on_____ | sur | *sewr* |
| under _____ | sous | *soo* |
| against _____ | contre | *kawntr* |
| opposite_____ | en face de | *ohn fahs duh* |
| next to _____ | à côté de | *ah koatay duh* |
| near_____ | près de | *preh duh* |
| in front of_____ | devant | *devohn* |
| in the centre _____ | au milieu de | *oa meelyuh duh* |
| forward_____ | en avant | *ohn nahvohn* |
| down_____ | en bas | *ohn bah* |
| up_____ | en haut | *ohn oa* |
| inside _____ | à l'intérieur | *ah lahntayryuhr* |
| outside _____ | à l'extérieur | *ah lehxtayryuhr* |
| behind _____ | derrière | *dehryehr* |
| at the front _____ | à l'avant | *ah lahvohn* |
| at the back_____ | à l'arrière | *ah lahryehr* |
| in the north _____ | au nord | *oa nor* |
| to the south_____ | vers le sud | *vehr luh sewd* |
| from the west_____ | venant de l'ouest | *vuhnohn duh lwehst* |
| from the east _____ | venant de l'est | *vuhnohn duh lehst* |
| ...of _____ | à...de | *ah...duh* |

# .7 What does that sign say?

**See 5.4 Traffic signs**

| | | |
|---|---|---|
| à louer | entrée gratuite | ne pas déranger s'il |
| **for hire** | **admission free** | vous plaît |
| à vendre | entrée interdite | **do not disturb please** |
| **for sale** | **no entry** | ouvert/fermé |
| accueil | escalier roulant | **open/closed** |
| **reception** | **escalator** | peinture fraîche |
| animaux interdits | escalier | **wet paint** |
| **no pets allowed** | **stairs** | pelouse interdite |
| ascenseur | escalier de secours | **keep off the grass** |
| **elevator** | **fire escape** | premiers soins |
| attention à la marche | ...étage | **first aid** |
| **watch your step** | **...floor** | propriété privée |
| attention chien | frein de secours | **private (property)** |
| méchant | **emergency brake** | renseignements |
| **beware of the dog** | haute tension | **information** |
| caisse | **high voltage** | réservé |
| **pay here** | heures d'ouverture | **reserved** |
| complet | **opening hours** | risque d'incendie |
| **full** | interdit d'allumer un | **fire hazard** |
| dames | feu | soldes |
| **ladies** | **no open fires** | **sale** |
| danger | interdit de fumer | sortie |
| **danger** | **no smoking** | **exit** |
| défense de toucher | interdit de | sortie de secours |
| **please do not touch** | photographier | **emergency exit** |
| eau non potable | **no photographs** | pousser/tirer |
| **not drinking water** | liquidation de stock | **push/pull** |
| en panne | **close-out sale** | toilettes, wc |
| **out of order** | messieurs | **toilets** |
| entrée | **gents/gentlemen** | |
| **entrance** | | |

# .8 Telephone alphabet

| a | _____ | *ah* | comme Anatole | *kom ahnnahtol* |
|---|---|---|---|---|
| b | _____ | *bay* | comme Berthe | *kom behrt* |
| c | _____ | *say* | comme Célestin | *kom saylehstahn* |
| d | _____ | *day* | comme Désiré | *kom dayzeeray* |
| e | _____ | *uh* | comme Eugène | *kom uhjhehn* |
| f | _____ | *ehf* | comme François | *kom frohnswah* |
| g | _____ | *jhay* | comme Gaston | *kom gahstawn* |
| h | _____ | *ash* | comme Henri | *kom ohnree* |
| i | _____ | *ee* | comme Irma | *kom eermah* |
| j | _____ | *jhee* | comme Joseph | *kom jhosehf* |
| k | _____ | *kah* | comme Kléber | *kom klaybehr* |
| l | _____ | *ehl* | comme Louis | *kom looee* |
| m | _____ | *ehm* | comme Marcel | *kom mahrsehl* |
| n | _____ | *ehn* | comme Nicolas | *kom neekolah* |
| o | _____ | *oh* | comme Oscar | *kom oskahr* |
| p | _____ | *pay* | comme Pierre | *kom pyehr* |
| q | _____ | *kew* | comme Quintal | *kom kahntahl* |

**Useful lists**

| | | | |
|---|---|---|---|
| r _____ehr | comme Raoul | *kom rahool* |
| s _____ehs | comme Suzanne | *kom sewzahnn* |
| t _____tay | comme Thérèse | *kom tayrehz* |
| u _____ew | comme Ursule | *kom ewrsewl* |
| v _____vee | comme Victor | *kom veektor* |
| w _____doobluhvay | comme William | *kom weelyahm* |
| x _____eex | comme Xavier | *kom gsahvyay* |
| y _____eegrehk | comme Yvonne | *kom eevon* |
| z _____zee | comme Zoé | *kom zoa-ay* |

 **.9 Personal details**

| | |
|---|---|
| surname_____ | nom |
| | *nawn* |
| christian/given name(s) ____ | prénom(s) |
| | *praynawn* |
| initials_____ | initiales |
| | *eeneesyahl* |
| address (street/number) ___ | adresse (rue/numéro) |
| | *ahdrehs (rew/newmayroa)* |
| postal/zip code/town_____ | code postal/ville |
| | *kod postahl/veel* |
| sex (male/female) _____ | sexe (m/f) |
| | *sehx (ehm/ehf)* |
| nationality _____ | nationalité |
| | *nahsyonahleetay* |
| date of birth _____ | date de naissance |
| | *daht duh nehsohns* |
| place of birth_____ | lieu de naissance |
| | *lyuh duh nehsohns* |
| occupation_____ | profession |
| | *profehsyawn* |
| married/single/divorced____ | marié(e) /célibataire/divorcé(e) |
| | *mahreeay/sayleebahtehr/deevorsay* |
| widowed _____ | veuf/veuve |
| | *vuhf/vuhv* |
| (number of) children_____ | (nombre d')enfants |
| | *(nawnbr d)ohnfohn* |
| identity card/passport/ _____ | numéro de carte d'identité/ |
| driving license number | passeport/permis de conduire |
| | *newmayroa duh kahrt deedohnteetay/* |
| | *pahspor/pehrmee duh kawndweer* |
| place and date of issue ____ | lieu et date de délivrance |
| | *lyuh ay daht duh dayleevrohns* |

**2**

# Courtesies

**2.1**  Greetings                    18

**2.2**  How to ask a question        19

**2.3**  How to reply                 20

**2.4**  Thank you                    21

**2.5**  Sorry                        22

**2.6**  What do you think?           22

# Courtesies

● **It is usual in France** to shake hands on meeting and parting company. Female friends and relatives may kiss each other on both cheeks when meeting and parting company. With men this varies according to the region. It is also polite to say monsieur and madame quite systematically as part of a greeting, i.e. Bonjour, monsieur; au revoir, madame. Remember please (seel voo play) and thank you (mehrsee) where indicated.

● **The English** "you" is expressed in French by either "tu" or "vous". "Tu" is the more familiar form of address, used to talk to someone close or used between young people or when adults are talking to young children. "Vous" is the more formal and polite form of address and should always be used with the above exceptions. "On" is the generalised form of "nous" meaning people in general ("one" and "we" in English).

## .1 Greetings

| | |
|---|---|
| Hello, Mr Smith | Bonjour monsieur Smith<br>*bawnjhoor muhsyuh dewpawn* |
| Hello, Mrs Jones | Bonjour madame Jones<br>*bawnjhoor mahdahm dewrohn* |
| Hello, Peter | Salut, Pierre<br>*sahlew, pyehr* |
| Hi, Helen | Ça va, Hélène?<br>*sah vah, aylehn?* |
| Good morning, madam | Bonjour madame<br>*bawnjhoor mahdahm* |
| Good afternoon, sir | Bonjour monsieur<br>*bawnjhoor muhsyuh* |
| Good evening | Bonsoir<br>*bawhnswahr* |
| How are you? | Comment allez-vous?<br>*komohn tahlay voo?* |
| Fine, thank you, and you? | Très bien et vous?<br>*treh byahn ay voo?* |
| Very well | Très bien<br>*treh byahn* |
| Not very well | Pas très bien<br>*pah treh byahn* |
| Not too bad | Ça va<br>*sah vah* |
| I'd better be going | Je m'en vais<br>*jhuh mohn veh* |
| I have to be going | Je dois partir<br>*jhuh dwah pahrteer* |
| Someone's waiting for me | On m'attend<br>*awn mahtohn* |
| Bye! | Salut!<br>*sahlew!* |
| Good-bye | Au revoir<br>*oa ruhvwahr* |

| | |
|---|---|
| See you soon _____ | A bientôt |
| | *ah byahntoa* |
| See you later _____ | A tout à l'heure |
| | *ah too tah luhr* |
| See you in a little while ____ | A tout de suite |
| | *ah toot sweet* |
| Sleep well _____ | Dormez bien/dors bien |
| | *dormay byahn, dor byahn* |
| Good night _____ | Bonne nuit |
| | *bon nwee* |
| Have fun_____ | Amuse-toi bien |
| | *ahmewz twah byahn* |
| Good luck_____ | Bonne chance |
| | *bon shahns* |
| Have a nice vacation _____ | Bonnes vacances |
| | *bon vahkohns* |
| Have a good trip _____ | Bon voyage |
| | *bawn vwahyahjh* |
| Thank you, you too_____ | Merci, de même |
| | *mehrsee, duh mehm* |
| Say hello to...for me_____ | Mes amitiés à... |
| | *may zahmeetyay ah...* |

 ## .2 How to ask a question

| | |
|---|---|
| Who?_____ | Qui? |
| | *kee?* |
| Who's that? _____ | Qui est-ce? |
| | *kee ehs?* |
| What? _____ | Quoi? |
| | *kwah?* |
| What's there to_____ | Qu'est-ce qu'on peut voir ici? |
| see here? | *kehsk awn puh vwahr eesee?* |
| What kind of hotel_____ | C'est quelle sorte d'hôtel? |
| is that? | *seh kehl sort doatehl?* |
| Where?_____ | Où? |
| | *oo?* |
| Where's the bathroom? ____ | Où sont les toilettes? |
| | *oo sawn lay twahleht?* |
| Where are you going? _____ | Où allez-vous? |
| | *oo ahlay voo?* |
| Where are you from? _____ | D'où venez-vous? |
| | *doo vuhnay voo?* |
| How?_____ | Comment? |
| | *komohn?* |
| How far is that? _____ | C'est loin? |
| | *seh lwahn?* |
| How long does that take? __ | Combien de temps faut-il? |
| | *kawnbyahn duh tohn foa teel?* |
| How long is the trip? _____ | Combien de temps dure le voyage? |
| | *kawnbyahn duh tohn dewr luh vwahyahjh?* |
| How much? _____ | Combien? |
| | *kawnbyahn?* |
| How much is this?_____ | C'est combien? |
| | *seh kawnbyahn?* |
| What time is it? _____ | Quelle heure est-il? |
| | *kehl uhr eh teel?* |

**Courtesies**

| | |
|---|---|
| Which? _____ | Quel? Quels?/Quelle? Quelles? |
| | *kehl?* |
| Which glass is mine? _____ | Quel est mon verre? |
| | *kehl eh mawn vehr?* |
| When? _____ | Quand? |
| | *kohn?* |
| When are you leaving? ____ | Quand partez-vous? |
| | *kohn pahrtay voo?* |
| Why?_____ | Pourquoi? |
| | *poorkwah?* |
| Could you...me?_____ | Pouvez-vous me...? |
| | *poovay voo muh...?* |
| Could you help me, _____ please? | Pouvez-vous m'aider s'il vous plaît? |
| | *poovay voo mayday seel voo pleh?* |
| Could you point that_____ out to me? | Pouvez-vous me l'indiquer? |
| | *poovay voo muh lahndeekay?* |
| Could you come _____ with me, please? | Pouvez-vous m'accompagner s'il vous plaît? |
| | *poovay voo mahkawnpahnnyay seel voo pleh?* |
| Could you..._____ | Voulez-vous...? |
| | *voolay voo...?* |
| Could you reserve some ___ tickets for me, please? | Voulez-vous me réserver des places s'il vous plaît? |
| | *voolay voo muh rayzehrvay day plahs seel voo pleh?* |
| Do you know...? _____ | Connaissez-vous...? |
| | *konehssay voo...?* |
| Do you know another_____ hotel, please? | Vous connaissez peut-être un autre hôtel? |
| | *voo konehssay puh tehtr uhn noatr oatehl?* |
| Do you know whether...?___ | Savez-vous si...? |
| | *sahvay voo see...?* |
| Do you have a...?_____ | Avez-vous un...? |
| | *ahvay voo zuhn...?* |
| Do you have a _____ vegetarian dish, please? | Vous avez peut-être un plat sans viande? |
| | *voo zahvay puh tehtr uhn plah sohn vyohnd?* |
| I'd like... _____ | Je voudrais... |
| | *jhuh voodreh...* |
| I'd like a kilo of apples, ____ please | Je voudrais un kilo de pommes |
| | *jhuh voodreh zuhn keeloa duh pom* |
| Can I...?_____ | Puis-je...? |
| | *pwee jhuh...?* |
| Can I take this?_____ | Puis-je prendre ceci? |
| | *pwee jhuh prohndr suhsee?* |
| Can I smoke here? _____ | Puis-je fumer ici? |
| | *pwee jhuh fewmay eesee?* |
| Could I ask you _____ something? | Puis-je vous demander quelque chose? |
| | *pwee jhuh voo duhmohnday kehlkuh shoaz?* |

## 2 .3 How to reply

| | |
|---|---|
| Yes, of course_____ | Oui, bien sûr |
| | *wee, byahn sewr* |
| No, I'm sorry_____ | Non, je suis désolé |
| | *nawn, jhuh swee dayzolay* |
| Yes, what can I do_____ for you? | Oui, que puis-je faire pour vous? |
| | *wee, kuh pwee jhuh fehr poor voo?* |

| | |
|---|---|
| Just a moment, please _____ | Un moment s'il vous plaît |
| | *uhn momohn seel voo pleh* |
| No, I don't have _____ time now | Non, je n'ai pas le temps en ce moment |
| | *nawn, jhuh nay pah luh tohn ohn suh momohn* |
| No, that's impossible _____ | Non, c'est impossible |
| | *nawn, seh tahnposseebl* |
| I think so _____ | Je le crois bien |
| | *jhuh luh krwah byahn* |
| I agree _____ | Je le pense aussi |
| | *jhuh luh pohns oasee* |
| I hope so too _____ | Je l'espère aussi |
| | *jhuh lehspehr oasee* |
| No, not at all _____ | Non, absolument pas |
| | *nawn, ahbsolewmohn pah* |
| No, no one _____ | Non, personne |
| | *nawn, pehrson* |
| No, nothing _____ | Non, rien |
| | *nawn, ryahn* |
| That's (not) right _____ | C'est (ce n'est pas) exact |
| | *seht (suh neh pahz) ehgzah* |
| I (don't) agree _____ | Je suis (je ne suis pas) d'accord avec vous |
| | *jhuh swee (jhuh nuh swee pah) dahkor ahvehk voo* |
| All right _____ | C'est bien |
| | *seh byahn* |
| Okay _____ | D'accord |
| | *dahkor* |
| Perhaps _____ | Peut-être |
| | *puh tehtr* |
| I don't know _____ | Je ne sais pas |
| | *jhuh nuh seh pah* |

## .4 Thank you

| | |
|---|---|
| Thank you _____ | Merci/merci bien |
| | *mehrsee/mehrsee byahn* |
| You're welcome _____ | De rien/avec plaisir |
| | *duh ryahn/ahvehk playzeer* |
| Thank you very much _____ | Merci beaucoup |
| | *mehrsee boakoo* |
| Very kind of you _____ | C'est aimable de votre part |
| | *seh taymahbl duh votr pahr* |
| I enjoyed it very much _____ | C'était un réel plaisir |
| | *sayteh tuhn rayehl playzeer* |
| Thank you for your trouble _____ | Je vous remercie pour la peine |
| | *jhuh voo ruhmehrsee poor lah pehn* |
| You shouldn't have _____ | Vous n'auriez pas dû |
| | *voo noaryay pah dew* |
| That's all right _____ | Pas de problème |
| | *pah duh problehm* |

**Courtesies**

### .5 Sorry

| | |
|---|---|
| Excuse me_____ | Excusez-moi |
| | *ehxkewzay mwah* |
| Sorry! _____ | Pardon! |
| | *pahrdawn!* |
| I'm sorry, I didn't know...___ | Pardon, je ne savais pas que... |
| | *pahrdawn jhuh nuh sahveh pah kuh...* |
| I do apologize_____ | Excusez-moi |
| | *ehxkewzay mwah* |
| I'm sorry_____ | Je suis désolé |
| | *jhuh swee dayzolay* |
| I didn't do it on purpose, | Je ne l'ai pas fait exprès, c'était un |
| it was an accident | accident |
| | *jhuh ne lay pah feh ehxpreh, sayteh tuhn* |
| | *nahxeedohn* |
| That's all right_____ | Ce n'est pas grave |
| | *suh neh pah grahv* |
| Never mind_____ | Ça ne fait rien |
| | *sah nuh feh ryahn* |
| It could've happened to____ | Ça peut arriver à tout le monde |
| anyone | *sah puh ahreevay ah too luh mawnd* |

### .6 What do you think?

| | |
|---|---|
| Which do you prefer?_____ | Qu'est-ce que vous préférez? |
| | *kehs kuh voo prayfayray?* |
| What do you think?_____ | Qu'en pensez-vous? |
| | *kohn pohnsay-voo?* |
| Don't you like dancing?____ | Vous n'aimez pas danser? |
| | *voo nehmay pah dohnsay?* |
| I don't mind_____ | Ça m'est égal |
| | *sah meh taygahl* |
| Well done!_____ | Très bien! |
| | *treh byahn!* |
| Not bad!_____ | Pas mal! |
| | *pah mahl!* |
| Great!_____ | Génial! |
| | *jhaynyahl!* |
| Wonderful!_____ | Super! |
| | *sewpehr!* |
| It's really nice here!_____ | C'est drôlement agréable ici! |
| | *seh droalmohn ahgrayahbl eesee!* |
| How nice!_____ | Pas mal, chouette! |
| | *pah mahl, shweht!* |
| How nice for you!_____ | C'est formidable! |
| | *seh formeedahbl!* |
| I'm (not) very happy_____ | Je suis (ne suis pas) très satisfait(e) de... |
| with... | *jhuh swee (nuh swee pah) treh sahteesfeh(t)* |
| | *duh...* |
| I'm glad..._____ | Je suis content(e) que... |
| | *jhuh swee kawntohn(t) kuh...* |
| I'm having a great time____ | Je m'amuse beaucoup |
| | *jhuh mahmewz boakoo* |

| | |
|---|---|
| I'm looking forward to it | Je m'en réjouis |
| | *jhuh mohn rayjhwee* |
| I hope it'll work out | J'espère que cela réussira |
| | *jhehspehr kuh suhlah rayewseerah* |
| That's ridiculous! | C'est nul! |
| | *seh newl!* |
| That's terrible! | Quelle horreur! |
| | *kehl oruhr!* |
| What a pity! | C'est dommage! |
| | *seh domahjh!* |
| That's filthy! | C'est dégoûtant! |
| | *seh daygootohn!* |
| What nonsense! | C'est ridicule/C'est absurde! |
| | *seh reedeekewl/seh tahbsewrd!* |
| I don't like... | Je n'aime pas... |
| | *jhuh nehm pah...* |
| I'm bored to death | Je m'ennuie à mourir |
| | *jhuh mohnnwee ah mooreer* |
| I've had enough | J'en ai assez/ras le bol |
| | *jhohn nay ahsay/rahl bol* |
| This is no good | Ce n'est pas possible |
| | *suh neh pah posseebl* |
| I was expecting something completely different | Je m'attendais à quelque chose de très différent |
| | *jhuh mahtohndeh ah kehlkuh shoaz duh treh deefayrohn* |

**3**

# **C**onversation

**3.1**   **I** beg your pardon?              25

**3.2**   **I**ntroductions                  26

**3.3**   **S**tarting/ending a
           conversation                  28

**3.4**   **C**ongratulations and
           condolences                   28

**3.5**   **A** chat about the weather 28

**3.6**   **H**obbies                     29

**3.7**   **B**eing the host(ess)         29

**3.8**   **I**nvitations                 29

**3.9**   **P**aying a compliment         30

**3.10**  **I**ntimate comments/
           questions                     31

**3.11**  **A**rrangements                32

**3.12**  **S**aying good-bye             32

# Conversation

## 3 .1 I beg your pardon?

| | |
|---|---|
| I don't speak any/ _____ I speak a little... | Je ne parle pas/je parle un peu... *jhuh nuh pahrl pah/jhuh pahrl uhn puh..* |
| I'm American _____ | Je suis américain/américaine *jhuh swee zamayreekan/amayreekehn* |
| Do you speak _____ English/French/German? | Parlez-vous anglais/français/allemand? *pahrlay voo ohngleh/ frohnseh/ahlmohn?* |
| Is there anyone who _____ speaks...? | Y a-t-il quelqu'un qui parle...? *ee yah teel kehlkuhn kee pahrl...?* |
| I beg your pardon? _____ | Que dites-vous? *kuh deet voo?* |
| I (don't) understand _____ | Je (ne) comprends (pas) *jhuh (nuh) kawnprohn (pah)* |
| Do you understand me? ___ | Me comprenez-vous? *me kawnpruhnay voo?* |
| Could you repeat that, _____ please? | Voulez-vous répéter s'il vous plaît? *voolay voo raypaytay seel voo pleh?* |
| Could you speak more_____ slowly, please? | Pouvez-vous parler plus lentement s'il vous plaît? *poovay voo pahrlay plew lohntmohn seel voo pleh?* |
| What does that word _____ mean? | Qu'est-ce que ce mot veut dire? *kehs kuh suh moa vuh deer?* |
| Is that similar to/the _____ same as...? | Est-ce (environ) la même chose que...? *ehs (ohnveerawn) lah mehm shoaz kuh...?* |
| Could you write that_____ down for me, please? | Pouvez-vous me l'écrire? *poovay voo muh laykreer?* |
| Could you spell that _____ for me, please? | Pouvez-vous me l'épeler? *poovay voo muh laypuhlay?* |

*(See 1.8 Telephone alphabet)*

| | |
|---|---|
| Could you point that_____ out in this phrase book, please? | Pouvez-vous me le montrer dans ce guide de conversation? *poovay voo muh luh mawntray dohn suh gueed duh kawnvehrsahsyawn?* |
| One moment, please,_____ I have to look it up | Un moment, je dois le chercher *uhn momohn, jhuh dwah luh shehrshay* |
| I can't find the word/the ___ sentence | Je ne trouve pas le mot/la phrase *jhuh nuh troov pah luh moa/lah frahz* |
| How do you say_____ that in...? | Comment dites-vous cela en...? *komohn deet voo suhlah ohn...?* |
| How do you pronounce_____ that? | Comment prononcez-vous cela? *komohn pronawnsay voo suhlah?* |

### 3 .2 Introductions

| | |
|---|---|
| May I introduce myself? ___ | Puis-je me présenter? |
| | *pwee jhuh muh prayzohntay?* |
| My name's... ___ | Je m'appelle... |
| | *jhuh mahpehl...* |
| I'm... ___ | Je suis... |
| | *jhuh swee...* |
| What's your name? ___ | Comment vous appelez-vous? |
| | *komohn voo zahpuhlay voo?* |
| May I introduce...? ___ | Puis-je vous présenter? |
| | *pwee jhuh voo prayzohntay?* |
| This is my wife/ ___ | Voici ma femme/fille/mère/mon amie |
| daughter/mother/ | *vwahsee mah fahm/feey/mehr/mawn* |
| girlfriend | *nahmee* |
| – my husband/son/ ___ | Voici mon mari/fils/père/ami |
| father/boyfriend | *vwahsee mawn mahree/fees/pehr/ahmee* |
| How do you do ___ | Enchanté(e). |
| | *ohnshohntay* |
| Pleased to meet you ___ | Je suis heureux(se) de faire votre |
| | connaissance |
| | *jhuh swee zuhruh(z) duh fehr votr* |
| | *kohnehssohns* |
| Where are you from? ___ | D'où venez-vous? |
| | *doo vuhnay voo?* |
| I'm from ___ | Je viens de Les États Unis |
| the United States | *jhuh vyahn duh layz ehtahz oonee* |
| What city do you live in? __ | Vous habitez dans quelle ville? |
| | *voo zahbeetay dohn kehl veel?* |
| In..., It's near... ___ | A...C'est à côté de... |
| | *ah...seh tah koatay duh...* |
| Have you been here ___ | Etes-vous ici depuis longtemps? |
| long? | *eht voo zeesee duhpwee lawntohn?* |
| A few days ___ | Depuis quelques jours |
| | *depwee kehlkuh jhoor* |
| How long are you ___ | Combien de temps restez-vous ici? |
| staying here? | *kawnbyahn duh tohn rehstay voo zeesee?* |
| We're (probably) leaving ___ | Nous partirons (probablement) |
| tomorrow/in two weeks | demain/dans quinze jours |
| | *noo pahrteerawn (probahbluhmohn)* |
| | *duhmahn/dohn kahnz jhoor* |
| Where are you staying? ___ | Où logez-vous? |
| | *oo lojhay voo?* |
| In a hotel/an apartment ___ | Dans un hôtel/appartement |
| | *dohn zuhn noatehl/ahpahrtuhmohn* |
| On a camp site ___ | Dans un camping |
| | *dohn zuhn kohnpeeng* |
| With friends/relatives ___ | Chez des amis/chez de la famille |
| | *shay day zahmee/shay duh lah fahmeey* |
| Are you here on your ___ | Etes-vous ici seul/avec votre famille? |
| own/with your family? | *eht voo zeesee suhl/ahvehk votr* |
| | *fahmeey?* |
| I'm on my own ___ | Je suis seul(e) |
| | *jhuh swee suhl* |

Conversation

26

| | |
|---|---|
| I'm with my partner/wife/husband | Je suis avec mon ami(e)/ma femme/mon mari<br>*jhu swee zahvehk mawn nahmee/mah fahm/mawn mahree* |
| – with my family | Je suis avec ma famille<br>*jhuh swee zahvehk mah fahmeey* |
| – with relatives | Je suis avec de la famille<br>*jhuh swee zahvehk duh lah fahmeey* |
| – with a friend/friends | Je suis avec un ami/une amie /des amis<br>*jhuh swee zahvehk uhn nahmee/ewn ahmee/day zahmee* |
| Are you married? | Etes-vous marié(e)?<br>*eht voo mahreeay?* |
| Do you have a steady boyfriend/girlfriend? | As-tu un petit ami (une petite amie)?<br>*ah tew uhn puhtee tahmee (ewn puhteet ahmee)?* |
| That's none of your business | Cela ne vous regarde pas<br>*suhlah nuh voo ruhgahrd pah* |
| I'm married | Je suis marié(e)<br>*jhuh swee mahreeay* |
| – single | Je suis célibataire<br>*jhuh swee sayleebahtehr* |
| – separated | Je suis séparé(e)<br>*jhuh swee saypahray* |
| – divorced | Je suis divorcé(e)<br>*jhuh swee deevorsay* |
| – a widow/widower | Je suis veuf/veuve<br>*jhuh swee vuhf/vuhv* |
| I live alone/with someone | J'habite tout(e) seul(e)/avec quelqu'un<br>*jhahbeet too suhl(toot suhl)/ahvehk kehlkuhn* |
| Do you have any children/grandchildren? | Avez-vous des enfants/petits-enfants?<br>*ahvay voo day zohnfohn/puhtee zohnfohn?* |
| How old are you? | Quel âge avez-vous?<br>*kehl ahjh ahvay voo?* |
| How old is he/she? | Quel âge a-t-il/a-t-elle?<br>*kehl ahjh ah teel/ah tehl?* |
| I'm...years old | J'ai...ans<br>*jhay...ohn* |
| He's/she's...years old | Il/elle a...ans<br>*eel/ehl ah...ohn* |
| What do you do for a living? | Quel est votre métier?<br>*kehl eh votr maytyay?* |
| I work in an office | Je travaille dans un bureau<br>*jhuh trahvahy dohn zuhn bewroa* |
| I'm a student/ I'm at school | Je fais des études/je vais à l'école<br>*jhuh feh day zaytewd/jhuh veh zah laykol* |
| I'm unemployed | Je suis au chômage<br>*jhuh swee zoa shoamajh* |
| I'm retired | Je suis retraité(e)<br>*jhuh swee ruhtrehtay* |
| I'm on a disability pension | Je suis en invalidité<br>*jhuh swee zohn nahnvahleedeetay* |
| I'm a housewife | Je suis femme au foyer<br>*jhuh swee fahm oa fwahyay* |
| Do you like your job? | Votre travail vous plaît?<br>*votr trahvahy voo pleh?* |

| Most of the time | Ça dépend |
| | *sah daypohn* |
| I prefer vacations | J'aime mieux les vacances |
| | *Jhehm myuh lay vahkohns* |

## .3 Starting/ending a conversation

| Could I ask you something? | Puis-je vous poser une question? |
| | *pwee jhuh voo poazay ewn kehstyawn?* |
| Excuse me | Excusez-moi |
| | *ehxkewsay mwah* |
| Excuse me, could you help me? | Pardon, pouvez-vous m'aider? |
| | *pahrdawn, poovay voo mayday?* |
| Yes, what's the problem? | Oui, qu'est-ce qui se passe? |
| | *wee, kehs kee suh pahss?* |
| What can I do for you? | Que puis-je faire pour vous? |
| | *kuh pwee jhuh fehr poor voo?* |
| Sorry, I don't have time now | Excusez-moi, je n'ai pas le temps maintenant |
| | *ehxkewzay mwah, jhuh nay pah luh tohn mahntuhnohn* |
| Do you have a light? | Vous avez du feu? |
| | *voo zahvay dew fuh?* |
| May I join you? | Puis-je m'asseoir à côté de vous? |
| | *pwee jhuh mahsswahr ah koatay duh voo?* |
| Could you take a picture of me/us? Press this button. | Voulez-vous me/nous prendre en photo? Appuyez sur ce bouton. |
| | *voolay voo muh/noo prohndr ohn foatoa? ahpweeyay sewr suh bootawn* |
| Leave me alone | Laissez-moi tranquille |
| | *laysay mwah trohnkeey* |
| Get lost | Fichez le camp |
| | *feeshay luh kohn* |
| Go away or I'll scream | Si vous ne partez pas, je crie |
| | *see voo nuh pahrtay pah, jhuh kree* |

## .4 Congratulations and condolences

| Happy birthday/many happy returns | Bon anniversaire/bonne fête |
| | *bohn nahnneevehrsehr/bon feht* |
| Please accept my condolences | Mes condoléances |
| | *may kawndolayohns* |
| I'm very sorry for you | Cela me peine beaucoup pour vous |
| | *suhlah muh pehn boakoo poor voo* |

## .5 A chat about the weather

***See also 1.5 The weather***

| It's so hot/cold today! | Qu'est-ce qu'il fait chaud/froid aujourd'hui! |
| | *kehs keel feh shoa/frwah oajhoordwee!* |
| Nice weather, isn't it? | Il fait beau, n'est-ce pas? |
| | *eel feh boa, nehs pah?* |
| What a wind/storm! | Quel vent/orage! |
| | *kehl vohn/orahjh!* |

| All that rain/snow! _____ | Quelle pluie/neige! |
| | *kehl plwee/nehjh!* |
| All that fog! _____ | Quel brouillard! |
| | *kehl brooy-yahr!* |
| Has the weather been _____ like this for long here? | Fait-il ce temps-là depuis longtemps? |
| | *feh teel suh tohn lah duhpwee lawntohn?* |
| Is it always this hot/cold ___ here? | Fait-il toujours aussi chaud/froid ici? |
| | *feh teel toojhoor oasee shoa/frwah eesee?* |
| Is it always this dry/wet ____ here? | Fait-il toujours aussi sec/humide ici? |
| | *feh teel toojhoor oasee sehk/ewmeed eesee?* |

 **.6 H**obbies

| Do you have any _____ hobbies? | Avez-vous des passe-temps? |
| | *ahvay voo day pahs tohn?* |
| I like painting/_____ reading/photography | J'aime peindre/lire/la photo |
| | *jhehm pahndr/leer/lah foatoa* |
| I like music _____ | J'aime la musique |
| | *jhehm lah mewzeek* |
| I like playing the _____ guitar/piano | J'aime jouer de la guitare/du piano |
| | *jhehm jhooay duh lah gueetahr/dew pyahnoa* |
| I like going to the _____ movies | J'aime aller au cinéma |
| | *jhehm ahlay oa seenaymah* |
| I like travelling/playing____ sports/fishing/walking | J'aime voyager/faire du sport/la pêche/me promener |
| | *jhehm vwahyahjhay/fehr dew spor/lah pehsh/ muh promuhnay* |

 **.7 B**eing the host(ess)

*See also 4 Eating out*

| Can I offer you a drink? ____ | Puis-je vous offrir quelque chose à boire? |
| | *pwee jhuh voo zofreer kehlkuh shoaz ah bwahr?* |
| What would you like _____ to drink? | Que désires-tu boire? |
| | *kuh dayzeer tew bwahr?* |
| Something non-_____ alcoholic, please. | De préférence quelque chose sans alcool |
| | *duh prayfayrohns kehlkuh shoaz sohn zahlkol* |
| Would you like a _____ cigarette/cigar? | Voulez-vous une cigarette/un cigare? |
| | *voolay voo zewn seegahreht/uhn seegahr?* |
| I don't smoke _____ | Je ne fume pas |
| | *jhuh nuh fewm pah* |

**.8 I**nvitations

| Are you doing anything____ tonight? | Faites-vous quelque chose ce soir? |
| | *feht voo kehlkuh shoaz suh swahr?* |
| Do you have any plans _____ for today/this afternoon/tonight? | Avez-vous déjà fait des projets pour aujourd'hui/cet après-midi/ce soir? |
| | *ahvay voo dayjhah feh day projheh poor oa-jhoordwee/seht ahpreh meedee/suh swahr?* |
| Would you like to go _____ out with me? | Voulez-vous sortir avec moi? |
| | *voolay voo sorteer ahvehk mwah?* |

29

| | |
|---|---|
| Would you like to go _____ dancing with me? | Voulez-vous aller danser avec moi? |
| | *voolay voo zahlay dohnsay ahvehk mwah?* |
| Would you like to have ____ lunch/dinner with me? | Voulez-vous déjeuner/dîner avec moi? |
| | *voolay voo dayjhuhnay/deenay ahvehk mwah?* |
| Would you like to come____ to the beach with me? | Voulez-vous aller à la plage avec moi? |
| | *voolay voo zahlay ah lah plahjh ahvehk mwah?* |
| Would you like to come____ into town with us? | Voulez-vous aller en ville avec nous? |
| | *voolay voo zahlay ohn veel ahvehk noo?* |
| Would you like to come____ and see some friends with us? | Voulez-vous aller chez des amis avec nous? |
| | *voolay voo zahlay shay day zahmee ahvehk noo?* |
| Shall we dance?_____ | On danse? |
| | *awn dohns?* |
| – sit at the bar? _____ | On va s'asseoir au bar? |
| | *awn vah saswahr oa bahr?* |
| – get something to drink? __ | On va boire quelque chose? |
| | *awn vah bwahr kehlkuh shoaz?* |
| – go for a walk/drive?_____ | On va marcher un peu/on va faire un tour en voiture? |
| | *awn vah mahrshay uhn puh/awn vah fehr uhn toor ohn vwahtewr?* |
| Yes, all right _____ | Oui, d'accord |
| | *wee, dahkor* |
| Good idea _____ | Bonne idée |
| | *bon eeday* |
| No (thank you) _____ | Non (merci) |
| | *nawn (mehrsee)* |
| Maybe later_____ | Peut-être tout à l'heure |
| | *puh tehtr too tah luhr* |
| I don't feel like it _____ | Je n'en ai pas envie |
| | *jhuh nohn nay pah zohnvee* |
| I don't have time _____ | Je n'ai pas le temps |
| | *jhuh nay pah luh tohn* |
| I already have a date _____ | J'ai déjà un autre rendez-vous |
| | *jhay dayjhah uhn noatr rohnday voo* |
| I'm not very good at_____ dancing/volleyball/ swimming | Je ne sais pas danser/jouer au volley/nager |
| | *jhuh nuh seh pah dohnsay/jhooay oa volay/nahjhay* |

### 3 .9 Paying a compliment

| | |
|---|---|
| You look wonderful! _____ | Vous avez l'air en pleine forme! |
| | *voo zahvay lehr ohn plehn form!* |
| I like your car! _____ | Quelle belle voiture! |
| | *kehl behl vwahtewr!* |
| I like your ski outfit! _____ | Quelle belle combinaison de ski! |
| | *kehl behl kawnbeenehzawn duh skee!* |
| You're a nice boy/girl _____ | Tu es un garçon/une fille sympathique |
| | *tew eh zuhn gahrsohn/ewn feey sahnpahteek* |
| What a sweet child! _____ | Quel adorable enfant! |
| | *kehl ahdorahbl ohnfohn!* |

| You're a wonderful _____ dancer! | Vous dansez très bien! |
| | *voo dohnsay treh byahn!* |
| You're a wonderful _____ cook! | Vous faites très bien la cuisine! |
| | *voo feht treh byahn lah kweezeen!* |
| You're a terrific soccer _____ player! | Vous jouez très bien au football! |
| | *voo jhooay treh byahn oa footbol!* |

## .10 Intimate comments/questions

| I like being with you _____ | J'aime bien être près de toi |
| | *jhehm byahn ehtr preh duh twah* |
| I've missed you so much___ | Tu m'as beaucoup manqué |
| | *tew mah boakoo mohnkay* |
| I dreamt about you _____ | J'ai rêvé de toi |
| | *jhay rehvay duh twah* |
| I think about you all day ___ | Je pense à toi toute la journée |
| | *jhuh pohns ah twah toot lah jhoornay* |
| You have such a sweet _____ smile | Tu souris si gentiment |
| | *tew sooree see jhohnteemohn* |
| You have such beautiful ___ eyes | Tu as de si jolis yeux |
| | *tew ah duh see jhoalee zyuh* |
| I'm in love with you _____ | Je suis amoureux/se de toi |
| | *jhuh swee zahmooruh(z) duh twah* |
| I'm in love with you too ___ | Moi aussi de toi |
| | *mwah oasee duh twah* |
| I love you_____ | Je t'aime |
| | *jhuh tehm* |
| I love you too _____ | Je t'aime aussi |
| | *jhuh tehm oasee* |
| I don't feel as strongly _____ about you | Je n'ai pas d'aussi forts sentiments pour toi |
| | *jhuh nay pah doasee for sohnteemohn poor twah* |
| I already have a _____ boyfriend/girlfriend | J'ai déjà un ami/une amie |
| | *jhay dayjhah uhn nahmee/ewn ahmee* |
| I'm not ready for that _____ | Je n'en suis pas encore là |
| | *jhuh nohn swee pah zohnkor lah* |
| This is going too fast _____ for me. | Ça va un peu trop vite |
| | *sah vah uhn puh troa veet* |
| Take your hands off me_____ | Ne me touche pas |
| | *nuh muh toosh pah* |
| Okay, no problem _____ | D'accord, pas de problème |
| | *dahkor, pah duh problehm* |
| Will you stay with me _____ tonight? | Tu restes avec moi cette nuit? |
| | *tew rehst ahvehk mwah seht nwee?* |
| I'd like to go to bed _____ with you | J'aimerais coucher avec toi |
| | *jhehmuhreh kooshay ahvehk twah* |
| Only if we use a_____ condom | Seulement en utilisant un préservatif |
| | *suhlmohn ohn newteeleezohn uhn prayzehrvahteef* |
| We have to be careful _____ about AIDS | Il faut être prudent à cause du sida |
| | *eel foa tehtr prewdohn ah koaz dew seedah* |
| That's what they all say_____ | Ils disent tous pareil |
| | *eel deez toos pahrehy* |
| We shouldn't take any _____ risks | Ne prenons aucun risque |
| | *nuh pruhnawn zoakuhn reesk* |

Conversation

| | |
|---|---|
| Do you have a condom? ___ | Tu as un préservatif? |
| | *tew ah zuhn prayzehrvahteef?* |
| No? In that case we _____ won't do it | Non? Alors je ne veux pas |
| | *nawn? ahlor jhuh nuh vuh pah* |

## .11 Arrangements

| | |
|---|---|
| When will I see _____ you again? | Quand est-ce que je te revois? |
| | *kohn tehs kuh jhuh tuh ruhvwah?* |
| Are you free over the _____ weekend? | Vous êtes/tu es libre ce week-end? |
| | *voozeht/tew eh leebr suh week-ehnd?* |
| What shall we do? _____ | Que décidons-nous? |
| | *kuh dayseedawn noo?* |
| Where shall we meet? _____ | Où nous retrouvons-nous? |
| | *oo noo ruhtroovawn noo?* |
| Will you pick me/us up? ___ | Vous venez me/nous chercher? |
| | *voo vuhnay muh/noo shehrshay?* |
| Shall I pick you up? _____ | Je viens vous/te chercher? |
| | *jhuh vyahn voo/tuh shehrshay?* |
| I have to be home by... ____ | Je dois être à la maison à...heures |
| | *jhuh dwah zehtr ah lah mehzawn ah...uhr* |

## .12 Saying good-bye

| | |
|---|---|
| I don't want to see _____ you anymore | Je ne veux plus vous revoir |
| | *jhuh nuh vuh plew voo ruhvwahr* |
| Can I take you home? _____ | Puis-je vous raccompagner à la maison? |
| | *pwee jhuh voo rahkawnpahnyay ah lah mehzawn?* |
| Can I write/call you? _____ | Puis-je vous écrire/téléphoner? |
| | *pwee jhuh voo zaykreer/taylayfonay?* |
| Will you write/call me? ___ | M'écrirez-vous/me téléphonerez-vous? |
| | *maykreeray voo/muh taylayfonuhray voo?* |
| Can I have your _____ address/phone number? | Puis-je avoir votre adresse/numéro de téléphone? |
| | *pwee jhavwahr votr ahdrehs/newmayroa duh taylayfon?* |
| Thanks for everything _____ | Merci pour tout |
| | *mehrsee poor too* |
| It was very nice _____ | C'était très agréable |
| | *sayteh treh zahgrayahbl* |
| Say hello to... _____ | Présentez mes amitiés à... |
| | *prayzohntay may zahmeetyay ah...* |
| Good luck _____ | Bonne chance |
| | *bon shohns* |
| When will you be back? ____ | Quand est-ce que tu reviens? |
| | *kohn tehs kuh tew ruhvyahn?* |
| I'll be waiting for you _____ | Je t'attendrai |
| | *jhuh tahtohndray* |
| I'd like to see you again ____ | Je voudrais te revoir |
| | *jhehvoodray tuh ruhvwahr* |
| I hope we meet _____ again soon | J'espère que nous nous reverrons bientôt |
| | *jjheh voodray kuh noo noo ruhvehrawn byahntoa* |
| You are welcome _____ | Vous êtes le/la bienvenu(e) |
| | *voozeht luh/lah byahnvuhnew* |

# Eating out

**4.1** On arrival                              34

**4.2** Ordering                                35

**4.3** The bill                                37

**4.4** Complaints                              38

**4.5** Paying a compliment                     39

**4.6** The menu                                39

**4.7** Alphabetical list of drinks
         and dishes                             39

 **E**ating out

● **In France** people usually have three meals:

1 *Le petit déjeuner* (breakfast) approx. between 7.30 and 10am. Breakfast is light and consists of café noir, *café au lait* (white coffee), or lemon tea, a croissant, or slices of baguette (French bread), with butter and jam.

2 *Le déjeuner* (lunch) approx. between midday and 2pm. Lunch always includes a hot dish and is the most important meal of the day. Offices and shops often close and lunch is taken at home, in a restaurant or canteen (in some factories and schools). It usually consists of four courses:

– starter
– main course
– cheese
– dessert

3 *Le dîner* (dinner) between 7.30 and 9pm. Dinner is a light hot meal, usually taken with the family.

At around 5pm, a special snack (*le goûter*) is served to children, usually a roll or slices of baguette and biscuits with some chocolate.

### 4.1 On arrival

| | |
|---|---|
| I'd like to reserve a table ___ for seven o'clock, please? | Puis-je réserver une table pour sept heures? |
| | *pwee jhuh rayzehrvay ewn tahbl poor seht uhr?* |
| I'd like a table for two, ____ please | Une table pour deux personnes s'il vous plaît |
| | *ewn tahbl poor duh pehrson seel voo pleh* |
| We've/we haven't _____ reserved | Nous (n')avons (pas) réservé |
| | *noo zahvawn/noo nahvawn pah rayzehrvay* |
| Is the restaurant open ____ yet? | Le restaurant est déjà ouvert? |
| | *luh rehstoarohn eh dayjhah oovehr?* |
| What time does the _____ restaurant open/close? | A quelle heure ouvre/ferme le restaurant? |
| | *ah kehl uhr oovr/fehrm luh rehstoarohn?* |
| Can we wait for a _____ table? | Pouvons-nous attendre qu'une table soit libre? |
| | *poovawn noo zahtohndr kewn tahbl swah leebr?* |
| Do we have to wait long? __ | Devons-nous attendre longtemps? |
| | *devawn noo zahtohndr lawntohn?* |

| | |
|---|---|
| Vous avez réservé?_____ | Do you have a reservation? |
| A quel nom?_____ | What name, please? |
| Par ici, s'il vous plaît._____ | This way, please |
| Cette table est réservée._____ | This table is reserved |
| Nous aurons une table de libre _____ dans un quart d'heure. | We'll have a table free in fifteen minutes. |
| Voulez-vous attendre (au bar)?_____ | Would you like to wait (at the bar)? |

| | |
|---|---|
| Is this seat taken? _____ | Est-ce que cette place est libre? |
| | *ehs kuh seht plahs eh leebr?* |
| Could we sit here/there? \_\_\_ | Pouvons-nous nous asseoir ici/là-bas? |
| | *poovawn noo noo zahswahr eesee/lahbah?* |
| Can we sit by the_____ window? | Pouvons-nous nous asseoir près de la fenêtre? |
| | *poovawn noo noo zahswahr preh duh lah fuhnehtr?* |
| Can we eat outside? _____ | Pouvons-nous aussi manger dehors? |
| | *poovawn noo zoasee mohnjhay duh-ohr?* |
| Do you have another \_\_\_\_\_ chair for us? | Avez-vous encore une chaise? |
| | *ahvay voo zohnkor ewn shehz?* |
| Do you have a highchair? \_\_ | Avez-vous une chaise haute? |
| | *ahvay voo zewn shehz oat?* |
| Is there a socket for \_\_\_\_\_ this bottle-warmer? | Y a-t-il une prise pour ce chauffe-biberon? |
| | *ee ya teel ewn preez poor suh shoaf beebuhrawn?* |
| Could you warm up _____ this bottle/jar for me? | Pouvez-vous me réchauffer ce biberon/ce petit pot? |
| | *poovay voo muh rayshoafay suh beebuhrawn/suh puhtee poa?* |
| Not too hot, please_____ | Pas trop chaud s'il vous plaît |
| | *pah troa shoa seel voo pleh* |
| Is there somewhere I \_\_\_\_\_ can change the baby's diaper? | Y a-t-il ici une pièce où je peux m'occuper du bébé? |
| | *ee ya teel eesee ewn pyehs oo jhuh puh mokewpay dew baybay?* |
| Where are the restrooms/\_\_ bathrooms? | Où sont les toilettes? |
| | *oo sawn lay twahleht?* |

## 4 .2 Ordering

| | |
|---|---|
| Waiter! _____ | Garçon! |
| | *gahrsawn!* |
| Madam! _____ | Madame! |
| | *mahdahm!* |
| Sir!_____ | Monsieur! |
| | *muhsyuh!* |
| We'd like something to \_\_\_ eat/a drink | Nous voulons manger/boire quelque chose |
| | *noo voolawn mohnjhay/bwahr kehlkuh shoaz* |
| Could I have a quick \_\_\_\_\_ meal? | Puis-je rapidement manger quelque chose? |
| | *pwee jhuh rahpeedmohn mohnjhay kehlkuh shoaz?* |
| We don't have much_____ time | Nous avons peu de temps |
| | *noo zavawn puh duh tohn* |
| We'd like to have a _____ drink first | Nous voulons d'abord boire quelque chose |
| | *noo voolawn dahbor bwahr kehlkuh shoaz* |
| Could we see the_____ menu/wine list, please? | Pouvons-nous avoir la carte/la carte des vins? |
| | *poovawn noo zahvwahr lah kahrt/lah kahrt day vahn?* |
| Do you have a menu \_\_\_\_\_ in English? | Vous avez un menu en anglais? |
| | *voo zahvay zuhn muhnew ohn nohngleh?* |

| | |
|---|---|
| Do you have a dish _____ of the day? | Vous avez un plat du jour? *voo zahvay zuhn plah dew jhoor?* |
| We haven't made a _____ choice yet | Nous n'avons pas encore choisi *noo nahvawn pah zohnkor shwahzee* |
| What do you _____ recommend? | Qu'est-ce que vous nous conseillez? *kehs kuh voo noo kawnsayay?* |
| What are the specialities _____ of the region/the house? | Quelles sont les spécialités de cette région/de la maison? *kehl sawn lay spaysyahleetay duh seht rayjhyawn/duh lah mehzawn?* |
| I like strawberries/olives _____ | J'aime les fraises/les olives *jhehm lay frehz/lay zoleev* |
| I don't like meat/fish/... _____ | Je n'aime pas la viande/le poisson/... *jhuh nehm pah lah vyohnd/luh pwahssawn/...* |
| What's this? _____ | Qu'est-ce que c'est? *kehs kuh seh?* |
| Does it have...in it? _____ | Y a-t-il du/de la/des...dedans? *ee ya teel dew/duh lah/day...duhdohn?* |
| What does it taste like? _____ | A quoi cela goute-t-il? *ah kwah suhlah goot teel?* |
| Is this a hot or a _____ cold dish? | Ce plat, est-il chaud ou froid? *suh plah, eh teel shoa oo frwah?* |
| Is this sweet? _____ | Ce plat, est-il sucré? *suh plah, eh teel sewkray?* |
| Is this spicy? _____ | Ce plat, est-il épicé? *suh plah, eh teel aypeesay?* |
| Do you have anything _____ else, please? | Vous avez peut-être autre chose? *voo zahvay puh tehtr oatr shoaz?* |
| I'm on a salt-free diet _____ | Le sel m'est interdit *luh sehl meh tahntehrdee* |
| I can't eat pork _____ | La viande de porc m'est interdite *lah vyohnd duh por meh tahntehrdeet* |
| – sugar _____ | Le sucre m'est interdit *luh sewkr meh tahntehrdee* |
| – fatty foods _____ | Le gras m'est interdit *luh grah meh tahntehrdee* |
| – (hot) spices _____ | Les épices (fortes) me sont interdites *lay zaypees (fort) muh sawn tahntehrdeet* |

| | |
|---|---|
| Vous désirez prendre un apéritif? _____ | Would you like a drink first? |
| Vous avez déjà fait votre choix? _____ | Have you decided? |
| Que désirez-vous boire? _____ | What would you like to drink? |
| Bon appétit _____ | Enjoy your meal |
| Vous désirez votre viande saignante, _____ à point ou bien cuite? | Would you like your steak rare, medium or well done? |
| Vous désirez un dessert/du café? _____ | Would you like a dessert/coffee? |

| | |
|---|---|
| I'll have what those _____ people are having | J'aimerais la même chose que ces personnes-là |
| | *jhehmuhreh lah mehm shoaz kuh say pehrson lah* |
| I'd like... _____ | Je veux... |
| | *jheh veh...* |
| We're not having a _____ starter | Nous ne prenons pas d'entrée |
| | *noo nuh pruhnawn pah dohntray* |
| The child will share _____ what we're having | L'enfant partagera notre menu |
| | *lohnfohn pahrtahjhuhrah notr muhnew* |
| Could I have some _____ more bread, please? | Encore du pain s'il vous plaît |
| | *ohnkor dew pahn seel voo pleh* |
| – a bottle of water/wine ____ | Une autre bouteille d'eau/de vin |
| | *ewn oatr bootehy doa/duh vahn* |
| – another helping of... ____ | Une autre portion de... |
| | *ewn oatr porsyawn duh...* |
| – some salt and pepper ____ | Pouvez-vous apporter du sel et du poivre? |
| | *poovay voo zahportay dew sehl ay dew pwahvr?* |
| – a napkin _____ | Pouvez-vous apporter une serviette? |
| | *poovay voo zahportay ewn sehrvyeht?* |
| – a spoon _____ | Pouvez-vous apporter une cuillère? |
| | *poovay voo zahportay ewn kweeyehr?* |
| – an ashtray _____ | Pouvez-vous apporter un cendrier? |
| | *poovay voo zahportay uhn sohndryay?* |
| – some matches _____ | Pouvez-vous apporter des allumettes? |
| | *poovay voo zahportay day zahlewmeht?* |
| – some toothpicks _____ | Pouvez-vous apporter des cure-dents? |
| | *poovay voo zahportay day kewr dohn?* |
| – a glass of water _____ | Pouvez-vous apporter un verre d'eau? |
| | *poovay voo zahportay uhn vehr doa?* |
| – a straw (for the child) ____ | Pouvez-vous apporter une paille (pour l'enfant)? |
| | *poovay voo zahportay ewn paheey (poor lohnfohn)?* |
| Enjoy your meal! _____ | Bon appétit! |
| | *bohn nahpaytee!* |
| You too! _____ | De même vous aussi |
| | *duh mehm voo zoasee* |
| Cheers! _____ | Santé! |
| | *sohntay!* |
| The next round's on me ___ | La prochaine tournée est pour moi |
| | *lah proshehn toornay eh poor mwah* |
| Could we have a doggy ___ bag, please? | Pouvons-nous emporter les restes pour notre chien? |
| | *poovawn noo zohnportay lay rehst poor notr shyahn?* |

## 4 .3 The bill

*See also 8.2 Settling the bill*

| | |
|---|---|
| How much is this dish? ____ | Quel est le prix de ce plat? |
| | *kehl eh luh pree duh suh plah?* |
| Could I have the bill, _____ please? | L'addition s'il vous plaît |
| | *lahdeesyawn seel voo pleh* |

| All together _____ | Tout ensemble |
| | *too tohnsohnbl* |
| Everyone pays separately __ | Chacun paye pour soi |
| | *shahkuhn pehy poor swah* |
| Could we have the menu __ again, please? | Pouvons-nous revoir la carte? |
| | *poovawn noo ruhvwahr lah kahrt?* |
| The...is not on the bill _____ | Le...n'est pas sur l'addition |
| | *luh...neh pah sewr lahdeesyawn* |

## .4 Complaints

| It's taking a very _____ long time | C'est bien long |
| | *seh byahn lawn* |
| We've been here an _____ hour already. | Nous sommes ici depuis une heure |
| | *noo som zeesee duhpwee zewn uhr* |
| This must be a mistake ____ | Cela doit être une erreur |
| | *suhlah dwah tehtr ewn ehruhr* |
| This is not what I _____ ordered. | Ce n'est pas ce que j'ai commandé |
| | *suh neh pah suh kuh jhay komohnday* |
| I ordered... _____ | J'ai commandé un... |
| | *jhay komohnday uhn...* |
| There's a dish missing _____ | Il manque un plat |
| | *eel mohnk uhn plah* |
| This is broken/not clean ___ | C'est cassé/ce n'est pas propre |
| | *seh kahssay/suh neh pah propr* |
| The food's cold _____ | Le plat est froid |
| | *luh plah eh frwah* |
| – not fresh _____ | Le plat n'est pas frais |
| | *luh plah neh pah freh* |
| – too salty/sweet/spicy _____ | Le plat est trop salé/sucré/épicé |
| | *luh plah eh troa sahlay/sewkray/aypeesay* |
| The meat's not done _____ | La viande n'est pas cuite |
| | *lah vyohnd neh pah kweet* |
| – overdone _____ | La viande est trop cuite |
| | *lah vyohnd eh troa kweet* |
| – tough _____ | La viande est dure |
| | *lah vyohnd eh dewr* |
| – off _____ | La viande est avariée |
| | *lah vyohnd eh tahvahryay* |
| Could I have something __ else instead of this? | Vous pouvez me donner autre chose à la place? |
| | *voo poovay muh donay oatr shoaz ah lah plahs?* |
| The bill/this amount is _____ not right | L'addition/cette somme n'est pas exacte |
| | *lahdeesyawn/seht som neh pah zehgzahkt* |
| We didn't have this _____ | Ceci nous ne l'avons pas eu |
| | *suhsee noo nuh lahvawn pah zew* |
| There's no toilet paper in __ the restroom | Il n'y a plus de papier hygiénique dans les toilettes |
| | *eel nee yah plew duh pahpyay eejhyayneek dohn lay twahleht* |
| Do you have a _____ complaints book? | Avez-vous un registre de réclamations? |
| | *ahvay voo zuhn ruhjheestr duh rayklahmahsyawn?* |
| Will you call the _____ manager, please? | Voulez-vous appeler le directeur s'il vous plaît? |
| | *voolay voo zahpuhlay luh deerehktuhr seel voo pleh?* |

## 4.5 Paying a compliment

| | |
|---|---|
| That was a wonderful _____ meal | Nous avons très bien mangé |
| | _noo zahvawn treh byahn mohnjhay_ |
| The food was excellent _____ | Le repas était succulent |
| | _luh ruhpah ayteh sewkewlohn_ |
| The...in particular was _____ delicious | Le...surtout était délicieux |
| | _luh...sewrtoo ayteh dayleesyuh_ |

## 4.6 The menu

| | | |
|---|---|---|
| apéritifs | gibier | plat principal |
| **aperitifs** | **game** | **main course** |
| boissons alcoolisées | hors d'oeuvres | potages |
| **alcoholic beverages** | **starters** | **soups** |
| boissons chaudes | légumes | service compris |
| **hot beverages** | **vegetables** | **tip included** |
| carte des vins | plats chauds | spécialités |
| **wine list** | **hot dishes** | régionales |
| coquillages | plats froids | **regional specialities** |
| **shellfish** | **cold dishes** | viandes |
| desserts | plat du jour | **meat dishes** |
| **sweets** | **dish of the day** | volailles |
| fromages | pâtisserie | **poultry** |
| **cheese** | **pastry** | |

## 4.7 Alphabetical list of drinks and dishes

| | | |
|---|---|---|
| agneau | beurre | caille |
| **lamb** | **butter** | **quail** |
| ail | biftec | calmar |
| **garlic** | **steak** | **squid** |
| amandes | bière (bière | canard |
| **almonds** | pression) | **duck** |
| ananas | **beer (draught beer)** | câpres |
| **pineapple** | biscuit | **capers** |
| anchois | **biscuit** | carpe |
| **anchovy** | boeuf | **carp** |
| anguille | **beef** | carte des vins |
| **eel** | boissons alcoolisées | **wine list** |
| anis | **alcoholic beverages** | céleri |
| **aniseed** | boissons chaudes/ | **celery** |
| apéritif | froides | cerises |
| **aperitif** | **hot/cold beverages** | **cherries** |
| artichaut | boudin noir | champignons |
| **artichoke** | **black sausage pudding** | **mushrooms** |
| asperge | brochet | crème chantilly |
| **asparagus** | **pike** | **cream (whipped)** |
| baguette | cabillaud | châtaigne |
| **french bread** | **cod** | **chestnut** |
| banane | café (noir/au lait) | chausson aux |
| **banana** | **coffee (black/white)** | pommes |
| | | **apple turnover** |

Eating out

chou-fleur
cauliflower
choucroute
sauerkraut
chou
cabbage
choux de Bruxelles
Brussels sprouts
citron
lemon
civet de lièvre
jugged hare
clou de girofle
clove
cocktails
cocktails
cognac
brandy
concombre
cucumber
confiture
jam
consommé
broth
coquillages
shellfish
coquilles
  Saint-Jacques
scallops
cornichon
gherkin
côte/côtelette
chop
côte de boeuf
T-bone steak
côte de porc
pork chop
côtelette d'agneau
lamb chop
côtelettes dans
  l'échine
spare rib
couvert
cutlery
crabe
crab
crêpes
pancakes
crevettes grises
shrimps
crevettes roses
prawns
croissant
croissant

croque monsieur
grilled ham and
  cheese sandwich
cru
raw
crustacés
seafood
cuisses de
  grenouilles
frog's legs
cuit(à l'eau)
boiled
dattes
dates
daurade
sea bream
dessert
dessert
eau minérale
  gazeuse/non
  gazeuse
sparkling/still
  mineral water
échalote
shallot
écrevisse
crayfish
endives
chicory
entrecôte
sirloin steak
entrées
first course
épices
spices
épinards
spinach
escargots
snails
farine
flour
fenouil
fennel
fèves
broad beans
figues
figs
filet de boeuf
fillet
filet mignon
fillet steak
filet de porc
pork tenderloin

fines herbes
herbs
foie gras
goose liver
fraises
strawberries
framboises
raspberries
frit
fried
friture
deep-fried
fromage
cheese
fruit de la passion
passion fruit
fruits de la saison
seasonal fruits
gaufres
waffles
gigot d'agneau
leg of lamb
glace
ice cream
glaçons
ice cubes
grillé
grilled
groseilles
red currants
hareng
herring
haricots blancs
haricot beans
haricots verts
french beans
homard
lobster
hors d'oeuvre
starters
huîtres
oysters
jambon
  blanc/cru/fumé
ham(cooked/Parma
  style/smoked)
jus de citron
lemon juice
jus de fruits
fruit juice
jus d'orange
orange juice

lait/écrémé/
  entier
**milk/skimmed/
  whole**
langouste
**crayfish**
langoustine
**scampi**
langue
**tongue**
lapin
**rabbit**
légumes
**vegetables**
lentilles
**lentils**
liqueur
**liqueur**
lotte
**monkfish**
loup de mer
**sea bass**
macaron
**macaroon**
maïs
**sweetcorn**
épis de maïs
**corn (on the cob)**
marron
**chestnut**
melon
**melon**
menu du jour/à la
  carte
**menu of the day/à la
  carte**
morilles
**morels**
moules
**mussels**
mousse au chocolat
**chocolate mousse**
moutarde
**mustard**
myrtilles
**bilberries**
noisette
**hazelnut**
noix
**walnut**
noix de veau
**fillet of veal**
oeuf à la
  coque/dur/au plat
**egg soft/hard
  boiled/fried**

oignon
**onion**
olives
**olives**
omelette
**omelette**
origan
**oregano**
pain au chocolat
**chocolate bun**
part
**portion**
pastis
**pastis**
pâtisserie
**pastry**
pêche
**peach**
petite friture
**fried fish(whitebait
  or similar)**
petits (biscuits) salés
**saltines (crackers)**
petit pain
**roll**
petits pois
**green peas**
pigeon
**pigeon**
pintade
**guinea fowl**
plat du jour
**dish of the day**
plats froids/chauds
**cold/hot courses**
poire
**pear**
pois chiches
**chick peas**
poisson
**fish**
poivre
**pepper**
poivron
**green/red pepper**
pomme
**apple**
pommes de terre
**potatoes**
pommes frites
**French fries (or fried
  potatoes)**
poulet(blanc)
**chicken(breast)**
prune
**plum**

pruneaux
**prunes**
queue de boeuf
**oxtail**
ragoût
**stew**
ris de veau
**sweetbread**
riz
**rice**
rôti de boeuf (rosbif)
**roast beef**
rouget
**red mullet**
saignant
**rare**
salade verte
**lettuce**
salé/sucré
**salted/sweet**
sandwich
**sandwich**
saumon
**salmon**
sel
**salt**
service compris/non
  compris
**tip (not) included**
sole
**sole**
soupe
**soup**
soupe à l'oignon
**onion soup**
spécialités
  régionales
**regional specialities**
sucre
**sugar**
thon
**tuna**
thym
**thyme**
tripes
**tripe**
truffes
**truffles**
truite
**trout**
truite saumonée
**salmon trout**
turbot
**turbot**
vapeur (à la)
**steamed**

| | | |
|---|---|---|
| venaison | vin rosé | xérès |
| **venison** | **rosé wine** | **sherry** |
| viande hachée | vin rouge | |
| **ground meat** | **red wine** | |
| vin blanc | vinaigre | |
| **white wine** | **vinegar** | |

**4**

**Eating out**

# **O**n the road

| | | |
|---|---|---|
| **5.1** | **A**sking for directions | 44 |
| **5.2** | **C**ustoms | 45 |
| **5.3** | **L**uggage | 46 |
| **5.4** | **T**raffic signs | 47 |
| **5.5** | **T**he car | 48 |
| | *The parts of a car* | *50–51* |
| **5.6** | **T**he gas station | 48 |
| **5.7** | **B**reakdown and repairs | 49 |
| **5.8** | **T**he bicycle/moped | 52 |
| | *The parts of a bicycle* | *54–55* |
| **5.9** | **R**enting a vehicle | 53 |
| **5.10** | **H**itchhiking | 56 |

## **5** **O**n the road

### **5** .1 **A**sking for directions

| | |
|---|---|
| Excuse me, could I ask you something? | Pardon, puis-je vous demander quelque chose? |
| | *pahrdawn, pwee jhuh voo duhmohnday kehlkuh shoaz?* |
| I've lost my way | Je me suis égaré(e) |
| | *jhuh muh swee zaygahray* |
| Is there a(n)... around here? | Connaissez-vous un...dans les environs? |
| | *konehssay voo zuhn... dohn lay zohnveerawn?* |
| Is this the way to...? | Est-ce la route vers...? |
| | *ehs lah root vehr...?* |
| Could you tell me how to get to...? | Pouvez-vous me dire comment aller à...? |
| | *poovay voo muh deer komohn tahlay ah...?* |
| What's the quickest way to...? | Comment puis-je arriver le plus vite possible à...? |
| | *komohn pwee jhuh ahreevay luh plew veet pohseebl ah...?* |
| How many kilometers is it to...? | Il y a encore combien de kilomètres jusqu'à...? |
| | *eel ee yah ohnkor kohnbyahn duh keeloamehtr jhewskah...?* |
| Could you point it out on the map? | Pouvez-vous me l'indiquer sur la carte? |
| | *poovay voo muh lahndeekay sewr lah kahrt?* |

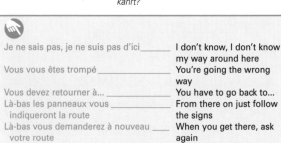

| | |
|---|---|
| Je ne sais pas, je ne suis pas d'ici | I don't know, I don't know my way around here |
| Vous vous êtes trompé | You're going the wrong way |
| Vous devez retourner à... | You have to go back to... |
| Là-bas les panneaux vous indiqueront la route | From there on just follow the signs |
| Là-bas vous demanderez à nouveau votre route | When you get there, ask again |

| | | |
|---|---|---|
| tout droit | le carrefour | l'immeuble |
| **straight ahead** | **the intersection** | **the building** |
| à gauche | la rue | à l'angle, au coin |
| **left** | **the street** | **at the corner** |
| à droite | le feu (de signalisation) | la rivière, le fleuve |
| **right** | | **the river** |
| tourner | **the traffic light** | l'autopont |
| **turn** | le tunnel | **the overpass** |
| suivre | **the tunnel** | le pont |
| **follow** | le panneau `cédez la priorité' | **the bridge** |
| traverser | | le passage à niveau |
| **cross** | **the yield sign** | **the grade crossing** |

| la barrière | le panneau direction... | la flèche |
|---|---|---|
| **barrier** | **the sign pointing to...** | **the arrow** |

## .2 Customs

● **Border documents** (France, Belgium, Luxembourg): valid passport, visa. For car and motorbike: valid US driving licence and registration document, insurance document, green card, US registration plate. Trailer/Motorhome: must be entered on the green card and driven with the same registration number. A warning cone, headlight convertors and extra headlight bulbs must be carried. Insurance should also be upgraded.

Import and export specifications:

– Foreign currency: no restrictions

– Alcohol (aged 17 and above): 10 litres of spirits and 90 litres of wine.

– Tobacco (aged 17 and above): 800 cigarettes, 200 cigars or a kilo of tobacco. Restricted to personal consumption only.

| | |
|---|---|
| Votre passeport s'il vous plaît _____ | Your passport, please |
| La carte verte s'il vous plaît _____ | Your green card, please |
| La carte grise s'il vous plaît _____ | Your vehicle documents, please |
| Votre visa s'il vous plaît _____ | Your visa, please |
| Où allez-vous? _____ | Where are you heading? |
| Combien de temps pensez-vous _____ rester? | How long are you planning to stay? |
| Avez-vous quelque chose à déclarer? ____ | Do you have anything to declare? |
| Voulez-vous l'ouvrir? _____ | Open this, please |

| | |
|---|---|
| My children are entered ___ on this passport | Mes enfants sont inscrits dans ce passeport |
| | *may zohnfohn sawn tahnskree dohn suh pahspor* |
| I'm travelling through _____ | Je suis de passage |
| | *jhuh swee duh pahsahjh* |
| I'm going on vacation to... _ | Je vais en vacances en... |
| | *jhuh veh zohn vahkohns ohn...* |
| I'm on a business trip _____ | Je suis en voyage d'affaires |
| | *jhuh swee zohn vvahyahjh dahfehr* |
| I don't know how long_____ I'll be staying yet | Je ne sais pas encore combien de temps je reste |
| | *jhuh nuh seh pah zohnkor kawnbyahn duh tohn jhuh rehst* |
| I'll be staying here for _____ a weekend | Je reste un week-end ici |
| | *jhuh rehst uhn weekehnd eesee* |
| – for a few days _____ | Je reste quelques jours ici |
| | *jhuh rehst kehlkuh jhoor eesee* |
| – for a week_____ | Je reste une semaine ici |
| | *jhuh rehst ewn suhmehn eesee* |

On the road

| | |
|---|---|
| –for two weeks | Je reste quinze jours ici |
| | *jhuh rehst kahnz jhoor eesee* |
| I've got nothing to declare | Je n'ai rien à déclarer |
| | *jhuh nay ryahn nah dayklahray* |
| I've got...with me | J'ai... avec moi |
| | *jhay... ahvehk mwah* |
| – ...cartons of cigarettes | J'ai des cartouches de cigarettes |
| | *jhay day kahrtoosh duh seegahreht* |
| – ...bottles of... | J'ai des bouteilles de... |
| | *jhay day bootehy duh...* |
| – some souvenirs | J'ai quelques souvenirs |
| | *jhay kehlkuh soovneer* |
| These are personal effects | Ce sont des affaires personnelles |
| | *suh sawn day zahfehr pehrsonehl* |
| These are not new | Ces affaires ne sont pas neuves |
| | *say zahfehr nuh sawn pah nuhv* |
| Here's the receipt | Voici la facture |
| | *vwahsee lah fahktewr* |
| This is for private use | C'est pour usage personnel |
| | *seh poor ewzahjh pehrsonehl* |
| How much import duty do I have to pay? | Combien de droits d'importation dois-je payer? |
| | *kawnbyahn duh drwah dahnpohrtasyawn dwah jhuh payay?* |
| Can I go now? | Puis-je partir maintenant? |
| | *pwee jhuh pahrteer mahntuhnohn?* |

## 5 .3 Luggage

| | |
|---|---|
| Porter! | Porteur! |
| | *portuhr!* |
| Could you take this luggage to...? | Voulez-vous porter ces bagages à... s'il vous plaît? |
| | *voolay voo portay say bahgahjh ah... seel voo pleh?* |
| How much do I owe you? | Combien vous dois-je? |
| | *kawnbyahn voo dwah jhuh?* |
| Where can I find a luggage cart? | Où puis-je trouver un chariot pour les bagages? |
| | *oo pwee jhuh troovay uhn shahryoa poor lay bahgahjh?* |
| Could you store this luggage for me? | Puis-je mettre ces bagages en consigne? |
| | *pwee jhuh mehtr say bahgahjh ohn kawnseenyuh?* |
| Where are the luggage lockers? | Où est la consigne automatique? |
| | *oo eh lah kawnseenyuh oatoamahteek?* |
| I can't get the locker open | Je n'arrive pas à ouvrir la consigne |
| | *jhuh nahreev pah zah oovreer lah kawnseenyuh* |
| How much is it per item per day? | Combien cela coûte-t-il par bagage par jour? |
| | *kawnbyahn suhlah koot-uh teel pahr bahgahjh pahr jhoor?* |
| This is not my bag/ suitcase | Ce n'est pas mon sac/ma valise |
| | *suh neh pah mawn sahk/mah vahleez* |

| There's one item/bag/_____ | Il manque encore une chose/un sac/une |
| suitcase missing still | valise |
| | *eel mohnk ohnkor ewn shoaz/uhn sahk/ewn* |
| | *vahleez* |
| My suitcase is damaged ___ | Ma valise est abîmée |
| | *mah vahleez eh tahbeemay* |

 **.4 Traffic signs**

| | | |
|---|---|---|
| accès interdit à tous les véhicules | déviation | sens unique |
| **no entry** | **detour** | **one-way traffic** |
| accotement non stabilisé | fin de... | serrez à droite |
| **soft shoulder** | **end of...** | **keep right** |
| allumez vos feux | fin d'allumage des feux | sortie |
| **turn on lights** | **end of need for lights** | **exit** |
| autoroute | | sortie de camions |
| **motorway** | | **trucks exit** |
| barrière de dégel | fin de chantier | interdiction de stationner |
| **road closed** | **end of road works** | **no parking** |
| bison fûté | interdiction de dépasser | taxis |
| **recommended route** | **no passing** | **taxis** |
| brouillard fréquent | interdiction de klaxonner | travaux (sur...km) |
| **beware fog** | **do not blow horn** | **roadwork ahead** |
| cédez le passage | interdiction sauf riverains | véhicules lents |
| **yield** | **access only** | **slow traffic** |
| chaussée à gravillons | limite de vitesse | véhicules transportant des matières dangereuses |
| **loose gravel** | **speed limit** | **vehicles transporting dangerous substances** |
| chaussée déformée | passage à niveau | |
| **uneven road surface** | **grade crossing** | |
| chaussée glissante | passage d'animaux | verglas fréquent |
| **slippery road** | **animals crossing** | **ice on road** |
| circulation alternée | passage pour piétons | virages sur...km |
| **alternate route** | **pedestrian crossing** | **winding road for...km** |
| danger | péage | vitesse limite |
| **danger** | **toll** | **maximum speed** |
| carrefour dangereux | poids lourds | zone bleue |
| **dangerous crossing** | **heavy trucks** | **parking permit required** |
| priorité à droite | rappel | zone piétonne |
| **priority to vehicles from right** | **reminder** | **pedestrian zone** |
| descente dangereuse | remorques et semi-remorques | |
| **steep hill** | **trucks and semis** | |

**On the road**

47

**.5 T**he car

*See the diagram on page 51.*

● **Particular traffic regulations:**
– maximum speed for cars:
  130km/h on toll roads
  110km/h on other motorways
  90km/h outside town centers
  60km/h in town centers
– yield: all traffic from the right has the right of way, including slow
vehicles, except for major roads.

 **.6 T**he gas station

| How many kilometers to ___ the next gas station, please? | Il y a combien de kilomètres jusqu'à la prochaine station-service? |
| | *eel ee yah kawnbyahn duh keeloamehtr jhewskah lah proshehn stasyawn sehrvees?* |
| I would like...liters of..., ___ please | Je voudrais ... litres |
| | *jhuh voodreh ... leetr* |
| – 4-star ___ | Je voudrais ... litres de super |
| | *jhuh voodreh ... leetr duh sewpehr* |
| – leaded ___ | Je voudrais ... litres d'essence ordinaire |
| | *jhuh voodreh ... leetr dehssohns ohrdeenehr* |
| – unleaded ___ | Je voudrais ... litres d'essence sans plomb |
| | *jhuh voodreh ... leetr dehssohns sohn plawn* |
| – diesel ___ | Je voudrais ... litres de gazoil |
| | *jhuh voodreh ... leetr duh gahzwahl* |
| I would like...francs ___ worth of gas, please. | Je voudrais pour ... francs d'essence s'il vous plaît |
| | *jhuh voodreh poor ... frohn dehssohns seel voo pleh* |
| Fill it up, please ___ | Le plein s'il vous plaît |
| | *luh plahn seel voo pleh* |
| Could you check...? ___ | Vous voulez contrôler...? |
| | *voo voolay kawntroalay...?* |
| – the oil level ___ | Vous voulez contrôler le niveau d'huile? |
| | *voo voolay kawntroalay luh neevoa dweel?* |
| – the tire pressure ___ | Vous voulez contrôler la pression des pneus? |
| | *voo voolay kawntroalay lah prehsyawn day pnuh?* |
| Could you change the ___ oil, please? | Vous pouvez changer l'huile? |
| | *voo poovay shohnjhay lweel?* |
| Could you clean the ___ windows/the windshield, please? | Vous pouvez nettoyer les vitres/le pare-brise? |
| | *voo poovay nehtwahyay lay veetr/luh pahrbreez?* |
| Could you wash the car, ___ please? | Vous pouvez faire laver la voiture? |
| | *voo poovay fehr lahvay lah vwahtewr?* |

| | |
|---|---|
| I'm having car trouble. Could you give me a hand? | Je suis en panne. Vous pouvez m'aider? *jhuh swee zohn pahnn. voo poovay mayday?* |
| I've run out of gas | Je n'ai plus d'essence *jhuh neh plew dehssohns* |
| I've locked the keys in the car | J'ai laissé les clefs dans la voiture fermée *jhay layssay lay klay dohn lah vwahtewr fehrmay* |
| The car/motorcycle/ moped won't start | La voiture/la moto/le vélomoteur ne démarre pas *lah vwahtewr/lah moatoa/luh vayloamotuhr nuh daymahr pah* |
| Could you contact the road service for me, please? | Vous pouvez m'appeler l'assistance routière? *voo poovay mahpuhlay lahseestohns rootyehr?* |
| Could you call a garage for me, please? | Vous pouvez m'appeler un garage? *voo poovay mahpuhlay uhn gahrahjh?* |
| Could you give me a lift to...? | Puis-je aller avec vous jusqu'à ...? *pwee jhahlay ahvehk voo jhewskah ...?* |
| – a garage/into town? | Puis-je aller avec vous jusqu'à un garage/la ville? *pwee jhahlay ahvehk voo jhewskah uhn gahrahjh/lah veel?* |
| – a phone booth? | Puis-je aller avec vous jusqu'à une cabine téléphonique? *pwee jhahlay ahvehk voo jhewskah ewn kahbeen taylayfoneek?* |
| – an emergency phone? | Puis-je aller avec vous jusqu'à un téléphone d'urgence? *pwee jhalay ahvehk voo jhewskah uhn taylayfon dewrjhohns?* |
| Can we take my bicycle/moped? | Est-ce que vous pouvez également prendre mon vélo(moteur)? *ehs kuh voo poovay aygahlmohn prohndr mawn vayloa(motuhr)?* |
| Could you tow me to a garage? | Vous pouvez me remorquer jusqu'à un garage? *voo poovay muh ruhmorkay jhewskah uhn gahrahjh?* |
| There's probably something wrong with...(See page 50) | Le ... a certainement quelque chose de défectueux *luh ... ah sehrtehnemohn kehlkuh shoaz duh dayfehktewuh* |
| Can you fix it? | Vous pouvez le réparer? *voo poovay luh raypahray?* |
| Could you fix my tire? | Vous pouvez réparer mon pneu? *voo poovay raypahray mawn pnuh?* |
| Could you change this wheel? | Vous pouvez changer cette roue? *voo poovay shohnjhay seht roo?* |
| Can you fix it so it'll get me to...? | Vous pouvez le réparer pour que je puisse rouler jusqu'à...? *voo poovay luh raypahray poor kuh jhuh pwees roolay jhewskah...?* |

## The parts of a car
(the diagram shows the numbered parts)

| | | | |
|---|---|---|---|
| 1 | battery | la batterie | *lah bahtree* |
| 2 | rear light | le feu arrière | *luh fuh ahryehr* |
| 3 | rear-view mirror | le rétroviseur | *luh raytroaveezuhr* |
| | backup light | le phare de recul | *luh fahr duh ruhkewl* |
| 4 | aerial | l'antenne(f.) | *lohntehn* |
| | car radio | l'autoradio(m.) | *loatoarahdyoa* |
| 5 | gas tank | le réservoir d'essence | *luh rayzehrvwahr dehssohns* |
| | inside mirror | le rétroviseur intérieur | *luh raytroaveezuhr ahntayryuhr* |
| 6 | spark plugs | les bougies(f.) | *lay boojhee* |
| | fuel filter/pump | le filtre à carburant | *luh feeltr ah kahrbewrohn* |
| | | la pompe à carburant | *lah pawnp ah kahrbewrohn* |
| 7 | side mirror | le rétroviseur de côté | *luh raytroaveezuhr duh koatay* |
| 8 | bumper | le pare-chocs | *luh pahr shok* |
| | carburetor | le carburateur | *luh kahrbewrahtuhr* |
| | crankcase | le carter | *luh kahrtehr* |
| | cylinder | le cylindre | *luh seelahndr* |
| | ignition | l'allumage | *l'ahlewmahjh* |
| | warning light | la lampe témoin | *lah lohnp taymwahn* |
| | generator | la dynamo | *lah deenahmoa* |
| | accelerator | l'accélérateur | *lahksaylayrahtuhr* |
| | handbrake | le frein à main | *luh frahn ah mahn* |
| | valve | la soupape | *lah soopahp* |
| 9 | muffler | le silencieux | *luh seelohnsyuh* |
| 10 | trunk | le coffre | *luh kofr* |
| 11 | headlight | le phare | *luh fahr* |
| | crank shaft | le vilebrequin | *luh veelbruhkahn* |
| 12 | air filter | le filtre à air | *luh feeltr ah ehr* |
| | fog lamp | le phare anti-brouillard | *luh fahr ohntee brooy-yahr* |
| 13 | engine block | le bloc moteur | *luh blok motuhr* |
| | camshaft | l'arbre à cames | *lahrbr ah kahm* |
| | oil filter/pump | le filtre à huile | *luh feeltr ah weel* |
| | | la pompe à huile | *lah pawnp ah weel* |
| | dipstick | la jauge du niveau d'huile | *lah jhoajh dew neevoa dweel* |
| | pedal | la pédale | *lah paydahl* |
| 14 | door | la portière | *lah portyehr* |
| 15 | radiator | le radiateur | *luh rahdyahtuhr* |
| 16 | disc brake | le frein à disque | *luh frahn ah deesk* |
| | spare wheel | la roue de secours | *lah roo duh suhkoor* |
| 17 | indicator | le clignotant | *luh kleenyohtohn* |
| 18 | windshield wiper | l'essuie-glace(m.) | *lehswee glahs* |
| 19 | shock absorbers | les amortisseurs(m.) | *lay zahmorteesuhr* |
| | sunroof | le toit ouvrant | *luh twah oovrohn* |
| | starter motor | le démarreur | *luh daymahruhr* |
| 20 | steering column | la colonne de direction | *lah kolon duh deerehksyawn* |
| | steering wheel | le volant | *luh volohn* |

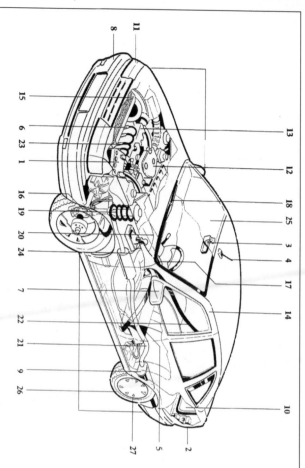

| 21 | exhaust pipe | le tuyau d'échappement | *luh tweeyoa dayshahpmohn* |
| 22 | seat belt | la ceinture de sécurité | *lah sahntewr duh saykewreetay* |
| | fan | le ventilateur | *luh vohnteelahtuhr* |
| 23 | distributor cable | le câble distributeur | *luh kahbl deestreebewtuhr* |
| 24 | gear shift | le levier de vitesses | *luh luhvyay duh veetehs* |
| 25 | windshield | le pare-brise | *luh pahrbreez* |
| | water pump | la pompe à eau | *lah pawnp ah oa* |
| 26 | wheel | la roue | *lah roo* |
| 27 | hubcap | l'enjoliveur | *lohnjholeevuhr* |
| | piston | le piston | *luh peestawn* |

| Which garage can _____ help me? | Quel garage pourrait m'aider? |
| | *kehl gahrahjh pooreh mayday?* |
| When will my car/bicycle __ be ready? | Quand est-ce que ma voiture/ma bicyclette sera prête? |
| | *kohn tehs kuh mah vvwahtewr/mah beeseekleht suhrah preht?* |
| Can I wait for it here? _____ | Je peux l'attendre ici? |
| | *jhuh puh lahtohndr eesee?* |
| How much will it cost? _____ | Combien cela va coûter? |
| | *kawnbyahn suhlah vah kootay?* |
| Could you itemize _____ the bill? | Vous pouvez me détailler la note? |
| | *voo poovay muh daytahyay lah not?* |
| Can I have a receipt for _____ the insurance? | Puis-je avoir un reçu pour l'assurance? |
| | *pwee jhahvvwahr uhn ruhsew poor lahsewrohns?* |

## 5 .8 The bicycle/moped

*See the diagram on page 55.*

● **Bicycle paths** are rare in France. Bikes can be hired at tourist centers (*vélo tout terrain* = mountain bike). Not much consideration for bikes should be expected on the roads. The maximum speed for mopeds is 45km/h both inside and outside town centers. A helmet is compulsory.

| Je n'ai pas les pièces détachées pour ___ votre voiture/bicyclette | I don't have parts for your car/bicycle |
| Je dois aller chercher les pièces _____ détachées ailleurs | I have to get the parts from somewhere else |
| Je dois commander les pièces _____ détachées | I have to order the parts |
| Cela prendra une demi-journée _____ | That'll take half a day |
| Cela prendra une journée_____ | That'll take a day |
| Cela prendra quelques jours _____ | That'll take a few days |
| Cela prendra une semaine _____ | That'll take a week |
| Votre voiture est bonne pour la ferraille _ | Your car is a write-off |
| Il n'y a plus rien à y faire _____ | It can't be repaired |
| La voiture/la moto/la mobylette/la_____ bicyclette sera prête à... heures | The car/motor bike/moped/bicycle will be ready at... o'clock |

## **.9 R**enting a vehicle

| | |
|---|---|
| I'd like to rent a... | J'aimerais louer un... |
| | *jhehmuhreh looay uhn...* |
| Do I need a (special) license for that? | Me faut-il un permis spécial? |
| | *muh foa teel uhn pehrmee spaysyal?* |
| I'd like to rent the...for... | Je voudrais louer le/la...pour |
| | *jhuh voodreh looay luh/lah...poor* |
| – one day | Je voudrais louer le/la...pour une journée |
| | *jhuh voodreh looay luh/lah...poor ewn jhoornay* |
| – two days | Je voodreh louer le/la...pour deux jours |
| | *jhuh voodreh looay luh/lah...poor duh jhoor* |
| How much is that per day/week? | C'est combien par jour/semaine? |
| | *seh kawnbyahn pahr jhoor/suhmehn?* |
| How much is the deposit? | De combien est la caution? |
| | *duh kawnbyahn eh lah koasyawn?* |
| Could I have a receipt for the deposit? | Puis-je avoir un reçu pour la caution? |
| | *pwee jhahvwahr uhn ruhsew poor lah koasyawn?* |
| How much is the surcharge per kilometer? | Quel est le supplément par kilomètre? |
| | *kehl eh luh sewplaymohn pahr keeloamehtr?* |
| Does that include gas? | Est-ce que l'essence est incluse? |
| | *ehs kuh lehsohns eh tahnklewz?* |
| Does that include insurance? | Est-ce que l'assurance est incluse? |
| | *ehs kuh lahsewrohns eh tahnklewz?* |
| What time can I pick the...up tomorrow? | Demain, à quelle heure puis-je venir chercher la...? |
| | *duhmahn ah kehl uhr pwee jhuh vuhneer shehrshay lah...?* |
| When does the...have to be back? | Quand dois-je rapporter la...? |
| | *kohn dwah jhuh rahportay lah...?* |
| Where's the gas tank? | Où est le réservoir? |
| | *oo eh luh rayzehrvwahr?* |
| What sort of fuel does it take? | Quel carburant faut-il utiliser? |
| | *kehl kahrbewrohn foa teel ewteeleezay?* |

**On the road**

5

## The parts of a bicycle

(the diagram shows the numbered parts)

| | | |
|---|---|---|
| 1 rear lamp | le feu arrière | *luh fuh ahryehr* |
| 2 rear wheel | la roue arrière | *lah roo ahryehr* |
| 3 (luggage) carrier | le porte-bagages | *luh port bahgahjh* |
| 4 bicycle fork | la tête de fourche | *lah teht duh foorsh* |
| 5 bell | la sonnette | *lah sohneht* |
| inner tube | la chambre à air | *lah shohnbr ah ehr* |
| tire | le pneu | *luh pnuh* |
| 6 crank | le pédalier | *luh paydahlyay* |
| 7 gear change | le changement de vitesse | *luh shohnjhmohn duh veetehs* |
| wire | le fil (électrique) | *luh feel (aylehktreek)* |
| generator | la dynamo | *lah deenahmoa* |
| bicycle trailer | la remorque de bicyclette | *lah ruhmork duh beeseekleht* |
| frame | le cadre | *luh kahdr* |
| 8 dress guard | le protège-jupe | *luh protehjh jhewp* |
| 9 chain | la chaîne | *lah shehn* |
| chainguard | le carter | *luh kahrtehr* |
| padlock | l'antivol (m.) | *lohnteevol* |
| odometer | le compteur kilométrique | *luh kawntuhr keeloamaytreek* |
| child's seat | le siège-enfant | *luh syehjh ohnfohn* |
| 10 headlight | le phare | *luh fahr* |
| bulb | l'ampoule (f.) | *lohnpool* |
| 11 pedal | la pédale | *lah paydahl* |
| 12 pump | la pompe | *lah pawnp* |
| 13 reflector | le réflecteur | *luh rayflehktuhr* |
| 14 brake shoe | les patins | *lay pahtahn* |
| 15 brake cable | le câble de frein | *luh kahbl duh frahn* |
| 16 wheel lock | le cadenas pour bicyclette | *lah kaduhnah poor beeseekleht* |
| 17 carrier straps | le tendeur | *luh tohnduhr* |
| tachometer | le compteur de vitesse | *luh kawntuhr duh veetehs* |
| 18 spoke | le rayon | *luh rayawn* |
| 19 mudguard | le garde-boue | *luh gahrd boo* |
| 20 handlebar | le guidon | *luh gueedawn* |
| 21 chain wheel | le pignon | *luh peenyawn* |
| toe clip | le câle-pied | *luh kahl pyay* |
| 22 crank axle | l'axe du pédalier (m.) | *lahx dew paydahlyay* |
| drum brake | le frein à tambour | *luh frahn ah tohnboor* |
| rim | la jante | *lah jhohnt* |
| 23 valve | la valve | *lah vahlv* |
| 24 valve tube | le raccord souple de la valve | *luh rahkor soopl duh lah vahlv* |
| 25 gear cable | la chaîne du dérailleur | *lah shehn dew dayrahyuhr* |
| 26 fork | la fourche | *lah foorsh* |
| 27 front wheel | la roue avant | *lah roo ahvohn* |
| 28 saddle | la selle | *lah sehl* |

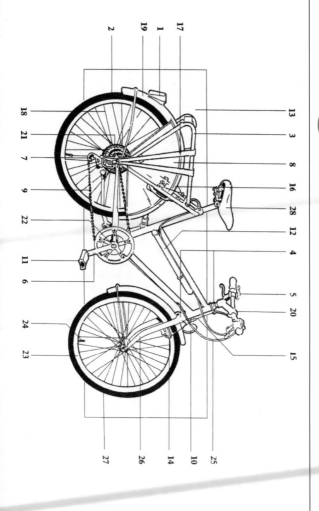

| | |
|---|---|
| Where are you heading? | Où allez-vous? |
| | *oo ahlay voo?* |
| Can I come along? | Pouvez-vous m'emmener en voiture? |
| | *poovay voo momuhnay ohn vwahtewr?* |
| Can my boyfriend/ girlfriend come too? | Mon ami(e), peut-il/peut-elle venir avec nous? |
| | *mawn nahmee, puh teel/puh tehl vuhneer ahvehk noo?* |
| I'm trying to get to... | Je dois aller à... |
| | *jhuh dwah zahlay ah...* |
| Is that on the way to...? | C'est sur la route de...? |
| | *seh sewr lah root duh...?* |
| Could you drop me off...? | Vous pouvez me déposer...? |
| | *voo poovay muh daypoazay...?* |
| – here? | Vous pouvez me déposer ici? |
| | *voo poovay muh daypoazay eesee?* |
| – at the...exit? | Vous pouvez me déposer à la sortie vers...? |
| | *voo poovay muh daypoazay ah lah sohrtee vehr...?* |
| – in the center? | Vous pouvez me déposer dans le centre? |
| | *voo poovay muh daypoazay dohn luh sohntr?* |
| – at the next rotary? | Vous pouvez me déposer au prochain rond-point? |
| | *voo poovay muh daypoazay oa proshahn rawnpwahn?* |
| Could you stop here, please? | Voulez-vous arrêter ici s'il vous plaît? |
| | *voolay voo zahrehtay eesee seel voo pleh?* |
| I'd like to get out here | Je voudrais descendre ici |
| | *jhuh voodreh duhsohndr eesee* |
| Thanks for the lift | Merci pour la route |
| | *mehrsee poor lah root* |

**5**

**On the road**

**6**

# Public transportation

| | | |
|---|---|---|
| **6.1** | **I**n general | 58 |
| **6.2** | **Q**uestions to passengers | 59 |
| **6.3** | **T**ickets | 60 |
| **6.4** | **I**nformation | 61 |
| **6.5** | **A**irplanes | 63 |
| **6.6** | **T**rains | 63 |
| **6.7** | **T**axis | 63 |

# 6 Public transportation

## 6.1 In general

● **You can check** departure times by telephone or minitel - a computerised information system widely available in France (for example in many post offices). Tickets for buses and the *métro* (Paris, Lyon and Marseille) are cheaper when bought in a *carnet* (book of ten), available at kiosks near some bus stops, at newsstands and in *métro* stations.

### Announcements

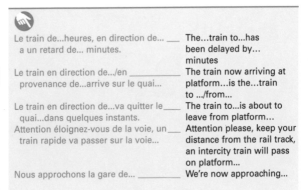

| | |
|---|---|
| Le train de...heures, en direction de... a un retard de... minutes. | The...train to...has been delayed by... minutes |
| Le train en direction de.../en provenance de...arrive sur le quai... | The train now arriving at platform...is the...train to .../from... |
| Le train en direction de...va quitter le quai...dans quelques instants. | The train to...is about to leave from platform... |
| Attention éloignez-vous de la voie, un train rapide va passer sur la voie... | Attention please, keep your distance from the rail track, an intercity train will pass on platform... |
| Nous approchons la gare de... | We're now approaching... |

| | |
|---|---|
| Where does this train go to? | Où va ce train? *oo vah suh trahn?* |
| Does this boat go to...? | Ce bateau, va-t-il à...? *suh bahtoa, vah teel ah...?* |
| Can I take this bus to...? | Puis-je prendre ce bus pour aller à...? *pwee jhuh prondr suh bews poor ahlay ah...?* |
| Does this train stop at...? | Ce train s'arrête-t-il à...? *suh trahn sahreht-uh-teel ah...?* |
| Is this seat taken/free/ reserved? | Est-ce que cette place est occupée/libre/réservée? *ehs kuh seht plahs eh tokewpay/leebr/rayzehrvay?* |
| I've reserved... | J'ai réservé... *jhay rayzehrvay...* |
| Could you tell me where I have to get off for... ? | Voulez-vous me dire où descendre pour...? *voolay voo muh deer oo duhsohndr poor...?* |
| Could you let me know when we get to...? | Voulez-me prévenir lorsque nous serons à...? *voolay voo muh prayvuhneer lorskuh noo suhrawn zah...?* |
| Could you stop at the next stop, please? | Voulez-vous vous arrêter au prochain arrêt s'il vous plaît? *voolay voo voo zahrehtay oa proshahn nahreht seel voo pleh?* |

| | |
|---|---|
| Where are we now? _____ | Où sommes-nous ici? |
| | *oo som noo zeesee?* |
| Do I have to get off _____ here? | Dois-je descendre ici? |
| | *dwah jhuh duhsohndr eesee?* |
| Have we already _____ passed...? | Avons-nous déjà dépassé...? |
| | *ahvawn noo dayjhah daypahsay...?* |
| How long have I been _____ asleep? | Combien de temps ai-je dormi? |
| | *kawnbyahn duh tohn ay jhuh dormee?* |
| How long does... _____ stop here? | Combien de temps...reste ici? |
| | *kawnbyahn duh tohn...rehst eesee?* |
| Can I come back on the ___ same ticket? | Puis-je revenir avec ce billet? |
| | *pwee jhuh ruhvuhneer ahvehk suh beeyeh?* |
| Can I change on this_____ ticket? | Puis-je prendre une correspondance avec ce billet? |
| | *pwee jhuh prondr ewn korehspawndohns ahvehk suh beeyeh?* |
| How long is this ticket _____ valid for? | Combien de temps ce billet reste-t-il valable? |
| | *kawnbyahn duh tohn suh beeyeh rehst-uh-teel vahlahbl?* |
| How much is the _____ extra fare for the TGV (high speed train)? | Combien coûte le supplément pour le TGV? |
| | *kawnbyahn koot luh sewplaymohn poor luh tayjhayvay?* |

##  .2 Questions to passengers

### Ticket types

| | |
|---|---|
| Première classe ou deuxième classe? ___ | First or second class? |
| Aller simple ou retour?_____ | Single or return? |
| Fumeurs ou non fumeurs?_____ | Smoking or nonsmoking? |
| Côté fenêtre ou côté couloir? _____ | Window or aisle? |
| A l'avant ou à l'arrière?_____ | Front or back? |
| Place assise ou couchette? _____ | Seat or berth? |
| Au-dessus, au milieu ou au-dessous? ___ | Top, middle or bottom? |
| Classe touriste ou classe affaires?_____ | Tourist class or business class? |
| Une cabine ou un fauteuil? _____ | Cabin or seat? |
| Une personne ou deux personnes? _____ | Single or double? |
| Vous êtes combien de personnes à_____ voyager? | How many are travelling? |

### Destination

| | |
|---|---|
| Où allez-vous?_____ | Where are you travelling? |
| Quand partez-vous?_____ | When are you leaving? |
| Votre...part à... _____ | Your...leaves at... |
| Vous devez prendre une_____ correspondance | You have to change trains |
| Vous devez descendre à... _____ | You have to get off at... |

**6**

**Public transportation**

| | |
|---|---|
| Vous devez passer par... _____ | You have to travel via... |
| L'aller est le... _____ | The outward journey is on... |
| Le retour est le... _____ | The return journey is on... |
| Vous devez être à bord au plus tard à... _____ | You have to be on board by... |

### On board

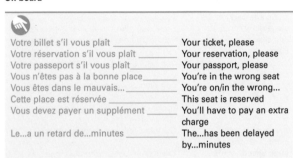

| | |
|---|---|
| Votre billet s'il vous plaît _____ | Your ticket, please |
| Votre réservation s'il vous plaît _____ | Your reservation, please |
| Votre passeport s'il vous plaît _____ | Your passport, please |
| Vous n'êtes pas à la bonne place _____ | You're in the wrong seat |
| Vous êtes dans le mauvais... _____ | You're on/in the wrong... |
| Cette place est réservée _____ | This seat is reserved |
| Vous devez payer un supplément _____ | You'll have to pay an extra charge |
| Le...a un retard de...minutes _____ | The...has been delayed by...minutes |

## 6 .3 Tickets

| | |
|---|---|
| Where can I...? _____ | Où puis-je...? |
| | *oo pwee jhuh...?* |
| – buy a ticket? _____ | Où puis-je acheter un billet? |
| | *oo pwee jhahshtay uhn beeyeh?* |
| – make a reservation? _____ | Où puis-je réserver une place? |
| | *oo pwee jhuh rayzehrvay ewn plahs?* |
| – reserve a flight? _____ | Où puis-je réserver un vol? |
| | *oo pwee jhuh rayzehrvay uhn vol?* |
| Could I have a...to..., please? _____ | Puis-je avoir...en direction de...? |
| | *pwee jhahvwahr...ohn deerehksyawn duh...?* |
| – a single _____ | Puis-je avoir un aller simple? |
| | *pwee jhahvwahr uhn nahlay sahnpl?* |
| – a return _____ | Puis-je avoir un aller-retour? |
| | *pwee jhahvwahr uhn nahlay ruhtoor?* |
| first class _____ | première classe |
| | *pruhmyehr klahs* |
| second class _____ | deuxième classe |
| | *duhzyehm klahs* |
| tourist class _____ | classe touriste |
| | *klahs tooreest* |
| business class _____ | classe affaires |
| | *klahs ahfehr* |
| I'd like to reserve a seat/berth/cabin _____ | Je voudrais réserver une place assise/couchette/cabine |
| | *jhuh voodreh rayzehrvay ewn plahs ahseez/koosheht/kahbeen* |
| I'd like to reserve a berth in the sleeping car _____ | Je voudrais réserver une place dans le wagon-lit |
| | *jhuh voodreh rayzehrvay ewn plahs dohn luh vahgawnlee* |

Public transportation

6

| | |
|---|---|
| top/middle/bottom _____ | au-dessus/au milieu/au-dessous |
| | *oaduhsew/ oa meelyuh/ oa duhsoo* |
| smoking/no smoking \_\_\_\_\_ | fumeurs/non fumeurs |
| | *fewmuhr/ nawn fewmuhr* |
| by the window _____ | à côté de la fenêtre |
| | *ah koatay duh lah fenehtr* |
| single/double _____ | une personne/deux personnes |
| | *ewn pehrson/duh pehrson* |
| at the front/back_____ | à l'avant/à l'arrière |
| | *ah lahvohn/ah lahryehr* |
| There are...of us_____ | Nous sommes...personnes |
| | *noo som...pehrson* |
| a car _____ | une voiture |
| | *ewn vwahtewr* |
| a trailer/RV_____ | une caravane |
| | *ewn kahrahvahnn* |
| ...bicycles_____ | ...bicyclettes |
| | *...beeseekleht* |
| Do you also have...? _____ | Avez-vous aussi...? |
| | *ahvay voo zoasee...?* |
| – season tickets? _____ | Avez-vous aussi une carte d'abonnement? |
| | *ahvay voo zoasee ewn kahrt dahbonmohn?* |
| – weekly tickets? _____ | Avez-vous aussi une carte hebdomadaire? |
| | *ahvay voo zoasee ewn kahrt ehbdomahdehr?* |
| – monthly season _____ tickets? | Avez-vous aussi une carte mensuelle? |
| | *ahvay voo zoasee ewn kahrt mohnsewehl?* |

## 6 .4 Information

| | |
|---|---|
| Where's? _____ | Où se trouve...? |
| | *oo suh troov...?* |
| Where's the information \_\_\_ desk? | Où se trouve le bureau de renseignements? |
| | *oo suh troov luh bewroa duh rohnsehnyuhmohn?* |
| Where can I find a_____ timetable? | Où se trouvent les horaires des départs/des arrivées? |
| | *oo se troov lay zorehr day daypahr/day zahreevay?* |
| Where's the...desk? _____ | Où se trouve la réception de...? |
| | *oo se troov lah raysehpsyawn duh...?* |
| Do you have a city map\_\_\_\_ with the bus/the subway routes on it? | Avez-vous un plan du réseau des bus/du métro? |
| | *ahvay voo zuhn plohn dew rayzoa day bews/dew maytroa?* |
| Do you have a _____ timetable? | Avez-vous un horaire des arrivées et des départs? |
| | *ahvay voo zuhn norehr day zahreevay ay day daypahr?* |
| I'd like to confirm/ _____ cancel/change my reservation for... | Je veux confirmer/annuler/changer ma réservation pour... |
| | *jhuh vuh kawnfeermay/ahnewlay/shohnjhay mah rayzehrvahsyawn poor...* |
| Will I get my money _____ back? | Mon argent me sera rendu? |
| | *mawn nahrjhohn muh suhrah rohndew?* |

Public transportation

| | |
|---|---|
| I want to go to... _____ | Je dois aller à...Comment puis-je y aller |
| How do I get there? | (le plus vite possible)? |
| (What's the quickest way | *jhuh dwah zahlay ah...komohn pwee jhee* |
| there?) | *ahlay (luh plew veet poseebl?)* |
| How much is a _____ | Combien coûte un aller simple/un aller- |
| single/return to...? | retour pour...? |
| | *kawnbyahn koot uhn nahlay sahnpl/uhn* |
| | *nahlay retoor poor...?* |
| Do I have to pay an_____ | Dois-je payer un supplément? |
| extra charge? | *dwah jheuh payay uhn sewplaymohn?* |
| Can I interrupt my _____ | Puis-je interrompre mon voyage avec ce |
| journey with this ticket? | billet? |
| | *pwee jhahntayrawnpr mawn vwahyahjh* |
| | *ahvehk suh beeyeh?* |
| How much luggage_____ | J'ai droit à combien de bagages? |
| am I allowed? | *jhay drwah ah kawnbyahn duh bahgahjh?* |
| Does this...travel direct? ___ | Ce...est direct? |
| | *suh...eh deerehkt?* |
| Do I have to change? _____ | Dois-je changer? Où? |
| Where? | *dwah jhuh shohnjhay? oo?* |
| Will this plane make any___ | L'avion fait escale? |
| stopovers? | *lahvyawn feh tehskahl?* |
| Does the boat stop at_____ | Est-ce que le bateau fait escale dans un |
| any ports on the way? | port pendant son trajet? |
| | *ehs kuh luh bahtoa feh tehskahl dohn zuhn* |
| | *por pohndohn sawn trahjheh?* |
| Does the train/ _____ | Est-ce que le train/le bus s'arrête à...? |
| bus stop at...? | *ehs kuh luh trahn/luh bews sahreht ah...?* |
| Where should I get off? ___ | Où dois-je descendre? |
| | *oo dwah jhuh duhsohndr?* |
| Is there a connection _____ | Y a-t-il une correspondance pour...? |
| to...? | *ee yah teel ewn korehspawndohns poor...?* |
| How long do I have to _____ | Combien de temps dois-je attendre? |
| wait? | *kawnbyahn duh tohn dwah jhahtohndr?* |
| When does...leave?_____ | Quand part...? |
| | *kohn pahr...?* |
| What time does the _____ | A quelle heure part le |
| first/next/last...leave? | premier/prochain/dernier...? |
| | *ah kehl uhr pahr luh* |
| | *pruhmyay/proshahn/dehrnyay...?* |
| How long does...take? ____ | Combien de temps met le...? |
| | *kawnbyahn duh tohn meh luh...?* |
| What time does...arrive ____ | A quelle heure arrive...à...? |
| in...? | *ah kehl uhr ahreev...ah...?* |
| Where does the...to... _____ | D'où part le...pour...? |
| leave from? | *doo pahr luh...poor...?* |
| Is this...to...? _____ | Est-ce le...pour...? |
| | *ehs luh...poor...?* |

## .5 Airplanes

● **At arrival** at a French airport (*aéroport*), you will find the following signs:

| arrivée | départ |
|---------|--------|
| **arrivals** | **departures** |

## .6 Trains

● **The rail network** is extensive. *La Société Nationale des Chemins de Fer Français (SNCF)* is responsible for the national rail traffic. Besides the normal train, there is also *le Train à Grande Vitesse (TGV)* for which you will have to pay an extra charge. Reservations before departure are cheaper. The *TGV* operates between the larger cities: Paris, Lyon, Marseille, and Nice. A train ticket has to be stamped (*composté*) before departure.

## .7 Taxis

● **In nearly all** large cities, there are plenty of taxis. French taxis have no standard color. Virtually all taxis have a meter. In the smaller towns, it is usual to agree a fixed price in advance. An extra charge is usual for luggage, a journey at night, on a Sunday or holiday, or to an airport. It is advisable in large cities such as Paris and Lyon to check that the meter has been returned to zero at the start of the journey.

| libre | occupé | station de taxis |
|-------|--------|------------------|
| **for hire** | **occupied** | **taxi stand** |

| | |
|---|---|
| Taxi! _____ | Taxi! |
| | *tahksee!* |
| Could you get me a taxi, ___ please? | Pouvez-vous m'appeler un taxi? |
| | *poovay voo mahpuhlay uhn tahksee?* |
| Where can I find a taxi_____ around here? | Où puis-je prendre un taxi par ici? |
| | *oo pwee jhuh prohndr uhn tahksee pahr eesee?* |
| Could you take me to..., ___ please? | Conduisez-moi à...s'il vous plaît. |
| | *kawndweezay mwah ah...seel voo pleh* |
| – this address _____ | Conduisez-moi à cette adresse. |
| | *kawndweezay mwah ah seht ahdrehs* |
| – the...hotel _____ | Conduisez-moi à l'hôtel... |
| | *kawndweezay mwah ah loatehl...* |
| – the town/center of _____ the city | Conduisez-moi dans le centre. |
| | *kawndweezay mwah dohn luh sohntr* |
| – the station _____ | Conduisez-moi à la gare. |
| | *kawndweezay mwah ah lah gahr* |
| – the airport_____ | Conduisez-moi à l'aéroport. |
| | *kawndweezay mwah ah layroapor.* |
| How much is the _____ trip to...? | Combien coûte un trajet jusqu'à...? |
| | *kawnbyahn koot uhn trahjheh jhewskah...?* |

Public transportation

|  |  |
|---|---|
| How far is it to...? _____ | C'est combien de kilomètres jusqu'à...? *seh kawnbyahn duh keeloamehtr jhewskah...?* |
| Could you turn on the _____ meter, please? | Voulez-vous mettre le compteur en marche s'il vous plaît? *voolay voo mehtr luh kawntuhr ohn mahrsh seel voo pleh?* |
| I'm in a hurry _____ | Je suis pressé. *jhuh swee prehssay* |
| Could you speed up/slow __ down a little? | Vous pouvez rouler plus vite/plus lentement? *voo poovay roolay plew veet/plew lohntmohn?* |
| Could you take a _____ different route? | Vous pouvez prendre une autre route? *voo poovay prohndr ewn oatr root?* |
| I'd like to get out here, _____ please | Je voudrais descendre ici *jhuh voodreh duhsohndr eesee* |
| You have to go...here _____ | Là vous allez... *lah voo zahlay...* |
| You have to go straight ____ here | Là vous allez tout droit *lah voo zahlay too drwah* |
| You have to turn left_____ here | Là vous allez à gauche *lah voo zahlay zah goash* |
| You have to turn right _____ here | Là vous allez à droite *lah voo zahlay zah drwaht* |
| This is it _____ | C'est ici *seht eesee* |
| Could you wait a minute___ for me, please? | Vous pouvez m'attendre un instant? *voo poovay mahtohndr uhn nahnstohn?* |

# Overnight accommodation

**7.1** **G**eneral 66

**7.2** **C**amping 67
*Camping equipment* *68–69*

**7.3** **H**otel/B&B/apartment/
holiday rental 70

**7.4** **C**omplaints 72

**7.5** **D**eparture 73

# 7  Overnight accommodation

## 7 .1 General

● **There is great variety** of overnight accommodation in France.
*Hôtels*: stars indicate the degree of comfort; from five stars, the most luxurious, to one star, very simple. Beside the star one often finds the letters *NN-Nouvelles Normes* (new classifications). This means that the star-classification is up-to-date. Most hotels offer *pension complète* (full board) or *demi-pension* (half board).
*Auberges et Relais de campagne:* luxurious; splendid view and lots of rest are guaranteed.
*Châteaux, Hôtels de France and Vieilles Demeures:* a very expensive tourist residence, always within a castle, country manor or an historic building.
*Logis de France:* an organization with many hotels with one or two stars, mostly outside the center of town. The hotel can be recognised by the yellow signboards with a green fireplace and the words: *logis de France*.
*Motels*: especially along the motorway, comparable to US motels.
*Auberges de jeunesse* (youth hostel): the number of nights is restricted to between three and seven.
*Camping:* free camping is allowed, except for forest areas with the sign *attention au feu* (fire hazard). Not all camping sites are guarded.
*Refuges et gîtes d'étape* (mountain huts): in the Alps and Pyrenees. These huts are owned by the *Club Alpin Français* and are inexpensive.

---

| | |
|---|---|
| Combien de temps voulez-vous _____ rester? | How long will you be staying? |
| Voulez-vous remplir ce questionnaire ___ s'il vous plaît? | Fill out this form, please |
| Puis-je avoir votre passeport? _____ | Could I see your passport? |
| Vous devez payer un acompte _____ | I'll need a deposit |
| Vous devez payer à l'avance _____ | You'll have to pay in advance |

---

| | |
|---|---|
| My name's...I've made a reservation over the phone/by mail | Mon nom est...J'ai réservé une place par téléphone/par lettre<br>*mawn nawn eh...jhay rayzehrvay ewn plahs pahr taylayfon/pahr lehtr* |
| How much is it per night/week/ month? | Quel est le prix pour une nuit/une semaine/un mois?<br>*kehl eh luh pree poor ewn nwee/ewn suhmehn/uhn mwah?* |
| We'll be staying at least...nights/weeks | Nous restons au moins...nuits/semaines.<br>*noo rehstawn zoa mwhan...nwee/suhmehn* |
| We don't know yet | Nous ne le savons pas encore exactement.<br>*noo nuh luh sahvawn pah zohnkor ehgzahktmohn* |
| Do you allow pets (cats/dogs)? | Est-ce que les animaux domestiques(chiens/chats) sont admis?<br>*ehs kuh lay zahneemoa domehsteek(shyahn/shah) sawn tahdmee?* |

| | |
|---|---|
| What time does the _____ gate/door open/close? | A quelle heure on ouvre/ferme le portail/la porte? |
| | *ah keh uhr awn noovr/fehrm luh portahy/lah port?* |
| Could you get me _____ a taxi, please? | Vous voulez m'appeler un taxi? |
| | *voo voolay mahplay uhn tahksee?* |
| Is there any mail _____ for me? | Y a-t-il du courrier pour moi? |
| | *ee yah teel dew kooryay poor mwah?* |

## 7 .2 Camping

*See the diagram on page 69*

| | |
|---|---|
| Vous pouvez vous-même choisir _____ votre emplacement. | You can pick your own site |
| Votre emplacement vous sera attribué. __ | You'll be allocated a site |
| Voici votre numéro d'emplacement._____ | This is your site number |
| Vous devez coller ceci sur votre_____ voiture. | Stick this on your car, please |
| Ne perdez surtout pas cette carte._____ | Please don't lose this card |

| | |
|---|---|
| Where's the manager? _____ | Où est le gardien? |
| | *oo eh luh gahrdyahn?* |
| Are we allowed to_____ camp here? | Pouvons-nous camper ici? |
| | *poovawn noo kohnpay eesee?* |
| There are...of us and _____ ...tents | Nous sommes...personnes et nous avons...tentes. |
| | *noo som...pehrson ay nooz ahvawn...tohnt* |
| Can we pick our _____ own place? | Pouvons-nous choisir nous-mêmes un emplacement? |
| | *poovawn noo shwahzeer noo mehm uhn nohnplahsmohn?* |
| Do you have a quiet _____ spot for us? | Avez-vous un endroit calme pour nous? |
| | *ahvay voo zuhn nohndrwah kahlm poor noo?* |
| Do you have any other _____ sites available? | Vous n'avez pas d'autre emplacement libre? |
| | *voo nahvay pah doatr ohnplahsmohn leebr?* |
| It's too windy/sunny/ _____ shady here. | Ici il y a trop de vent/soleil/ombre. |
| | *eesee eel ee yah troa duh vohn/sohlehy/awnbr* |
| It's too crowded here _____ | Il y a trop de monde ici. |
| | *eel ee yah troa duh mawnd eesee* |
| The ground's too _____ hard/uneven | Le sol est trop dur/irrégulier. |
| | *luh sohl eh troa dewr/eeraygewlyay* |
| Do you have a level _____ spot for the camper/ trailer/folding trailer? | Avez-vous un endroit plat pour le camping-car/la caravane/la caravane pliante? |
| | *ahvay voo zuhn nohndrwah plah poor luh kohnpeeng kahr/lah kahrahvahnn/lah kahrahvahnn plyohnt?* |
| Could we have _____ adjoining sites? | Pouvons-nous être l'un à côté de l'autre? |
| | *poovawn noo zehtr luhn nah koatay duh loatr?* |

## Camping equipment
(the diagram shows the numbered parts)

| | | |
|---|---|---|
| luggage space | l'espace (f.) bagages | *lehspahs bahgajh* |
| can opener | l'ouvre-boîte (m.) | *loovr bwaht* |
| butane gas bottle | la bouteille de butane | *lah bootehy duh bewtahnn* |
| 1 pannier | la sacoche de vélo | *lah sahkosh duh vayloa* |
| 2 gas cooker | le réchaud à gaz | *luh rayshoa ah gahz* |
| 3 groundsheet | le tapis de sol | *luh tahpee duh sol* |
| hammer | le marteau | *luh mahrtoa* |
| hammock | le hamac | *luh ahmahk* |
| 4 jerry can | le bidon d'essence | *luh beedawn dehssohns* |
| campfire | le feu de camp | *luh fuh duh kohn* |
| 5 folding chair | la chaise pliante | *lah shehz plyohnt* |
| 6 insulated picnic box | la glacière | *lah glahsyehr* |
| ice pack | le bac à glaçons | *luh bah kah glasawn* |
| compass | la boussole | *lah boosol* |
| wick | la mèche | *lah mehsh* |
| corkscrew | le tire-bouchon | *luh teer booshawn* |
| 7 airbed | le matelas pneumatique | *luh mahtuhlah pnuhmahteek* |
| 8 airbed plug | le bouchon du matelas pneumatique | *luh booshawn dew mahtuhlah pnemahteek* |
| pump | la pompe à air | *lah pawnp ah ehr* |
| 9 awning | l'auvent (m.) | *loavohn* |
| 10 mat | la natte | *lah naht* |
| 11 pan | la casserole | *lah kahsrol* |
| 12 pan handle | la poignée de casserole | *lah pwahnnyay duh kahsrol* |
| primus stove | le réchaud à pétrole | *luh rayshoa ah paytrol* |
| zip | la fermeture éclair | *lah fehrmuhtewr ayklehr* |
| 13 backpack | le sac à dos | *luh sahk ah doa* |
| 14 guy rope | la corde | *lah kord* |
| sleeping bag | le sac de couchage | *luh sahk duh kooshajh* |
| 15 storm lantern | la lanterne-tempête | *lah lohntehrn-tohnpeht* |
| camp bed | le lit de camp | *luh lee duh kohn* |
| table | la table | *lah tahbl* |
| 16 tent | la tente | *lah tohnt* |
| 17 tent peg | le piquet | *luh peekeh* |
| 18 tent pole | le mât | *luh mah* |
| vacuum | la bouteille thermos | *lah bootehy tehrmos* |
| 19 water bottle | la gourde | *lah goord* |
| clothes pin | la pince à linge | *lah pahns ah lahnjh* |
| windbreak | le pare-vent | *luh pahrvohn* |
| 20 flashlight | la torche électrique | *lah torsh aylehktreek* |
| pocket knife | le canif | *luh kahneef* |

Overnight accommodation

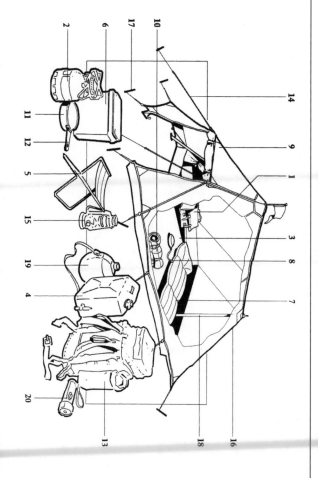

| Can we park the car next to the tent? | La voiture, peut-elle être garée à côté de la tente? |
| | *lah vwahtewr, puh tehl ehtr gahray ah koatay duh lah tohnt?* |
| How much is it per person/tent/trailer/car? | Quel est le prix par personne/tente/caravane/voiture? |
| | *kehl eh luh pree pahr pehrson/tohnt/kahrahvahnn/vwahtewr?* |
| Are there any...? | Y a-t-il...? |
| | *ee yah teel...?* |
| – any hot showers? | Y a-t-il des douches avec eau chaude? |
| | *ee yah teel day doosh ahvehk oa shoad?* |
| – washing machines? | Y a-t-il des machines à laver? |
| | *ee yah teel day mahsheen ah lahvay?* |
| Is there a...on the site? | Y a-t-il un...sur le terrain? |
| | *ee ayh teel uhn...sewr luh tehrahn?* |
| Is there a children's play area on the site? | Y a-t-il un terrain de jeux pour les enfants? |
| | *ee yah teel uhn tehrahn duh jhuh poor lay zohnfohn?* |
| Are there covered cooking facilities on the site? | Y a-t-il un endroit couvert pour cuisiner? |
| | *ee yah teel uhn nohndrwa koovehr poor kweezeenay?* |
| Can I rent a safe here? | Puis-je louer un coffre-fort ici? |
| | *pwee jhuh looay uhn kofr for eesee?* |
| Are we allowed to barbecue here? | Pouvons-nous faire un barbecue? |
| | *poovawn noo fehr uhn bahrbuhkew?* |
| Are there any power outlets? | Y a-t-il des prises électriques? |
| | *ee yah teel day preez aylehktreek?* |
| Is there drinking water? | Y a-t-il de l'eau potable? |
| | *ee yah teel duh loa potabl?* |
| When's the garbage collected? | Quand vide-t-on les poubelles? |
| | *kohn veed-uh-tawn lay poobehl?* |
| Do you sell gas bottles (butane gas/propane gas)? | Vendez-vous des bouteilles de gaz (butane/propane)? |
| | *vohnday voo day bootehuhy duh gahz (bewtahnn/propahnn)?* |

## 7 .3 Hotel/B&B/apartment/holiday rental

| Do you have a single/double room available? | Avez-vous une chambre libre pour une personne/deux personnes? |
| | *ahvay voo zewn shohnbr leebr poor ewn pehrson/duh pehrson?* |
| per person/per room | par personne/par chambre |
| | *pahr pehrson/pahr shohnbr* |
| Does that include breakfast/lunch/dinner? | Est-ce que le petit déjeuner/le déjeuner/le dîner est compris? |
| | *ehs kuh luh puhtee dayjhuhnay/luh dayjhuhnay/luh deenay eh kawnpree?* |
| Could we have two adjoining rooms? | Pouvons-nous avoir deux chambres contiguës? |
| | *poovawn noo zahvwahr duh shohnbr kawnteegew?* |
| with/without toilet/bath/shower | avec/sans toilettes/salle de bains/douche |
| | *ahvehk/sohn twahleht/sahl duh bahn/doosh* |

| | |
|---|---|
| (not) facing the street _____ | (pas) du côté rue |
| | *(pah) dew koatay rew* |
| with/without a view _____ of the sea | avec/sans vue sur la mer |
| | *ahvehk/sohn vew sewr lah mehr* |
| Is there...in the hotel? _____ | Y a-t-il...dans l'hôtel? |
| | *ee yah teel...dohn loatehl?* |
| Is there an elevator in _____ the hotel? | Y a-t-il un ascenseur dans l'hôtel? |
| | *ee yah teel uhn nahsohnsuhr dohn loatehl?* |
| Do you have room _____ service? | Y a-t-il un service de chambre dans l'hôtel? |
| | *ee yah teel uhn sehrvees duh shohnbr dohn loatehl?* |

| | |
|---|---|
| Les toilettes et la douche sont au _____ même étage/dans votre chambre | You can find the toilet and shower on the same floor/in the room |
| De ce côté, s'il vous plaît _____ | This way, please |
| Votre chambre est au...étage, c'est le _____ numéro... | Your room is on the... floor, number... |

| | |
|---|---|
| Could I see the room? _____ | Puis-je voir la chambre? |
| | *pwee jhuh vwhar lah shohnbr?* |
| I'll take this room _____ | Je prends cette chambre. |
| | *jhuh prohn seht shohnbr* |
| We don't like this one _____ | Celle-ci ne nous plaît pas. |
| | *sehl see nuh noo pleh pah* |
| Do you have a larger/_____ less expensive room? | Avez-vous une chambre plus grande/moins chère? |
| | *avay voo zewn shohnbr plew grohnd/mwahn shehr?* |
| Could you put in a cot? _____ | Pouvez-vous y ajouter un lit d'enfant? |
| | *poovay voo zee ahjhootay uhn lee dohnfohn?* |
| What time's breakfast? _____ | A quelle heure est le petit déjeuner? |
| | *ah kehl uhr eh luh puhtee dayjhuhnay?* |
| Where's the dining _____ room? | Où est la salle à manger? |
| | *oo eh lah sahl ah mohnjhay?* |
| Can I have breakfast _____ in my room? | Puis-je prendre le petit déjeuner dans la chambre? |
| | *pwee jhuh prohndr luh puhtee dayjhuhnay dohn lah shohnbr?* |
| Where's the emergency _____ exit/fire escape? | Où est la sortie de secours/l'escalier de secours? |
| | *oo eh lah sortee duh suhkoor/lehskahlyay duh suhkoor?* |
| Where can I park my _____ car (safely)? | Où puis-je garer ma voiture (en sécurité)? |
| | *oo pwee jhuh gahray mah vwahtewr (ohn saykewreetay)?* |
| The key to room..., _____ please | La clef de la chambre..., s'il vous plaît. |
| | *lah klay duh lah shohnbr...,seel voo pleh* |
| Could you put this in _____ the safe, please? | Puis-je mettre ceci dans votre coffre-fort? |
| | *pwee jhuh mehtr suhsee dohn votr kofr for?* |

| Could you wake me _____ at...tomorrow? | Demain voulez-vous me réveiller à...heures? |
|---|---|
| | *duhmahn voolay voo muh rayvehyay ah...uhr?* |
| Could you find a _____ babysitter for me? | Pouvez-vous m'aider à trouver une baby-sitter? |
| | *poovay voo mayday ah troovay ewn behbee seetehr?* |
| Could I have an extra _____ blanket? | Puis-je avoir une couverture supplémentaire? |
| | *pwee jhahvwahr ewn koovehrtewr sewplaymohntehr?* |
| What days do the _____ cleaners come in? | Quels jours fait-on le ménage? |
| | *kehl jhoor feh tawn luh maynahjh?* |
| When are the sheets/ _____ towels/dish towels changed? | Quand change-t-on les draps/les serviettes-éponge/les torchons? |
| | *kohn shohnjh tawn lay drah/lay sehrvyeht aypawnjh/lay tohrshawn?* |

 **.4 Complaints**

| We can't sleep for _____ the noise | Nous ne pouvons pas dormir à cause du bruit |
|---|---|
| | *noo nuh poovawn pah dormeer ah koaz dew brwee* |
| Could you turn the _____ radio down, please? | Est-ce que vous pouvez baisser un peu la radio? |
| | *ehs kuh voo poovay behssay uhn puh lah rahdyoa?* |
| We're out of toilet paper ___ | Il n'y a plus de papier hygiénique |
| | *eel nee yah plew duh pahpyay eejhyayneek* |
| There aren't any.../there's ___ not enough... | Il n'y a pas de/pas assez de... |
| | *eel nee yah pah duh/pah zahsay duh...* |
| The bed linen's dirty _____ | La literie est sale |
| | *lah leetree eh sahl* |
| The room hasn't been _____ cleaned | La chambre n'a pas été nettoyée |
| | *lah shohnbr nah pah zaytay nehtwahhay* |
| The kitchen is not clean ____ | La cuisine n'est pas propre |
| | *lah kweezeen neh pah propr* |
| The kitchen utensils are ____ dirty | Les ustensiles de cuisine sont sales |
| | *lay zewstohnseel duh kweezeen sawn sahl* |
| The heater's not _____ working | Le chauffage ne marche pas |
| | *luh shoafajh nuh marsh pah* |
| There's no (hot) _____ water/electricity | Il n'y a pas d'eau(chaude)/d'électricité |
| | *eel nee yah pah doa(shoad)/daylehktreeseetay* |
| ...is broken _____ | ...est cassé |
| | *...eh kahssay* |
| Could you have that _____ seen to? | Vous pouvez le faire réparer? |
| | *voo poovay luh fehr raypahray?* |
| Could I have another _____ room/camp site? | Puis-je avoir une autre chambre/un autre emplacement pour la tente? |
| | *pwee jhuh ahvwahr ewn oatr shohnbr/uhn noatr ohnplasmohn poor lah tohnt?* |
| The bed creaks terribly ____ | Le lit grince énormément |
| | *luh lee grahns aynormaymohn* |
| The bed sags _____ | Le lit s'affaisse |
| | *luh lee sahfehs* |

72

| | |
|---|---|
| There are bugs/insects ____ in our room | Nous sommes incommodés par des bestioles/insectes<br>_noo som zahnkomoday pahr day behstyol/day zahnsehkt_ |
| This place is full ____ of mosquitos | C'est plein de moustiques ici<br>_seh plahn duh moosteek eesee_ |
| – cockroaches ____ | C'est plein de cafards<br>_seh plahn duh kahfahr_ |

 **.5 D**eparture

*See also 8.2 Settling the bill*

| | |
|---|---|
| I'm leaving tomorrow. ____ Could I pay my bill, please? | Je pars demain. Puis-je payer maintenant?<br>_jhuh pahr duhmahn. pwee jhuh payay mahntuhnohn?_ |
| What time should we ____ check out? | A quelle heure devons-nous quitter la chambre?<br>_ah kehl uhr duhvawn noo keetay lah shohnbr?_ |
| Could I have my passport ____ back, please? | Pouvez-vous me rendre mon passeport?<br>_poovay voo muh rohndr mawn pahspor?_ |
| We're in a terrible hurry ____ | Nous sommes très pressés<br>_noo som treh prehssay_ |
| Could you forward ____ my mail to this address? | Pouvez-vous faire suivre mon courrier à cette adresse?<br>_poovay voo fehr sweevr mawn kooryay ah seht ahdrehs?_ |
| Could we leave our ____ luggage here until we leave? | Nos valises peuvent rester ici jusqu'à notre départ?<br>_noa vahleez puhv rehstay eesee jhewskah notr daypahr?_ |
| Thanks for your ____ hospitality | Merci pour votre hospitalité<br>_mehrsee poor votr ospeetahleetay_ |

**Overnight accommodation**

# Money matters

**8.1** Banks 75

**8.2** Settling the bill 76

# **M**oney matters

● **In general, banks are open** to the public between 9am and 12 noon and between 2 and 4pm; they are closed on Saturdays. In large city centers they are often open at lunchtime. In tourist areas, the bank can be closed on Monday morning and open on Saturday morning. To exchange currency a proof of identity is usually required. The sign *Change* indicates that money can be exchanged. Hotels and railway stations may also offer exchange facilities but at less favorable rates.

## .1 **B**anks

| | |
|---|---|
| Where can I find a bank/an exchange office around here? | Où puis-je trouver une banque/un bureau de change par ici? |
| | *oo pwee jhuh troovay ewn bohnk/uhn bewroa duh shohnjh pahr eesee?* |
| Where can I cash this traveler's check/giro check? | Où puis-je encaisser ce chèque de voyage/chèque postal? |
| | *oo pwee jhuh ohnkehssay suh shehk duh vwahyajh/shehk postahl?* |
| Can I cash this...here? | Puis-je encaisser ce...ici? |
| | *pweejh ohnkehssay suh...eesee?* |
| Can I withdraw money on my credit card here? | Puis-je retirer de l'argent avec une carte de crédit? |
| | *pwee jhuh ruhteeray duh lahrjhohn ahvehk ewn kahrt duh kraydee?* |
| What's the minimum/maximum amount? | Quel est le montant minimum/maximum? |
| | *kehl eh luh mohntohn meeneemuhm/mahxseemuhm?* |
| Can I take out less than that? | Puis-je retirer moins? |
| | *pwee jhuh ruhteeray mwahn?* |
| I've had some money transferred here. Has it arrived yet? | J'ai fait virer de l'argent par mandat télégraphique. Est-ce déjà arrivé? |
| | *jhay feh veeray duh lahrjhohn pahr mohndah taylaygrahfeek. ehs dayjhah ahreevay?* |
| These are the details of my bank in the United States | Voici les coordonnées de ma banque aux États Unis |
| | *vwahsee lay koa-ordonay duh mah bohnk ohz ehtahz oonee* |
| This is my bank/giro account number | Voici mon numéro de compte bancaire/numéro de chèque postal |
| | *vwahsee mawn newmayroa duh kawnt bohnkehr/newmayroa duh shehk postahl* |
| I'd like to change some money | J'aimerais changer de l'argent |
| | *jhehmuhreh shohnjhay duh lahrjhohn* |
| – pounds into... | des livres sterling contre... |
| | *day leevr stehrleeng kawntr...* |
| – dollars into... | des dollars contre... |
| | *day dolahr kawntr...* |
| What's the exchange rate? | Le change est à combien? |
| | *luh shohnjh eh tah kawnbyahn?* |
| Could you give me some small change with it? | Pouvez-vous me donner de la monnaie? |
| | *poovay voo muh donay duh lah moneh?* |
| This is not right | Ce n'est pas exact |
| | *suh neh pah zehgzah.* |

| Vous devez signer ici _____ | Sign here, please |
| Vous devez remplir ceci _____ | Fill this out, please |
| Puis-je voir votre passeport? _____ | Could I see your passport, please? |
| Puis-je voir une pièce d'identité? _____ | Could I see some identification, please? |
| Puis-je voir votre carte de chèque _____ postal? | Could I see your girobank card, please? |
| Puis-je voir votre carte bancaire? _____ | Could I see your bank card, please? |

## 8 .2 **S**ettling the bill

| Could you put it on _____ my bill? | Pouvez-vous le mettre sur mon compte? |
| | *poovay voo luh mehtr sewr mawn kawnt?* |
| Does this amount _____ include the tip? | Est-ce que le service est compris(dans la somme)? |
| | *ehs kuh luh sehrvees eh kawnpree(dohn lah som)?* |
| Can I pay by...? _____ | Puis-je payer avec...? |
| | *pwee jhuh payay ahvehk...?* |
| Can I pay by credit card? ___ | Puis-je payer avec une carte de crédit? |
| | *pwee jhuh payay ahvehk ewn kahrt duh kraydee?* |
| Can I pay by traveller's ____ cheque? | Puis-je payer avec un chèque de voyage? |
| | *pwee jhuh payay ahvehk uhn shehk duh vwahyajh?* |
| Can I pay with foreign _____ currency? | Puis-je vous payer en devises étrangères? |
| | *pwee jhuh voo payay ohn duhveez aytrohnjhehr?* |
| You've given me too _____ much/you haven't given me enough change | Vous m'avez trop/pas assez rendu |
| | *voo mahvay troa/pah zahsay rohndew* |
| Could you check this _____ again, please? | Voulez-vous refaire le calcul? |
| | *voolay voo ruhfehr luh kahlkewl?* |
| Could I have a receipt, _____ please? | Pouvez-vous me donner un reçu/le ticket de caisse? |
| | *poovay voo muh donay uhn ruhsew/luh teekeh duh kehs?* |
| I don't have enough _____ money on me | Je n'ai pas assez d'argent sur moi |
| | *jhuh nay pah zahsay dahrjhohn sewr mwah* |
| This is for you _____ | Voilà, c'est pour vous |
| | *vwahlah seh poor voo* |
| Keep the change _____ | Gardez la monnaie |
| | *gahrday lah moneh* |

| Nous n'acceptons pas les cartes de _____ crédit/les chèques de voyage/les devises étrangères | We don't accept credit cards/traveler's checks/foreign currency |

# Mail and telephone

**9.1** Mail 78

**9.2** Telephone 79

## **9** **M**ail and telephone

### **9** .1 **M**ail

*For giros, see 8 Money matters*

● **Post offices** are open from Monday to Friday between 8am and 7pm. In smaller towns the post office closes at lunch. On Saturday they are open between 8am and 12 noon.
Stamps *(timbres)* are also available in a *tabac* (café that sells cigarettes and matches).
The yellow letter box *(boîte aux lettres)* in the street and in the post office has two rates: *tarif normal* (normal rate) and *tarif réduit* (reduced rate).
It is advisable to opt for the *tarif normal*.

| | | |
|---|---|---|
| colis | télégrammes | timbres |
| parcels | telegrams | stamps |
| mandats | | |
| money orders | | |

| | |
|---|---|
| Where's...? | Où est...? |
| | *oo eh...?* |
| Where's the post office? | Où est la poste? |
| | *oo eh lah post?* |
| Where's the main post office? | Où est la poste centrale? |
| | *oo eh lah post sohntrahl?* |
| Where's the mailbox? | Où est la boîte aux lettres? |
| | *oo eh lah bwaht oa lehtr?* |
| Which counter should I go to...? | Quel est le guichet pour...? |
| | *kehl eh luh gueesheh poor...?* |
| – to send a fax | Quel est le guichet pour les fax? |
| | *kehl eh luh gueesheh poor lay fahx?* |
| – to change money | Quel est le guichet pour changer de l'argent? |
| | *kehl eh luh gueesheh poor shohnjhay duh lahrjhohn?* |
| -to change giro checks | Quel est le guichet pour les chèques postaux? |
| | *kehl eh luh gueesheh poor lay shehk postoa?* |
| -for a telegraph money order? | Quel est le guichet pour faire un virement postal télégraphique? |
| | *kehl eh luh gueesheh poor fehr uhn veermohn postahl taylaygrahfeek?* |
| General delivery | Poste restante |
| | *post rehstohnt* |
| Is there any mail for me? My name's... | Y a-t-il du courrier pour moi? Mon nom est... |
| | *ee yah teel dew kooryay poor mwah? mawn nawn eh...* |

### Stamps

| | |
|---|---|
| What's the postage _____ for a...to...? | Combien faut-il sur une...pour...? |
| | *kawnbyahn foa teel sewr ewn...poor...?* |
| Are there enough _____ stamps on it? | Y a-t-il suffisamment de timbres dessus? |
| | *ee yah teel sewfeezahmohn duh tahnbr duhsew?* |
| I'd like... ...franc stamps ____ | Je voudrais...timbres à... |
| | *jhuh voodreh...tahnbr ah...* |
| I'd like to send this..._____ | Je veux envoyer ce/cette... |
| | *jhuh vuh zohnvwahyay suh/seht...* |
| – express _____ | Je veux envoyer ce/cette...en express. |
| | *jhuh vuh zohnvwahyay suh/seht...ohn nehxprehs* |
| – by air mail _____ | Je veux envoyer ce/cette...par avion. |
| | *jhuh vuh zohnvwahyay suh/seht...pahr ahvyawn* |
| – by registered mail _____ | Je veux envoyer ce/cette...en recommandé. |
| | *jhuh vuh zohnvwahyay suh/seht...ohn ruhkomohnday* |

### Telegram / fax

| | |
|---|---|
| I'd like to send a_____ telegram to... | J'aimerais envoyer un télégramme à... |
| | *jhehmuhreh zohnvwahyay uhn taylaygrahm ah...* |
| How much is that _____ per word? | C'est combien par mot? |
| | *seh kawnbyahn pahr moa?* |
| This is the text I want_____ to send | Voici le texte que je veux envoyer. |
| | *vwahsee luh tehxt kuh jhuh vuh zohnvwahyay* |
| Shall I fill out the form____ myself? | Puis-je remplir le questionnaire moi-même? |
| | *pwee jhuh rohnpleer luh kehstyonehr mwah mehm?* |
| Can I make photocopies/___ send a fax here? | Puis-je faire des photocopies/envoyer un fax ici? |
| | *pwee jhuh fehr day foatoakopee/ohnvwahyay uhn fahx eesee?* |

## .2 Telephone

*See also 1.8 Telephone alphabet*

● **All phone booths** offer a direct international service to the UK or the US (00 + country code 44[UK] or 1[US]+ trunk code minus zero + number). In a few cases these are still payable with coins of 1, 5 and 10 francs, but most phone booths will only accept phone cards. These cards (*télécartes*), with 40 or 120 units (*unités*) can be bought at the post office or in a *tabac*. Phone booths do not take incoming calls. Charges can no longer be reversed in France. *A carte globéo* (special card) can be obtained from any office of the telephone company, on presentation of a credit card and identification. Charges are then deducted from the bank account.

When phoning someone in France, you will not be greeted with the subscriber's name, but with *allô* or *allô oui*?

| | |
|---|---|
| Is there a phone booth around here? | Y a-t-il une cabine téléphonique dans le coin? |
| | *ee ah teel ewn kahbeen taylayfoneek dohn luh kwahn?* |
| Could I use your phone, please? | Puis-je utiliser votre téléphone? |
| | *pwee jhuh ewteeleezay votr taylayfon?* |
| Do you have a (city/region)...phone directory? | Avez-vous un annuaire de la ville de.../de la région de...? |
| | *ahvay voo zuhn ahnnewehr duh lah veel duh.../duh lah rayjhyawn duh...?* |
| Where can I get a phone card? | Où puis-je acheter une télécarte? |
| | *oo pwee jhahshtay ewn taylaykahrt?* |
| Could you give me...? | Pouvez-vous me donner...? |
| | *poovay voo muh donay...?* |
| – the number for international directory assistance | Pouvez-vous me donner le numéro des renseignements pour l'étranger? |
| | *poovay voo muh donay luh newmayroa day rohnsehnyuhmohn poor laytrohnjhay?* |
| – the number of room... | Pouvez-vous me donner le numéro de la chambre...? |
| | *poovay voo muh donay luh newmayroa duh lah shohnbr...?* |
| – the international access code | Pouvez-vous me donner le numéro international? |
| | *poovay voo muh donay luh newmayroa ahntehrnahsyonahl?* |
| – the country code for... | Pouvez-vous me donner l'indicatif du pays pour...? |
| | *poovay voo muh donay lahndeekahteef dew payee poor...?* |
| – the area code for... | Pouvez-vous me donner l'indicatif de...? |
| | *poovay voo muh donay lahndeekahteef duh...?* |
| – the number of... | Pouvez-vous me donner le numéro d'abonné de...? |
| | *poovay voo muh donay luh newmayroa dahbonay duh...?* |
| Could you check if this number's correct? | Pouvez-vous vérifier si ce numéro est correct? |
| | *poovay voo vayreefyay see suh newmayroa eh korehkt?* |
| Can I dial international direct? | Puis-je téléphoner en automatique à l'étranger? |
| | *pwee jhuh taylayfonay ohn noatoamahteek ah laytrohnjhay?* |
| Do I have to go through the switchboard? | Dois-je appeler en passant par le standard? |
| | *dwah jhahpuhlay ohn pahsohn pahr luh stohndahr?* |
| Do I have to dial '0' first? | Dois-je d'abord faire le zéro? |
| | *dwah jhuh dahbor fehr luh zayroa?* |
| Do I have to reserve my calls? | Dois-je demander ma communication? |
| | *dwah jhuh duhmohnday mah komewneekahsyawn?* |
| Could you dial this number for me, please? | Voulez-vous m'appeler ce numéro? |
| | *voolay voo mahpuhlay suh newmayroa?* |

| | |
|---|---|
| Could you put me through to.../extension..., please? | Voulez-vous me passer.../le poste...? *voolay voo muh pahsay.../luh post...?* |
| What's the charge per minute? | Quel est le prix à la minute? *kehl eh luh pree ah lah meenewt?* |
| Have there been any calls for me? | Quelqu'un m'a-t-il appelé? *kehlkuhn mah teel ahpuhlay?* |

### The conversation

| | |
|---|---|
| Hello, this is... | Allô, ici... *ahloa, eesee...* |
| Who is this, please? | Qui est à l'appareil? *kee eh tah lahpahrehy?* |
| Is this...? | Je parle à...? *jhuh pahrl ah...?* |
| I'm sorry, I've dialed the wrong number | Pardon, je me suis trompé(e) de numéro *pahrdawn, jhuh muh swee trawnpay duh newmayroa.* |
| I can't hear you | Je ne vous entends pas *jhuh nuh voo zohntohn pah* |
| I'd like to speak to... | Je voudrais parler à... *jhuh voodreh pahrlay ah...* |
| Is there anybody who speaks English? | Y a-t-il quelqu'un qui parle l'anglais? *ee yah teel kehlkuhn kee pahrl lohngleh?* |
| Extension... please | Pouvez-vous me passer le poste...? *poovay voo muh pahsay luh post...?* |
| Could you ask him/her to call me back? | Voulez-vous demander qu'il/qu'elle me rappelle? *voolay voo duhmohnday keel/kehl muh rahpehl?* |
| My name's... My number's... | Mon nom est...Mon numéro est... *mawn nawn eh...mawn newmayroa eh...* |
| Could you tell him/her I called? | Voulez-vous dire que j'ai appelé? *voolay voo deer kuh jhay ahpuhlay?* |
| I'll call back tomorrow | Je rappellerai demain *jhuh rahpehluhray duhmahn* |

| | |
|---|---|
| On vous demande au téléphone | There's a phone call for you |
| Vous devez d'abord faire le zéro | You have to dial '0' first. |
| Vous avez un instant? | One moment, please |
| Je n'obtiens pas de réponse | There's no answer |
| La ligne est occupée | The line's busy |
| Vous voulez attendre? | Do you want to hold? |
| Je vous passe la communication | Connecting you |
| Vous vous êtes trompé de numéro | You've got a wrong number |
| Il/elle n'est pas ici en ce moment | He's/she's not here right now |
| Vous pouvez le/la rappeler à... | He'll/she'll be back... |
| C'est le répondeur automatique de... | This is the answering machine of... |

# **S**hopping

**10.1 S**hopping conversations  83

**10.2 F**ood  85

**10.3 C**lothing and shoes  86

**10.4 P**hotographs and video  87

**10.5 A**t the hairdresser's  89

_10_

# 10 **Shopping**

● **Opening times:** Tuesday to Saturday 8/9am-1pm and 2.30-7pm. On Mondays shops are closed in the morning or for the entire day. On Sunday mornings grocers and bakers are usually open, and markets are open until 1pm. Supermarkets and department stores in nearly all cities are open until 8pm once a week. Drugstores display the list of *pharmacies de garde* (those open on Sundays and after hours), but you may be charged double in some cities. You may be asked to pay in advance for shoe repairs and dry cleaning.

| | | |
|---|---|---|
| antiquités | grand magasin | magasin diététique |
| **antiques** | **department store** | **health food shop** |
| appareils électriques | laverie automatique | marché |
| **electrical appliances** | **launderette** | **market** |
| bijoutier | librairie | marché aux puces |
| **jeweler** | **bookshop** | **fleamarket** |
| blanchisserie | magasin | mercerie |
| **laundry** | **shop** | **notions** |
| boucherie | magasin | pâtisserie |
| **butcher** | d'ameublement | **cake shop** |
| boulangerie | **furniture shop** | pharmacie |
| **bakery** | magasin d'appareils | **drugstore** |
| centre commercial | photographiques | poissonnerie |
| **shopping center** | **camera shop** | **fishmonger** |
| charcuterie | magasin de | produits ménagers/ |
| **delicatessen** | bicyclettes | droguerie |
| coiffeur | **bicycle shop** | **household goods** |
| (femmes/hommes) | magasin de | quincaillerie |
| **hairdresser** | bricolage | **hardware shop** |
| (women/men) | **Do-it-yourself-store** | réparateur de |
| cordonnier | magasin de jouets | bicyclettes |
| **cobbler** | **toy shop** | **bicycle repairs** |
| crémerie | magasin de disques | salon de beauté |
| **dairy** | **record shop** | **beauty parlour** |
| épicerie | magasin de | salon de dégustation |
| **grocery store** | souvenirs | de glaces |
| fleuriste | **souvenir shop** | **ice-cream parlour** |
| **florist** | magasin de sport | supermarché |
| fruits et légumes | **sports shop** | **supermarket** |
| **greengrocer** | magasin de vins et | tabac |
| galerie marchande | spiritueux | **tobacconist** |
| **shopping arcade** | **liquor store** | teinturerie |
| | | **dry-cleaner** |

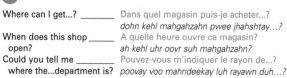

## 10 .1 **S**hopping conversations

| | |
|---|---|
| Where can I get...? | Dans quel magasin puis-je acheter...? |
| | *dohn kehl mahgahzahn pwee jhahshtay...?* |
| When does this shop open? | A quelle heure ouvre ce magasin? |
| | *ah kehl uhr oovr suh mahgahzahn?* |
| Could you tell me where the...department is? | Pouvez-vous m'indiquer le rayon de...? |
| | *poovay voo mahndeekay luh rayawn duh...?* |

Could you help me, _____ please? I'm looking for...
Pouvez-vous m'aider? Je cherche...
*poovay voo mayday? jhuh shehrsh...*

Do you sell English/ _____ American newspapers?
Vendez-vous des journaux anglais/américains?
*vohnday voo day jhoornoa ohngleh/ahmayreekahn?*

---

On s'occupe de vous? _____ **Are you being served?**

No, I'd like... _____
Non. J'aimerais...
*nawn. jhehmuhreh...*

I'm just looking, _____ if that's all right
Je jette un coup d'oeil, si c'est permis
*jhuh jheht uhn koo duhy, see seh pehrmee*

---

Vous désirez autre chose? _____ **Anything else?**

Yes, I'd also like... _____
Oui, donnez-moi aussi...
*wee, donay mwah oasee...*

No, thank you. That's all ___
Non, je vous remercie. Ce sera tout
*nawn, jhuh voo ruhmehrsee. suh suhrah too*

Could you show me...? ____
Pouvez-vous me montrer...?
*poovay voo muh mawntray...?*

I'd prefer... _____
Je préfère...
*jhuh prayfehr...*

This is not what I'm _____ looking for
Ce n'est pas ce que je cherche
*suh neh pah suh kuh jhuh shehrsh*

Thank you. I'll keep_____ looking
Merci. Je chercherai ailleurs
*mehrsee. jhuh shehrshuhray ahyuhr*

Do you have _____ something...?
Vous n'avez pas quelque chose de...?
*voo nahvay pah kehlkuh shoaz duh...?*

– less expensive?_____
Vous n'avez pas quelque chose de moins cher?
*voo nahvay pah kehlkuh shoaz duh mwahn shehr?*

– something smaller?_____
Vous n'avez pas quelque chose de plus petit?
*voo nahvay pah  kehlkuh shoaz duh plew puhtee?*

– something larger? _____
Vous n'avez pas quelque chose de plus grand?
*voo nahvay pah kehlkuh shoaz duh plew grohn?*

I'll take this one _____
Je prends celui-ci
*jhuh prohn suhlwee see*

Does it come with _____ instructions?
Y a-t-il un mode d'emploi avec?
*ee yah teel uhn mod dohnplwah ahvehk?*

It's too expensive_____
Je le trouve trop cher
*jhuh luh troov troa shehr*

I'll give you... _____
Je vous offre...
*jhuh voo zofr...*

| | |
|---|---|
| Could you keep this for ____ me? I'll come back for it later | Voulez-vous me le mettre de côté? Je reviendrai le chercher tout à l'heure |
| | *voolay voo muh luh mehtr duh koatay? jhuh ruhvyahndray luh shehrshay too tah luhr* |
| Have you got a bag _____ for me, please? | Vous avez un sac? |
| | *voo zahvay uhn sahk?* |
| Could you giftwrap _____ it, please? | Vous pouvez l'emballer dans un papier cadeau? |
| | *voo poovay lohnbahlay dohn zuhn pahpyay kahdoa?* |

| | |
|---|---|
| Je suis désolé, nous n'en avons pas____ | I'm sorry, we don't have that |
| Je suis désolé, le stock est épuisé _____ | I'm sorry, we're sold out |
| Je suis désolé, ce ne sera pas livré____ avant... | I'm sorry, that won't be in until... |
| Vous pouvez payer à la caisse _____ | You can pay at the cash desk |
| Nous n'acceptons pas les cartes de ____ crédit | We don't accept credit cards |
| Nous n'acceptons pas les chèques _____ de voyage | We don't accept traveler's checks |
| Nous n'acceptons pas les devises_____ étrangères | We don't accept foreign currency |

## 10 .2 Food

| | |
|---|---|
| I'd like a hundred_____ grams of..., please | Je voudrais cent grammes de... |
| | *jhuh voodreh sohn grahm duh...* |
| – five hundred grams/ ____ half a kilo of... | Je voudrais une livre de... |
| | *jhuh voodreh zewn leevr duh...* |
| – a kilo of... _____ | Je voudrais un kilo de... |
| | *jhuh voodreh zuhn keeloa duh...* |
| Could you...it for me, ____ please? | Vous voulez me le...? |
| | *voo voolay muh luh...?* |
| Could you slice it/_____ chop it for me, please? | Vous voulez me le couper en tranches/morceaux? |
| | *voo voolay muh luh koopay ohn trohnsh/mohrsoa?* |
| Could you grate it _____ for me, please? | Vous voulez me le râper? |
| | *voo voolay muh luh rahpay?* |
| Can I order it?_____ | Puis-je le commander? |
| | *pwee jhuh luh komohnday?* |
| I'll pick it up tomorrow/ ____ at... | Je viendrai le chercher demain/à...heures |
| | *jhuh vyahndray luh shehrshay duhmahn/ah...uhr* |
| Can you eat/drink this? ____ | Est-ce mangeable/buvable? |
| | *ehs mohnjhahbl/bewvahbl?* |
| What's in it? _____ | Qu'y a-t-il dedans? |
| | *kee yah teel duhdohn?* |

**Shopping**

**10**

| | |
|---|---|
| I saw something in the ____ window. Shall I point it out? | J'ai vu quelque chose dans la vitrine. Je vous le montre? *jhay vew kehlkuh shoaz dohn lah veetreen. jhuh voo lah mawntr?* |
| I'd like something to _____ go with this | J'aimerais quelque chose pour aller avec ceci *jhehmuhreh kehlkuh shoaz poor ahlay ahvehk suhsee* |
| Do you have shoes _____ to match this? | Avez-vous des chaussures de la même couleur que ça? *ahvay voo day shoasewr duh lah mehm kooluhr kuh sah?* |
| I'm a size...in the US_____ | Je fais du...aux États Unis *jhuh feh dew...ohz ehtahz oonee* |
| Can I try this on? _____ | Puis-je l'essayer? *pwee jhuh lehsayay?* |
| Where's the fitting room? __ | Où est la cabine d'essayage? *oo eh lah kahbeen dehsayahjh?* |
| It doesn't fit_____ | Cela ne me va pas *suhlah nuh muh vah pah* |
| This is the right size _____ | C'est la bonne taille *seh lah bon tahy* |
| It doesn't suit me_____ | Cela ne me convient pas *suhlah nuh muh kawnvyahn pah* |
| Do you have this in...? ____ | L'avez-vous aussi en...? *lahvay voo zoasee ohn...?* |
| The heel's too high/low ____ | Je trouve le talon trop haut/bas *jhuh troov luh tahlawn troa oa/bah* |
| Is this/are these _____ genuine leather? | Est-ce/sont-elles en cuir? *eh suh/sawn tehl ohn kweer?* |
| I'm looking for a..._____ for a...-year-old baby/child | Je cherche un...pour un bébé/enfant de...ans *jhuh shehrsh uhn...poor uhn baybay/ohnhfohn duh...ohn* |
| I'd like a... ... _____ | J'aurais aimé un...de... *jhoareh zaymay uhn... duh...* |
| – silk _____ | J'aurais aimé un...de soie *jhoareh zaymay uhn...duh swah* |
| – cotton _____ | J'aurais aimé un...de coton *jhoareh zaymay uhn...duh koatawn* |
| – woollen _____ | J'aurais aimé un...de laine *jhoareh zaymay uhn...duh lehn* |
| – linen_____ | J'aurais aimé un...de lin *jhoareh zaymay uhn...duh lahn* |
| What temperature _____ can I wash it at? | A quelle température puis-je le laver? *ah kehl tohnpayrahtewr pwee jhuh luh lahvay?* |
| Will it shrink in the _____ wash? | Cela rétrécit au lavage? *suhlah raytraysee oa lahvahjh?* |

| | | |
|---|---|---|
| Ne pas repasser | Étendre humide | Laver à la main |
| **Do not iron** | **Drip dry** | **Hand wash** |
| Ne pas essorer | Nettoyage à sec | Laver à la machine |
| **Do not spin dry** | **Dry clean** | **Machine wash** |

### At the cobbler

Could you mend _____ these shoes?
Pouvez-vous réparer ces chaussures?
*poovay voo raypahray say shoasewr?*

Could you put new _____ soles/heels on these?
Pouvez-vous y mettre de nouvelles semelles/nouveaux talons?
*poovay voo zee mehtr duh noovehl suhmehl/noovoa tahlawn?*

When will they be _____ ready?
Quand seront-elles prêtes?
*kohn suhrawn tehl preht?*

I'd like..., please _____
Je voudrais...
*jhuh voodreh...*

– a can of shoe polish _____
Je voudrais une boîte de cirage
*jhuh voodreh zewn bwaht duh seerahjh*

– a pair of shoelaces_____
Je voudrais une paire de lacets
*jhuh voodreh zewn pehr duh lahseh*

## 10 .4 Photographs and video

I'd like a film for this_____ camera, please
Je voudrais un rouleau de pellicules pour cet appareil
*jhuh voodreh zuhn rooloa duh payleekewl poor seht ahpahrehy*

– a 126 _____ cartridge
Je voudrais une cartouche de cent vingt-six
*jhuh voodreh zewn kahrtoosh duh sohn vahn sees*

– a slide film _____
Je voudrais un rouleau de pellicules pour diapositives
*jhuh voodreh zuhn rooloa duh payleekewl poor deeahpoaseeteev*

– a film _____
Je voudrais un rouleau de pellicules
*jhuh voodreh zuhn rooloa duh payleekewl*

– a videotape _____
Je voudrais une vidéocassette
*jhuh voodreh zewn veedayoakahseht*

color/black and white _____
couleur/noir et blanc
*kooluhr/nwahr ay blohn*

super eight _____
super huit mm
*sewpehr wee meeleemehtr*

12/24/36 exposures _____
douze/vingt-quatre/trente-six poses
*dooz/vahn kahtr/trohnt see poaz*

ASA/DIN number_____
nombre d'ASA/DIN
*nohnbr dahzah/deen*

daylight film _____
film pour la lumière du jour
*feelm poor lah lewmyehr dew joor*

film for artificial light _____
film pour la lumière artificielle
*feelm poor lah lewmyehr ahrteefeesyehl*

### Problems

| | |
|---|---|
| Could you load the _____ film for me, please? | Voulez-vous mettre le film dans l'appareil? *voolay voo mehtr luh feelm dohn lahpahrehy?* |
| Could you take the film ____ out for me, please? | Voulez-vous enlever le film de l'appareil-photo? *voolay voo zohnluhvay luh feelm duh lahpahrehy foatoa?* |
| Should I replace_____ the batteries? | Dois-je changer les piles? *dwah jhuh shohnjhay lay peel?* |
| Could you have a look_____ at my camera, please? It's not working | Voulez-vous jeter un coup d'oeil à mon appareil-photo? Il ne marche plus *voolay voo jhuhtay uhn koo duhy ah mawn nahpahrehy foatoa? eel nuh mahrsh plew* |
| The...is broken _____ | Le...est cassé *luh...eh kahssay* |
| The film's jammed _____ | La pellicule est bloquée *lah payleekewl eh blokay* |
| The film's broken_____ | La pellicule est cassée *lah payleekewl eh kahssay* |
| The flash isn't working ____ | Le flash ne marche pas *luh flahsh nuh mahrsh pah* |

### Processing and prints

| | |
|---|---|
| I'd like to have this film ____ developed/printed, please | Je voudrais faire développer/tirer ce film *jhuh voodreh fehr dayvuhlopay/teeray suh feelm* |
| I'd like...prints from _____ each negative | Je voudrais...tirages de chaque négatif *jhuh voodreh...teerahjh duh shahk naygahteef* |
| glossy/matte _____ | brillant/mat *breeyohn/maht* |
| 6x9_____ | six sur neuf *sees sewr nuhf* |
| I'd like to re-order _____ these photos | Je veux faire refaire cette photo *jhuh vuh fehr ruhfehr seht foatoa* |
| I'd like to have this _____ photo enlarged | Je veux faire agrandir cette photo *jhuh vuh fehr ahgrohndeer seht foatoa* |
| How much is_____ processing? | Combien coûte le développement? *kawnbyahn koot luh dayvuhlopmohn?* |
| – printing _____ | Combien coûte le tirage? *kawnbyahn koot luh teerahjh?* |
| – to reorder _____ | Combien coûte la commande supplémentaire? *kawnbyahn koot lah komohnd sewplaymohntehr?* |
| – the enlargement_____ | Combien coûte l'agrandissement? *kawnbyahn koot lahgrohndeesmohn?* |
| When will they_____ be ready? | Quand seront-elles prêtes? *kohn suhrawn tehl preht?* |

## 10 .5 At the hairdresser's

Do I have to make an _____ appointment?
Dois-je prendre un rendez-vous?
*dwah jhuh prohndr uhn rohnday voo?*

Can I come in right _____ now?
Pouvez-vous vous occuper de moi immédiatement?
*poovay voo voo zokewpay duh mwah eemaydyahtmohn?*

How long will I have_____ to wait?
Combien de temps dois-je attendre?
*kawnbyahn duh tohn dwah jhahtohndr?*

I'd like a shampoo/ _____ haircut
Je veux me faire laver/couper les cheveux
*jhuh vuh muh fehr lahvay/koopay lay shuhvuh*

I'd like a shampoo for_____ oily/dry hair, please
Je voudrais un shampooing pour cheveux gras/secs
*jhuh voodreh zuhn shohnpwahn poor shuhvuh grah/sehk*

an anti-dandruff_____ shampoo
Je voudrais un shampooing anti-pelliculaire
*jhuh voodreh zuhn shohnpwahn ohnteepayleekewlehr*

– a shampoo for_____ permed/colored hair
Je voudrais un shampooing pour cheveux permanentés/colorés
*jhuh voodreh zuhn shohnpwahn poor shuhvuh pehrmahnohntay/kohlohray*

– a color rinse shampoo ___
Je voudrais un shampooing colorant
*jhuh voodreh zuhn shohnpwahn kolorohn*

– a shampoo with _____ conditioner
Je voudrais un shampooing avec un soin traitant
*jhuh voodreh zuhn shohnpwahn ahvehk uhn swahn trehtohn*

– highlights _____
Je voudrais me faire faire des mèches
*jhuh voodreh muh fehr fehr day mehsh*

Do you have a color _____ chart, please?
Avez-vous une carte de coloration s'il vous plaît?
*ahvay voo zewn kahrt duh kolorahsyawn seel voo pleh?*

I want to keep it the _____ same color
Je veux garder la même couleur
*jhuh vuh gahrday lah mehm kooluhr*

I'd like it darker/lighter _____
Je les veux plus sombres/clairs
*jhuh lay vuh plew sawmbr/klehr*

I'd like/I don't want _____ hairspray
Je veux de la/ne veux pas de laque
*jhuh vuh duh la/nuh vuh pah duh lahk*

– gel_____
Je veux du/ne veux pas de gel
*jhuh vuh dew/ nuh vuh pah duh jhehl*

– lotion _____
Je veux de la/ne veux pas de lotion
*jhuh vuh duh lah/nuh vuh pah duh loasyawn*

I'd like short bangs _____
Je veux ma frange courte
*jhuh vuh mah frohnjh koort*

Not too short at the _____ back
Je ne veux pas la nuque trop courte
*jhuh nuh vuh pah lah newk troa koort*

Not too long here _____
Ici je ne les veux pas trop longs
*eesee jhuh nuh lay vuh pah troa lawn*

I'd like/I don't want _____ (many) curls
Je (ne) veux (pas) être (trop) frisée
*jhuh (nuh) vuh (pah) ehtr (troa) freezay*

Shopping

10

89

| It needs a little/_____ a lot taken off | Il faut en enlever une petite/grande quantité |
| | *eel foa ohn nohnluhvay ewn puhteet/grohnd kohnteetay* |
| I want a completely _____ different style | Je veux une toute autre coupe |
| | *jhuh vuh zewn toot oatr koop* |
| I'd like it like..._____ | Je veux mes cheveux comme... |
| | *jhuh vuh may shuhvuh kom...* |
| – the same as that lady's___ | Je veux la même coiffure que cette femme |
| | *jhuh vuh lah mehm kwahfewr kuh seht fahm* |
| – the same as in this photo | Je veux la même coiffure que sur cette photo |
| | *jhuh vuh lah mehm kwahfewr kuh sewr seht foatoa* |
| Could you put the _____ drier up/down a bit? | Pouvez-vous mettre le casque plus haut/plus bas? |
| | *poovay voo mehtr luh kahsk plew oa/plew bah?* |
| I'd like a facial_____ | J'aimerais un masque de beauté |
| | *jhehmuhreh zuhn mahsk duh boatay* |
| – a manicure_____ | J'aimerais qu'on me fasse les ongles |
| | *jhehmuhreh kawn muh fahs lay zawngl* |
| – a massage _____ | J'aimerais un massage |
| | *jhehmuhreh zuhn mahsahjh* |

| Quelle coupe de cheveux_____ désirez-vous? | How do you want it cut? |
| Quelle coiffure désirez-vous? _____ | What style did you have in mind? |
| Quelle couleur désirez-vous? _____ | What color do you want? |
| Est-ce la bonne température? _____ | Is the temperature all right for you? |
| Voulez-vous lire quelque chose? _____ | Would you like something to read? |
| Voulez-vous boire quelque chose? _____ | Would you like a drink? |
| C'est ce que vous vouliez?_____ | Is this what you had in mind? |

| Could you trim_____ my bangs? | Pouvez-vous égaliser ma frange? |
| | *poovay voo zaygahleezay mah frohnjh?* |
| – my beard? _____ | Pouvez-vous égaliser ma barbe? |
| | *poovay voo zaygahleezay mah bahrb?* |
| – my moustache? _____ | Pouvez-vous égaliser ma moustache? |
| | *poovay voo zaygahleezay mah moostahsh?* |
| I'd like a shave, please ____ | Pouvez-vous me raser s'il vous plaît? |
| | *poovay voo muh rahzay seel voo pleh?* |
| I'd like a wet shave,_____ please | Je veux être rasé au rasoir à main |
| | *jhuh vuh zehtr rahzay oa rahzwahr ah mahn* |

# **A**t the Tourist Information Center

**11.1** **P**laces of interest      92

**11.2** **G**oing out      94

**11.3** **R**eserving tickets      95

# 11 **A**t the Tourist Information Center

## 11 .1 **P**laces of interest

| | |
|---|---|
| Where's the Tourist Information, please? | Où est l'office de tourisme?<br>*oo eh lofees duh tooreesm?* |
| Do you have a city map? | Avez-vous un plan de la ville?<br>*ahvay voo zuhn plohn duh lah veel?* |
| Where is the museum? | Où est le musée?<br>*oo eh luh mewzay?* |
| Where can I find a church? | Où puis-je trouver une église?<br>*oo pwee jhuh troovay ewn aygleez?* |
| Could you give me some information about...? | Pouvez-vous me renseigner sur...?<br>*poovay voo muh rohnsehnyay sewr...?* |
| How much is that? | Combien ça coûte?<br>*kawnbyahn sah koot?* |
| What are the main places of interest? | Quelles sont les curiosités les plus importantes?<br>*kehl sawn lay kewryoseetay lay plewz ahnportohnt?* |
| Could you point them out on the map? | Pouvez-vous les indiquer sur la carte?<br>*poovay voo lay zahndeekay sewr lah kahrt?* |
| What do you recommend? | Que nous conseillez-vous?<br>*kuh noo kawnsehyay voo?* |
| We'll be here for a few hours | Nous restons ici quelques heures.<br>*noo rehstawn zeesee kehlkuh zuhr.* |
| – a day | Nous restons ici une journée.<br>*noo rehstawn zeesee ewn jhoornay.* |
| – a week | Nous restons ici une semaine.<br>*noo rehstawn zeesee ewn suhmehn.* |
| We're interested in... | Nous sommes intéressés par...<br>*noo som zahntayrehsay pahr...* |
| Is there a scenic walk around the city? | Pouvons-nous faire une promenade en ville?<br>*poovawn noo fehr ewn promuhnahd ohn veel?* |
| How long does it take? | Combien de temps dure-t-elle?<br>*kawnbyahn duh tohn dewr tehl?* |
| Where does it start/end? | Où est le point de départ/d'arrivée?<br>*oo eh luh pwahn duh daypahr/dahreevay?* |
| Are there any boat cruises here? | Y a-t-il des bateaux-mouches?<br>*ee yah teel day bahtoa moosh?* |
| Where can we board? | Où pouvons-nous embarquer?<br>*oo poovawn noo zohnbahrkay?* |
| Are there any bus tours? | Y a-t-il des promenades en bus?<br>*ee yah teel day promuhnahd ohn bews?* |
| Where do we get on? | Où devons-nous monter?<br>*oo devawn noo mawntay?* |
| Is there a guide who speaks English? | Y a-t-il un guide qui parle l'anglais?<br>*ee yah teel uhn gueed kee pahrl lohngleh?* |
| What trips can we take around the area? | Quelles promenades peut-on faire dans la région?<br>*kehl promuhnahd puh tawn fehr dohn lah rayjhyawn?* |

| | |
|---|---|
| Are there any excursions? | Y a-t-il des excursions? |
| | *ee yah teel day zehxkewrsyawn?* |
| Where do they go to? | Où vont-elles? |
| | *oo vawn tehl?* |
| We'd like to go to... | Nous voulons aller à... |
| | *noo voolawn zahlay ah...* |
| How long is the trip? | Combien de temps dure l'excursion? |
| | *kawnbyahn duh tohn dewr lehxkewrsyawn?* |
| How long do we stay in...? | Combien de temps restons-nous à...? |
| | *kawnbyahn duh tohn rehstawn noo zah...?* |
| Are there any guided tours? | Y a-t-il des visites guidées? |
| | *ee yah teel day veezeet gueeday?* |
| How much free time will we have there? | Combien de temps avons-nous de libre? |
| | *kawnbyahn duh tohn ahvawn noo duh leebr?* |
| We want to go hiking | Nous voulons faire une randonnée |
| | *noo voolawn fehr ewn rohndonay* |
| Can we hire a guide? | Pouvons-nous prendre un guide? |
| | *poovawn noo prohndr uhn gueed?* |
| Can I reserve mountain huts? | Puis-je réserver un refuge? |
| | *pwee jhuh rayzehrvay uhn ruhfewjhuh?* |
| What time does... open/close? | A quelle heure ouvre/ferme...? |
| | *ah kehl uhr oovr/fehrm...?* |
| What days is...open/ closed? | Quels sont les jours d'ouverture/de fermeture de...? |
| | *kehl sawn lay jhoor doovehrtewr/duh fehrmuhtewr duh...?* |
| What's the admission price? | Quel est le prix d'entrée? |
| | *kehl eh luh pree dohntray?* |
| Is there a group discount? | Y a-t-il une réduction pour les groupes? |
| | *ee yah teel ewn raydewksyawn poor lay groop?* |
| Is there a child discount? | Y a-t-il une réduction pour les enfants? |
| | *ee yah teel ewn raydewksyawn poor lay zohnfohn?* |
| Is there a discount for seniors? | Y a-t-il une réduction pour les personnes de plus de soixante-cinq ans? |
| | *ee yah teel ewn raydewksyawn poor lay pehrson duh plew duh swahssohnt sahnk ohn?* |
| Can I take (flash) photos/can I film here? | M'est-il permis de prendre des photos(avec flash)/filmer ici? |
| | *meh teel pehrmee duh prohndr day foatoa(ahvehk flahsh)/feelmay eesee?* |
| Do you have any postcards of...? | Vendez-vous des cartes postales de...? |
| | *vohnday voo day kahrt postahl duh...?* |
| Do you have an English...? | Avez-vous un...en anglais? |
| | *ahvay voo zuhn...ohn nohngleh?* |
| – an English catalogue? | Avez-vous un catalogue en anglais? |
| | *ahvay voo zuhn kahtahlog ohn nohngleh?* |
| – an English program? | Avez-vous un programme en anglais? |
| | *ahvay voo zuhn programh ohn nohngleh?* |
| – an English brochure? | Avez-vous une brochure en anglais? |
| | *ahvay voo zewn broshewr ohn nohngleh?* |

**At the Tourist Information Center**

● **In French theaters** you are usually shown to your seat by an usherette from whom you can buy a program. It is customary to tip. At the cinema most films are dubbed (*version française*). In large cities subtitled versions are often screened, advertised as *version originale* or *V.O.* If the publicity does not mention *V.O.*, the film will be dubbed. *L'Officiel des spectacles* (an entertainment guide) can be obtained from newspaper kiosks.

| | |
|---|---|
| Do you have this _____ week's/month's entertainment guide? | Avez-vous le journal des spectacles de cette semaine/de ce mois? *ahvay voo luh jhoornal day spehktahkl duh seht suhmehn/duh suh mwah?* |
| What's on tonight? _____ | Que peut-on faire ce soir? *kuh puh tawn fehr suh swahr?* |
| We want to go to... _____ | Nous voulons aller à... *noo voolawn zahlay oa...* |
| Which films are _____ showing? | Quels films passe-t-on? *kehl feelm pah stawn?* |
| What sort of film is that?___ | Qu'est-ce que c'est comme film? *kehs kuh seh kom feelm?* |
| suitable for all ages _____ | pour tous les âges *poor too lay zahjh* |
| not suitable for children under 12/16 years | pour les plus de douze ans/seize ans *poor lay plew duh dooz ohn/sehz ohn* |
| original version _____ | version originale *vehrsyawn oreejheenahl* |
| subtitled_____ | sous-titré *soo teetray* |
| dubbed_____ | doublé *dooblay* |
| Is it a continuous_____ showing? | Est-ce un spectacle permanent? *ehs uhn spehktahkl pehrmahnohn?* |
| What's on at...?_____ | Qu'y a-t-il au...? *kee yah teel oa...?* |
| – the theater? _____ | Qu'y a-t-il au théâtre? *kee yah teel oa tayahtr?* |
| – the concert hall? _____ | Qu'y a-t-il à la salle des concerts? *kee yah teel ah lah sahl day kawnsehr?* |
| – the opera? _____ | Qu'y a-t-il à l'opéra? *kee yah teel ah loapayrah?* |
| Where can I find a good ___ disco around here? | Où se trouve une bonne disco par ici? *oo suh troov ewn bon deeskoa pahr eesee?* |
| Is it members only? _____ | Exige-t-on une carte de membre? *ehgzeejh-tawn ewn kahrt duh mohnbr?* |
| Where can I find a good ___ nightclub around here? | Où se trouve une bonne boîte de nuit par ici? *oo suh troov ewn bon bwaht duh nwee pahr eesee?* |
| Is it evening wear only? ___ | La tenue de soirée, est-elle obligatoire? *lah tuhnew duh swahray, eh tehl obleegahtwahr?* |
| Should I/we dress up? _____ | La tenue de soirée, est-elle souhaitée? *lah tuhnew duh swahray ehtehl sooehtay?* |

| | |
|---|---|
| What time does the _____ show start? | A quelle heure commence la représentation? |
| | *ah kehl uhr komohns lah ruhprayzohntahsyawn?* |
| When's the next soccer _____ match? | Quand est le prochain match de football? |
| | *kohn teh luh proshahn mahtch duh footbohl?* |
| Who's playing? _____ | Qui joue contre qui? |
| | *kee jhoo kawntr kee?* |
| I'd like an escort for _____ tonight. Could you arrange that for me? | Je veux une hôtesse pour ce soir. Pouvez-vous arranger ça? |
| | *jhuh vuh zewn oatehs poor suh swahr. poovay voo zahrohnjhay sah?* |

## 11 .3 Reserving tickets

| | |
|---|---|
| Could you reserve some ___ tickets for us? | Pouvez-vous nous faire une réservation? |
| | *poovay voo noo fehr ewn rayzehrvahsyawn?* |
| We'd like to reserve... _____ seats/a table... | Nous voulons...places/une table... |
| | *noo voolawn...plahs/ewn tahbl...* |
| – in the orchestra_____ | Nous voulons...places à l'orchestre. |
| | *noo voolawn...plahs ah lorkehstr* |
| – in the balcony _____ | Nous voulons...places au balcon. |
| | *noo voolawn...plahs oa bahlkawn* |
| – box seats _____ | Nous voulons...places dans les loges. |
| | *noo voolawn...plahs dohn lay lojh* |
| – a table at the front_____ | Nous voulons...une table à l'avant. |
| | *noo voolawn...ewn tahbl ah lahvohn* |
| – in the middle _____ | Nous voulons...places au milieu. |
| | *noo voolawn...plahs oa meelyuh* |
| – at the back _____ | Nous voulons...places à l'arrière. |
| | *noo voolawn...plahs ah lahryehr* |
| Could I reserve...seats for _ the...o'clock performance? | Puis-je réserver...places pour la représentation de...heures? |
| | *pwee jhuh rayzehrvay...plahs poor lah ruhprayzohntahsyawn duh...uhr?* |
| Are there any seats left ____ for tonight? | Reste-t-il encore des places pour ce soir? |
| | *rehst-uh-teel ohnkor day plahs poor suh swahr?* |
| How much is a ticket? _____ | Combien coûte un billet? |
| | *kawnbyahn koot uhn beeyeh?* |
| When can I pick the _____ tickets up? | Quand puis-je venir chercher les billets? |
| | *kohn pwee jhuh vuhneer shehrshay lay beeyeh?* |
| I've got a reservation _____ | J'ai réservé |
| | *jhay rayzehrvay* |
| My name's... _____ | Mon nom est... |
| | *mawn nawn eh...* |

| | |
|---|---|
| Vous voulez réserver pour quelle représentation? _____ | Which performance do you want to reserve for? |
| Où voulez-vous vous asseoir? _____ | Where would you like to sit? |
| Tout est vendu_____ | Everything's sold out |
| Il ne reste que des places debout _____ | It's standing room only |
| Il ne reste que des places_____ au balcon | We've only got balcony seats left |
| Il ne reste que des places au_____ poulailler | We've only got seats left in the top balcony |
| Il ne reste que des places_____ d'orchestre | We've only got orchestra seats left |
| Il ne reste que des places à l'avant _____ | We've only got seats left at the front |
| Il ne reste que des places à l'arrière _____ | We've only got seats left at the back |
| Combien de places voulez-vous?_____ | How many seats would you like? |
| Vous devez venir chercher les billets _____ avant...heures | You'll have to pick up the tickets before...o'clock |
| Puis-je voir vos billets? _____ | Tickets, please |
| Voici votre place _____ | This is your seat |
| Vous n'êtes pas aux bonnes places_____ | You're in the wrong seats |

# Sports

**12.1** Sporting questions     98

**12.2** By the waterfront     98

**12.3** In the snow     99

## 12 Sports

### 12.1 Sporting questions

| | |
|---|---|
| Where can we... around here? | Où pouvons-nous...? |
| | *oo poovawn noo...?* |
| Is there a... around here? | Y a-t-il un...dans les environs? |
| | *ee yah teel uhn...dohn lay zohnveerawn?* |
| Can I hire a...here? | Puis-je louer un...ici? |
| | *pwee jhuh looay uhn...eesee?* |
| Can I take...lessons? | Puis-je prendre des cours de...? |
| | *pwee jhuh prohndr day koor duh...?* |
| How much is that per hour/per day/a turn? | Quel est le prix à l'heure/à la journée/à chaque fois? |
| | *kehl eh luh pree ah luhr/ah lah jhoornay/ah shahk fwah?* |
| Do I need a permit for that? | A-t-on besoin d'un permis? |
| | *ah tawn buhzwahn duhn pehrmee?* |
| Where can I get the permit? | Où puis-je obtenir le permis? |
| | *oo pwee jhuh obtuhneer luh pehrmee?* |

### 12.2 By the waterfront

| | |
|---|---|
| Is it a long way to the sea still? | La mer, est-elle encore loin? |
| | *lah mehr eh tehl ohnkor lwahn?* |
| Is there a...around here? | Y a-t-il un...dans les environs? |
| | *ee yah teel uhn...dohn lay zohnveerawn?* |
| – a public swimming pool | Y a-t-il une piscine dans les environs? |
| | *ee yah teel ewn peeseen dohn lay zohnveerawn?* |
| – a sandy beach | Y a-t-il une plage de sable dans les environs? |
| | *ee yah teel ewn plahjh duh sahbl dohn lay zohnveerawn?* |
| – a nudist beach | Y a-t-il une plage pour nudistes dans les environs? |
| | *ee yah teel ewn plahjh poor newdeest dohn lay zohnveerawn?* |
| – docking | Y a-t-il un embarcadère pour les bateaux dans les environs? |
| | *ee yah teel uhn nohnbahrkahdehr poor lay bahtoa dohn lay zohnveerawn?* |
| Are there any rocks here? | Y a-t-il aussi des rochers ici? |
| | *ee yah teel oasee day roshay eesee?* |
| When's high/low tide? | Quand est la marée haute/basse? |
| | *kohn teh lah mahray oat/bahs?* |
| What's the water temperature? | Quelle est la température de l'eau? |
| | *kehl eh lah tohnpayratewr duh loa?* |
| Is it (very) deep here? | Est-ce (très) profond ici? |
| | *ehs (treh) proafawn eesee?* |
| Can you stand here? | A-t-on pied ici? |
| | *ah tawn pyay eesee?* |
| Is it safe to swim here? | Peut-on nager en sécurité ici? |
| | *puh tawn nahjhay ohn saykewreetay eesee?* |
| Are there any currents? | Y a-t-il des courants? |
| | *ee yah teel day koorohn?* |

**Sports**

**12**

| | |
|---|---|
| Are there any rapids/_____ waterfalls in this river? | Est-ce que cette rivière a des courants rapides/des chutes d'eau? |
| | *ehs kuh seht reevyeer ah day koorohn rahpeed/day shewt doa?* |
| What does that flag/_____ buoy mean? | Que signifie ce drapeau/cette bouée là-bas? |
| | *kuh seenyeefee suh drahpoa/seht booway lah bah?* |
| Is there a life guard_____ on duty here? | Y a-t-il un maître nageur qui surveille? |
| | *ee yah teel uhn mehtr nahjhuhr kee sewrvehy?* |
| Are dogs allowed here?____ | Les chiens sont admis ici? |
| | *lay shyahn sawn tahdmee eesee?* |
| Is camping on the _____ beach allowed? | Peut-on camper sur la plage? |
| | *puh tawn kohnpay sewr lah plahjh?* |
| Are we allowed to_____ build a fire here? | Peut-on faire un feu ici? |
| | *puh tawn fehr uhn fuh eesee?* |

| | | |
|---|---|---|
| Danger | Pêche interdite | Baignade interdite |
| **Danger** | **No fishing** | **No swimming** |
| Pêche | Surf interdit | Seulement avec permis |
| **Fishing water** | **No surfing** | **Permits only** |

## 12 .3 In the snow

| | |
|---|---|
| Can I take ski lessons_____ here? | Puis-je prendre des leçons de ski? |
| | *pwee jhuh prohndr day luhsawn duh skee?* |
| for beginners/advanced____ | pour débutants/initiés |
| | *poor daybewtohn/eeneesyay* |
| How large are the _____ groups? | Quelle est la taille des groupes? |
| | *kehl eh lah tahy day groop?* |
| What language are _____ the classes in? | En quelle langue donne-t-on les leçons de ski? |
| | *ohn kehl lohng don tawn lay luhsawn duh skee?* |
| I'd like a lift pass, _____ please | Je voudrais un abonnement pour les remontées mécaniques. |
| | *jhuh voodreh zuhn nahbonmohn poor lay ruhmawntay maykahneek* |
| Must I give you a_____ passport photo? | Dois-je donner une photo d'identité? |
| | *dwah jhuh donay ewn foatoa deedohnteetay?* |
| Where can I have a _____ passport photo taken? | Où puis-je faire faire une photo d'identité? |
| | *oo pwee jhuh fehr fehr ewn foatoa deedohnteetay?* |
| Where are the_____ beginners' slopes? | Où sont les pistes de ski pour débutants? |
| | *oo sawn lay peest duh skee poor daybewtohn?* |
| Are there any runs for _____ cross-country skiing? | Y a-t-il des pistes de ski de fond dans les environs? |
| | *ee yah teel day peest duh skee duh fawn dohn lay zohnveerawn?* |

**Sports**

**12**

| | |
|---|---|
| Have the cross-country runs been marked? | Les pistes de ski de fond, sont-elles indiquées? |
| | *lay peest duh skee duh fawn, sawn tehl ahndeekay?* |
| Are the...in operation? | Est-ce que les...marchent? |
| | *ehs kuh lay...mahrsh?* |
| – the ski lifts | Est-ce que les remontées mécaniques marchent? |
| | *ehs kuh lay ruhmawntay maykahneek mahrsh?* |
| – the chair lifts | Est-ce que les télésièges marchent? |
| | *ehs kuh lay taylaysyehjh mahrsh?* |
| Are the slopes usable? | Est-ce que les pistes sont ouvertes? |
| | *ehs kuh lay peest sawn toovehrt?* |
| Are the cross-country runs usable? | Est-ce que les pistes de ski de fond sont ouvertes? |
| | *ehs kuh lay peest duh skee duh fawn sawn toovehrt?* |

# **S**ickness

**13.1 C**all (get) the doctor   102

**13.2 P**atient's ailments   102

**13.3 T**he consultation   103

**13.4 M**edication and
prescriptions   105

**13.5 A**t the dentist's   106

## 13 Sickness

### 13.1 Call (get) the doctor

| | |
|---|---|
| Could you call/get a _____ doctor quickly, please? | Voulez-vous vite appeler/aller chercher un médecin s'il vous plaît?<br>*voolay voo veet ahpuhlay/ahlay shehrshay uhn maydsahn seel voo pleh?* |
| When does the doctor _____ have office hours? | Quand est-ce que le médecin reçoit?<br>*kohn tehs kuh luh maydsahn ruhswah?* |
| When can the doctor _____ come? | Quand est-ce que le médecin peut venir?<br>*kohn tehs kuh luh maydsahn puh vuhneer?* |
| I'd like to make an _____ appointment to see the doctor | Pouvez-vous me prendre un rendez-vous chez le médecin?<br>*poovay voo muh prohndr uhn rohnday voo shay luh maydsahn?* |
| I've got an appointment ___ to see the doctor at... | J'ai un rendez-vous chez le médecin à...heures<br>*jhay uhn rohnday voo shay luh maydsahn a...uhr* |
| Which doctor/pharmacy ___ has night/weekend duty? | Quel médecin/Quelle pharmacie est de garde cette nuit/ce week-end?<br>*kehl maydsahn/kehl fahrmahsee eh duh gahrd seht nwee/suh week-ehnd?* |

### 13 .2 Patient's ailments

| | |
|---|---|
| I don't feel well _____ | Je ne me sens pas bien<br>*jhuh nuh muh sohn pah byahn* |
| I'm dizzy _____ | J'ai des vertiges<br>*jhay day vehrteejh* |
| – ill _____ | Je suis malade<br>*jhuh swee mahlahd* |
| – sick _____ | J'ai mal au coeur<br>*jhay mahl oa kuhr* |
| I've got a cold _____ | Je suis enrhumé(e)<br>*jhuh swee zohnrewmay* |
| It hurts here _____ | J'ai mal ici<br>*jhay mahl eesee* |
| I've been throwing up ____ | J'ai vomi<br>*jhay vomee* |
| I've got... _____ | Je souffre de...<br>*jhuh soofr duh...* |
| I'm running a _____ temperature | J'ai de la fièvre<br>*jhayduh lah fyehvr* |
| I've been stung by _____ a wasp. | J'ai été piqué(e) par une guêpe<br>*jhay aytay peekay pahr ewn gehp* |
| I've been stung by an _____ insect | J'ai été piqué(e) par un insecte<br>*jhay aytay peekay pahr uhn nahnsehkt* |
| I've been bitten by _____ a dog | J'ai été mordu(e) par un chien<br>*jhay aytay mordew pahr uhn shyahn* |
| I've been stung by _____ a jellyfish | J'ai été piqué(e) par une méduse<br>*jhay aytay peekay pahr ewn maydewz* |
| I've been bitten by _____ a snake | J'ai été mordu(e) par un serpent<br>*jhay aytay mordew pahr uhn sehrpohn* |

| | |
|---|---|
| I've been bitten by an animal | J'ai été mordu(e) par un animal |
| | *jhay aytay mordew pahr uhn nahneemahl* |
| I've cut myself | Je me suis coupé(e) |
| | *jhuh muh swee koopay* |
| I've burned myself | Je me suis brûlé(e) |
| | *jhuh muh swee brewlay* |
| I've grazed myself | Je me suis égratigné(e) |
| | *jhuh muh swee zaygrahteenyay* |
| I've had a fall | Je suis tombé(e) |
| | *jhuh swee tawnbay* |
| I've sprained my ankle | Je me suis foulé(e) la cheville |
| | *jhuh muh swee foolay lah shuhveey* |
| I've come for the morning-after pill | Je viens pour la pilule du lendemain |
| | *jhuh vyahn poor lah peelewl dew lohndmahn* |

## 🖐 .3 The consultation

| | |
|---|---|
| Quels sont vos symptômes? | What seems to be the problem? |
| Depuis combien de temps avez-vous ces symptômes? | How long have you had these symptoms? |
| Avez-vous eu ces symptômes auparavant? | Have you had this trouble before? |
| Avez-vous de la fièvre? | How high is your temperature? |
| Déshabillez-vous s'il vous plaît? | Get undressed, please |
| Pouvez-vous vous mettre torse nu? | Strip to the waist, please |
| Vous pouvez vous déshabiller là-bas. | You can undress there |
| Pouvez-vous remonter la manche de votre bras gauche/droit? | Roll up your left/right sleeve, please |
| Allongez-vous ici | Lie down here, please |
| Ceci vous fait mal? | Does this hurt? |
| Aspirez et expirez profondément | Breathe deeply |
| Ouvrez la bouche | Open your mouth |

### Patient's medical history

| | |
|---|---|
| I'm a diabetic | Je suis diabétique |
| | *jhuh swee dyahbayteek* |
| I have a heart condition | Je suis cardiaque |
| | *jhuh swee kahrdyahk* |
| I have asthma | J'ai de l'asthme |
| | *jhay duh lahsm* |
| I'm allergic to... | Je suis allergique à... |
| | *jhuh swee zahlehrjheek ah...* |
| I'm...months pregnant | Je suis enceinte de...mois |
| | *jhuh swee zohnsahnt duh...mwah* |
| I'm on a diet | Je suis au régime |
| | *jhuh swee zoa rayjheem* |
| I'm on medication/the pill | Je prends des médicaments/la pilule |
| | *jhuh prohn day maydeekahmohn/lah peelewl* |

| I've had a heart attack once before | J'ai déjà eu une crise cardiaque |
| | *jhay dayjhah ew ewn kreez kahrdyahk* |
| I've had a(n)...operation | J'ai été opéré(e) de... |
| | *jhay aytay oapayray duh...* |
| I've been ill recently | Je viens d'être malade |
| | *jhuh vyahn dehtr mahlahd* |
| I've got an ulcer | J'ai un ulcère à l'estomac |
| | *jhay uhn newlsehr ah lehstomah* |
| I've got my period | J'ai mes règles |
| | *jhay may rehgl* |

---

| Avez-vous des allergies? | Do you have any allergies? |
| Prenez-vous des médicaments? | Are you on any medication? |
| Suivez-vous un régime? | Are you on a diet? |
| Etes-vous enceinte? | Are you pregnant? |
| Etes-vous vacciné(e) contre le tétanos? | Have you had a tetanus injection? |

### The diagnosis

| Is it contagious? | Est-ce contagieux? |
| | *ehs kawntahjhyuh?* |
| How long do I have to stay...? | Combien de temps dois-je rester...? |
| | *kawnbyahn duh tohn dwah jhuh rehstay...?* |
| – in bed | Combien de temps dois-je rester au lit? |
| | *kawnbyahn duh tohn dwah jhuh rehstay oa lee?* |
| – in the hospital | Combien de temps dois-je rester à l'hôpital? |
| | *kawnbyahn duh tohn dwah jhuh rehstay ah loapeetahl?* |

---

| Ce n'est rien de grave | It's nothing serious |
| Vous vous êtes cassé le/la... | Your...is broken |
| Vous vous êtes foulé le/la... | You've sprained your... |
| Vous vous êtes déchiré le/la... | You've got a torn... |
| Vous avez une inflammation | You've got an infection |
| Vous avez une crise d'appendicite | You've got appendicitis |
| Vous avez une bronchite | You've got bronchitis |
| Vous avez une maladie vénérienne | You've got a venereal disease |
| Vous avez une grippe | You've got the flu |
| Vous avez eu une crise cardiaque | You've had a heart attack |
| Vous avez une infection (virale/bactérielle) | You've got an infection (viral/bacterial) |
| Vous avez une pneumonie | You've got pneumonia |

**Sickness**

**3**

| | |
|---|---|
| Vous avez un ulcère à l'estomac _____ | You've got an ulcer |
| Vous vous êtes froissé un muscle _____ | You've pulled a muscle |
| Vous avez une infection vaginale _____ | You've got a vaginal infection |
| Vous avez une intoxication alimentaire | You've got food poisoning |
| Vous avez une insolation _____ | You've got sunstroke |
| Vous êtes allergique à... _____ | You're allergic to... |
| Vous êtes enceinte _____ | You're pregnant |
| Je veux faire analyser votre sang/urine/vos selles | I'd like to have your blood/urine/stools tested |
| Il faut faire des points de suture _____ | It needs stitching |
| Je vous envoie à un spécialiste/l'hôpital | I'm referring you to a specialist/sending you to the hospital |
| Il faut faire des radios _____ | You'll need to have some x-rays taken |
| Voulez-vous reprendre place un petit instant dans la salle d'attente? | Could you wait in the waiting room, please? |
| Il faut vous opérer _____ | You'll need an operation |

| | |
|---|---|
| Do I have to go on a special diet? | Dois-je suivre un régime? *dwah jhuh sweevr uhn rayjheem?* |
| Am I allowed to travel? _____ | Puis-je voyager? *pwee jhuh vwahyahjhay?* |
| Can I make a new appointment? | Puis-je prendre un autre rendez-vous? *pwee jhuh prohndr uhn noatr rohnday voo?* |
| When do I have to come back? | Quand dois-je revenir? *kohn dwah jhuh ruhvuhneer?* |
| I'll come back tomorrow | Je reviendrai demain *jhuh ruhvyahndray duhmahn* |

| | |
|---|---|
| Vous devez revenir demain /dans...jours _____ | Come back tomorrow/in...days' time |

## 13 .4 Medication and prescriptions

| | |
|---|---|
| How do I take this medicine? | Comment dois-je prendre ces médicaments? *komohn dwah jhuh prohndr say maydeekahmohn?* |
| How many pills/drops/ injections/spoonfuls/ tablets each time? | Combien de capsules/gouttes/piqûres/ cuillères/comprimés à chaque fois? *kawnbyahn duh kahpsewl/goot/peekewr/ kweeyehr/kawnpreemay ah shahk fwah?* |
| How many times a day? _____ | Combien de fois par jour? *kawnbyahn duh fwah pahr jhoor?* |
| I've forgotten my medication. At home I take... | J'ai oublié mes médicaments. A la maison je prends... *jhay oobleeay may maydeekahmohn. ah lah mehzawn jhuh prohn...* |
| Could you write a prescription for me? | Pouvez-vous me faire une ordonnance? *poovay voo muh fehr ewn ordonohns?* |

| Je vous prescris un antibiotique/un ___ sirop/un tranquillisant/un calmant | I'm prescribing antibiotics/a mixture/a tranquillizer/pain killer |
|---|---|
| Vous devez rester au calme___ | Have lots of rest |
| Vous ne devez pas sortir ___ | Stay indoors |
| Vous devez rester au lit___ | Stay in bed |

| | | |
|---|---|---|
| avaler entièrement | cuillerées (...à | pendant...jours |
| **swallow whole** | soupe/...à café) | **for...days** |
| avant chaque repas | **spoonfuls** | piqûres |
| **before meals** | **(tablespoons/** | **injections** |
| capsules | **teaspoons)** | pommade |
| **pills** | dissoudre dans l'eau | **ointment** |
| la prise de ce | **dissolve in water** | prendre |
| médicament peut | enduire | **take** |
| rendre dangereuse | **rub on** | toutes les...heures |
| la conduite | finir le traitement | **every...hours** |
| automobile | **finish the course** | uniquement pour |
| **this medication** | ...fois par jour | usage externe |
| **impairs your driving** | **...times a day** | **not for internal use** |
| comprimés | gouttes | |
| **tablets** | **drops** | |

## 🔟.5 At the dentist's

| Do you know a good ___ dentist? | Connaissez-vous un bon dentiste? *konehsay voo zuhn bawn dohnteest?* |
|---|---|
| Could you make a___ dentist's appointment for me? It's urgent | Pouvez-vous me prendre un rendez-vous chez le dentiste? C'est urgent *poovay voo muh prohndr uhn rohnday voo shay luh dohnteest? seh tewrjhohn* |
| Can I come in today,___ please? | Puis-je venir aujourd'hui s'il vous plaît? *pwee jhuh vuhneer oajhoordwee seel voo pleh?* |
| I have (terrible)___ toothache | J'ai une rage de dents/un mal de dents(épouvantable) *jhay ewn rahjh duh dohn/uhn mahl duh dohn (aypoovohntahbl)* |
| Could you prescribe/ ___ give me a painkiller? | Pouvez-vous me prescrire/donner un calmant? *poovay voo muh prehskreer/donay uhn kahlmohn?* |
| A piece of my tooth ___ has broken off | Ma dent s'est cassée *mah dohn seh kahssay* |
| My filling's come out ___ | Mon plombage est parti *mawn plawnbahjh eh pahrtee* |
| I've got a broken crown___ | Ma couronne est cassée *mah kooron eh kahssay* |
| I'd like/I don't want a ___ local anaesthetic | Je (ne) veux (pas) une anesthésie locale *jhuh (nuh) vuh (paz) ewn ahnehstayzee lokahl* |

**Sickness**

**3**

| | |
|---|---|
| Can you do a temporary ___ repair job? | Pouvez-vous me soigner de façon provisoire? |
| | *poovay voo muh swahnyay duh fahsawn proveezwahr?* |
| I don't want this tooth ___ pulled | Je ne veux pas que cette dent soit arrachée |
| | *jhuh nuh vuh pah kuh seht dohn swaht ahrahshay* |
| My dentures are broken. ___ Can you fix them? | Mon dentier est cassé. Pouvez-vous le réparer? |
| | *mawn dohntyay eh kahssay. poovay voo luh raypahray?* |

---

| | |
|---|---|
| Quelle dent/molaire vous fait mal? ___ | Which tooth hurts? |
| Vous avez un abcès ___ | You've got an abscess |
| Je dois faire une dévitalisation ___ | I'll have to do a root canal |
| Je vais vous faire une anesthésie ___ locale | I'm giving you a local anaesthetic |
| Je dois plomber/extraire/polir cette ___ dent | I'll have to fill/pull/file down this tooth |
| Je dois utiliser la roulette ___ | I'll have to drill |
| Ouvrez bien la bouche ___ | Open wide, please |
| Fermez la bouche ___ | Close your mouth, please |
| Rincez ___ | Rinse, please |
| Sentez-vous encore la douleur? ___ | Does it hurt still? |

# 14

# In trouble

**14.1 A**sking for help     109

**14.2 L**oss     110

**14.3 A**ccidents     110

**14.4 T**heft     111

**14.5 M**issing person     111

**14.6 T**he police     112

# 14 In trouble

## 14 .1 Asking for help

| Help! | Au secours! |
| | *oa suhkoor!* |
| Fire! | Au feu! |
| | *oa fuh!* |
| Police! | Police! |
| | *pohlees!* |
| Quick! | Vite! |
| | *veet!* |
| Danger! | Danger! |
| | *dohnjhay* |
| Watch out! | Attention! |
| | *ahtohnsyawn!* |
| Stop! | Stop! |
| | *stop!* |
| Be careful! | Prudence! |
| | *prewdohns!* |
| Don't! | Arrêtez! |
| | *ahrehtay!* |
| Let go! | Lâchez! |
| | *lahshay!* |
| Stop that thief! | Au voleur! |
| | *oa voluhr!* |
| Could you help me, please? | Voulez-vous m'aider? |
| | *voolay voo mayday?* |
| Where's the police station/emergency exit/fire escape? | Où est le poste de police/la sortie de secours/l'escalier de secours? |
| | *oo eh luh post duh polees/lah sortee duh suhkoor/lehskahlyay duh suhkoor?* |
| Where's the nearest fire extinguisher? | Où y a-t-il un extincteur? |
| | *oo ee yah teel uhn nehxtahnktuhr?* |
| Call the fire department! | Prévenez les sapeurs-pompiers! |
| | *prayvuhnay lay sahpuhr pawnpyay!* |
| Call the police! | Appelez la police! |
| | *ahpuhlay lah polees!* |
| Call an ambulance! | Appelez une ambulance! |
| | *ahpuhlay ewn ohnbewlohns!* |
| Where's the nearest phone? | Où est le téléphone le plus proche? |
| | *oo eh luh taylayfon luh plew prosh?* |
| Could I use your phone? | Puis-je utiliser votre téléphone? |
| | *pwee jhuh ewteeleezay votr taylayfon?* |
| What's the emergency number? | Quel est le numéro d'urgence? |
| | *kehl eh luh newmayroa dewrjhohns?* |
| What's the number for the police? | Quel est le numéro de téléphone de la police? |
| | *kehl eh luh newmayroa duh taylayfon duh lah polees?* |

In trouble

14

## 14.2 Loss

I've lost my purse/_____
wallet
J'ai perdu mon porte-monnaie/
portefeuille
*jhay pehrdew mawn port moneh/portfuhy*

I lost my...yesterday _____
Hier j'ai perdu mon/ma...
*yehr jhay pehrdew mawn/mah...*

I left my...here_____
J'ai laissé mon/ma...ici
*jhay layssay mawn/mah...eesee*

Did you find my...? _____
Avez-vous trouvé mon/ma...?
*ahvay voo troovay mawn/mah...?*

It was right here_____
Il était là
*eel ayteh lah*

It's quite valuable _____
C'est un objet de valeur
*seh tuhn nobjheh duh vahluhr*

Where's the lost _____
and found?
Où est le bureau des objets trouvés?
*oo eh luh bewroa day zobjheh troovay?*

## 14.3 Accidents

There's been an accident____
Il y a eu un accident
*eel ee yah ew uhn nahkseedohn*

Someone's fallen into_____
the water
Quelqu'un est tombé dans l'eau
*kehlkuhn eh tawnbay dohn loa*

There's a fire _____
Il y a un incendie.
*eel ee yah uhn nahnsohndee*

Is anyone hurt? _____
Y a-t-il quelqu'un de blessé?
*ee yah teel kehlkuhn duh blehssay?*

Some people have _____
been/no one's been
injured
Il (n)y a des(pas de) blessés
*eel (n)ee yah day(pah duh) blehssay*

There's someone in _____
the car/train still
Il y a encore quelqu'un dans la voiture/le
train
*eel ee ah ohnkor kehlkuhn dohn lah
vwahtewr/luh trahn*

It's not too bad. Don't_____
worry
Ce n'est pas si grave. Ne vous inquiétez
pas
*suh neh pah see grahv. nuh voo zahnkyaytay
pah*

Leave everything the _____
way it is, please
Ne touchez à rien s'il vous plaît
*nuh tooshay ah ryahn seel voo pleh*

I want to talk to the_____
police first
Je veux d'abord parler à la police
*jhuh vuh dahbor pahrlay ah lah polees*

I want to take a _____
photo first
Je veux d'abord prendre une photo
*jhuh vuh dahbor prohndr ewn foatoa*

Here's my name_____
and address
Voici mon nom et mon adresse
*vwahsee mawn nawn ay mawn nahdrehs*

Could I have your _____
name and address?
Puis-je connaître votre nom et votre
adresse?
*pwee jhuh konehtr votr nawn ay votr
ahdrehs?*

**In trouble**

**4**

| | |
|---|---|
| Could I see some_____ identification/your insurance papers? | Puis-je voir vos papiers d'identité/papiers d'assurance? |
| | *pwee jhuh vwahr voa pahpyay deedohnteetay/pahpyay dahsewrohns?* |
| Will you act as a _____ witness? | Voulez-vous être témoin? |
| | *voolay voo zehtr taymwahn?* |
| I need the details for _____ the insurance | Je dois avoir les données pour l'assurance. |
| | *jhuh dwah zahvwahr lay donay poor lahsewrohns* |
| Are you insured?_____ | Etes-vous assuré? |
| | *eht voo zahsewray?* |
| Third party or all _____ inclusive? | Responsabilité civile ou tous risques? |
| | *rehspawnsahbeeleetay seeveel oo too reesk?* |
| Could you sign here, _____ please? | Voulez-vous signer ici? |
| | *voolay voo seenyay eesee?* |

## 14 .4 Theft

| | |
|---|---|
| I've been robbed _____ | On m'a volé. |
| | *awn mah volay* |
| My...has been stolen _____ | Mon/ma...a été volé(e). |
| | *mawn/mah...ah aytay volay* |
| My car's been _____ broken into | On a cambriolé ma voiture. |
| | *awn nah kohnbreeolay mah vwahtewr* |

## 14 .5 Missing person

| | |
|---|---|
| I've lost my child/_____ grandmother | J'ai perdu mon enfant/ma grand-mère |
| | *jhay pehrdew mawn nohnfohn/mah grohnmehr* |
| Could you help me _____ find him/her? | Voulez-vous m'aider à le/la chercher? |
| | *voolay voo mayday ah luh/lah shehrshay?* |
| Have you seen a _____ small child? | Avez-vous vu un petit enfant? |
| | *ahvay voo vew uhn puhtee tohnfohn?* |
| He's/she's...years old_____ | Il/elle a...ans. |
| | *eel/ehl ah...ohn* |
| He's/she's got _____ short/long/blond/red/ brown/black/gray/curly/ straight/frizzy hair | Il/elle a les cheveux courts/longs/blonds/ roux/bruns/noirs/gris/bouclés/raides/frisés |
| | *eel/ehl ah lay shuhvuh koor/lawn/blawn/roo/bruhn/nwahr/gree rehd/freezay* |
| with a ponytail _____ | avec une queue de cheval |
| | *ahvehk ewn kuh duh shuhvahl* |
| with braids _____ | avec des nattes |
| | *ahvehk day naht* |
| in a bun _____ | avec un chignon |
| | *ahvehk uhn sheenyawn* |
| He's/she's got _____ blue/brown/green eyes | Il/elle a les yeux bleus/bruns/verts |
| | *eel/ehl ah lay zyuh bluh/bruhn/vehr* |
| He's wearing swimming ___ trunks/mountaineering boots | Il porte un maillot de bain/des chaussures de montagne. |
| | *eel port uhn mahyoa duh bahn/day shoasewr duh mawntahnyuh* |

| | |
|---|---|
| with/without glasses/ a bag | avec/sans lunettes/un sac *ahvehk/sohn lewneht/uhn sahk* |
| tall/short | grand(e)/petit(e) *grohn(d)/puhtee(t)* |
| This is a photo of him/her | Voici une photo de lui/d'elle. *vwahsee ewn foatoa duh lwee/dehl* |
| He/she must be lost | Il/elle s'est certainement égaré(e). *eel/ehl seh sehrtehnmohn aygahray* |

## 14 .6 The police

### An arrest

| | |
|---|---|
| Vos papiers de voiture s'il vous plaît. | Your registration papers, please |
| Vous rouliez trop vite | You were speeding |
| Vous êtes en stationnement interdit | You're not allowed to park here |
| Vous n'avez pas mis d'argent dans le parcmètre | You haven't put money in the meter |
| Vos phares ne marchent pas | Your lights aren't working |
| Vous avez une contravention de...francs | That's a...franc fine |
| Vous voulez payer immédiatement? | Do you want to pay now? |
| Vous devez payer immédiatement | You'll have to pay now |

| | |
|---|---|
| I don't speak French | Je ne parle pas français. *jhuh nuh pahrl pah frohnseh* |
| I didn't see the sign | Je n'ai pas vu ce panneau. *jhuh nay pah vew suh pahnoa* |
| I don't understand what it says | Je ne comprends pas ce qu'il y est écrit. *jhuh nuh kawnprohn pah suh keel ee yeh taykree* |
| I was only doing... kilometres an hour | Je ne roulais qu'à...kilomètres à l'heure. *jhuh nuh rooleh kah...keeloamehtr ah luhr* |
| I'll have my car checked | Je vais faire réviser ma voiture. *jhuh veh fehr rayveezay mah vwahtewr* |
| I was blinded by oncoming lights | J'ai été aveuglé(e) par une voiture en sens inverse. *jhay aytay ahvuhglay pahr ewn vwahtewr ohn sohns ahnvehrs* |

In trouble

4

### At the police station

| | |
|---|---|
| Où est-ce arrivé? | Where did it happen? |
| Qu'avez-vous perdu? | What's missing? |
| Qu'a-t-on volé? | What's been taken? |
| Puis-je voir vos papiers d'identité? | Could I see some identification? |
| A quelle heure est-ce arrivé? | What time did it happen? |
| Qui est en cause? | Who was involved? |
| Y a-t-il des témoins? | Are there any witnesses? |
| Voulez-vous remplir ceci? | Fill this out, please |
| Signez ici s'il vous plaît | Sign here, please |
| Voulez-vous un interprète? | Do you want an interpreter? |

I want to report a collision/missing person/rape
Je viens faire la déclaration d'une collision/d'une disparition/d'un viol
*jhuh vyahn fehr lah dayklahrasyawn dewn koleezyawn/dewn deespahreesyawn/duhn vyol*

Could you make out a report, please?
Voulez-vous faire un rapport?
*voolay voo fehr uhn rahpor?*

Could I have a copy for the insurance?
Puis-je avoir une copie pour l'assurance?
*pwee jhahvwahr ewn kopee poor lahsewrohns?*

I've lost everything
J'ai tout perdu
*jhay too pehrdew*

I'd like an interpreter
J'aimerais un interprète
*jhehmuhreh zuhn nahntehrpreht*

I'm innocent
Je suis innocent(e)
*jhuh swee zeenosohn(t)*

I don't know anything about it
Je ne sais rien
*jhuh nuh seh ryahn*

I want to speak to someone from the American consulate
Je veux parler à quelqu'un du consulat américain
*jhuh vuh pahrlay ah kehlkuhn dew kawnsewlah amayreekan*

I need to see someone from the American embassy
Je dois parler à quelqu'un de l'ambassade américaine
*jhuh dwah pahrlay ah kehlkuhn duh lohnbahsahd amayreekehn*

I want a lawyer who speaks English
Je veux un avocat qui parle anglais
*jhuh vuh uhn nahvokah kee pahrl ohngleh*

**In trouble**

**14**

# 15

## **W**ord list

# Word list English - French

● **This word list** is meant to supplement the previous chapters.
Nouns are always accompanied by the French definite article in order
to indicate whether it is a masculine (le) or feminine (la) word. In the
case of an abbreviated article (l'), the gender is indicated by (m.) or (f.).
In a number of cases, words not contained in this list can be found
elsewhere in this book, namely alongside the diagrams of the car, the
bicycle and the tent. Many food terms can be found in the French-
English list in 4.7.

## A

| | | |
|---|---|---|
| about | environ | ohnveerawn |
| above | au-dessus | oadsew |
| abroad | l'étranger (m.) | laytrohnjhay |
| accident | l'accident (m.) | lahkseedohn |
| adder | la vipère | lah veepehr |
| addition | l'addition (f.) | lahdeesyawn |
| address | l'adresse (f.) | lahdrehs |
| admission | l'entrée (f.) | lohntray |
| admission price | le prix d'entrée | luh pree dohntray |
| advice | le conseil | luh kawnsehy |
| after | après | ahpreh |
| afternoon | l'après-midi (m., f.) | lahpreh meedee |
| aftershave | la lotion après-rasage | lah loasyawn ahpreh rahzahjh |
| again | à nouveau | ah noovoa |
| against | contre | kawntr |
| age | l'âge (m.) | lahjh |
| AIDS | le sida | luh seedah |
| air conditioning | l'air conditionné (m.) | lehr kawndeesyonay |
| air mattress | le matelas pneumatique | luh mahtlah pnuhmahteek |
| air sickness bag | le petit sac à vomissements | luh puhtee sahk ah vomeesmohn |
| airplane | l'avion (m.) | lahvyawn |
| airport | l'aéroport (m.) | lahayroapor |
| alarm | l'alarme (f.) | lahlahrm |
| alarm clock | le réveil | luh rayvehy |
| alcohol | l'alcool (m.) | lahlkol |
| a little | un peu | uhn puh |
| allergic | allergique | ahlehrjheek |
| alone | seul | suhl |
| always | toujours | toojhoor |
| ambulance | l'ambulance (f.) | lohnbewlohns |
| American | l'américain (m.) | lamayreekan |
| | l'américaine (f.) | lamayreekehn |
| amount | le montant | luh mawntohn |
| amusement park | le parc d'attractions | luh pahrk dahtrahksyawn |
| anaesthetize | anesthésier | ahnehstayzyay |
| anchovy | l'anchois (m.) | lohnshwah |
| and | et | ay |
| angry | en colère | ohn kolehr |
| animal | l'animal (m.) | lahneemahl |
| answer | la réponse | lah raypawns |
| ant | la fourmi | lah foormee |

| antibiotics | l'antibiotique (m.) | *lohnteebyoteek* |
|---|---|---|
| antifreeze | l'antigel (m.) | *lohnteejhehl* |
| antique | ancien | *ohnsyahn* |
| antiques | antiquités (f.) | *ohnteekeetay* |
| anus | l'anus (m.) | *lahnews* |
| apartment | l'appartement (m.) | *lahpahrtuhmohn* |
| aperitif | l'apéritif (m.) | *lahpayreeteef* |
| apologies | les excuses | *lay zehxkewz* |
| apple | la pomme | *lah pom* |
| apple juice | le jus de pommes | *luh jhew duh pom* |
| apple pie | la tarte aux pommes | *lah tahrt oa pom* |
| apple sauce | la compote de | *lah kawnpot* |
| | pommes | *duh pom* |
| appointment | le rendez-vous | *luh rohndayvoo* |
| apricot | l'abricot (m.) | *lahbreekoa* |
| April | avril | *ahvreel* |
| archbishop | l'archevêque (m.) | *lahrshuhvehk* |
| architecture | l'architecture (f.) | *lahrsheetehktewr* |
| area | les environs | *lay zohnveerawn* |
| area code | l'indicatif (m.) | *lanndeekateef* |
| arm | le bras | *luh brah* |
| arrive | arriver | *ahreevay* |
| arrow | la flèche | *lah flehsh* |
| art | l'art (m.) | *lahr* |
| artery | l'artère (f.) | *lahrtehr* |
| artichoke | l'artichaut (m.) | *lahrteeshoa* |
| article | l'article (m.) | *lahrteekl* |
| artificial respiration | la respiration | *lah rehspeerahsyawn* |
| | artificielle | *ahrteefeesyehl* |
| arts and crafts | l'artisanat d'art | *lahrteezahnah dahr* |
| ashtray | le cendrier | *luh sohndreeay* |
| ask | demander | *duhmohnday* |
| ask (request) | prier | *preeay* |
| asparagus | les asperges | *lay zahspehrjh* |
| aspirin | l'aspirine (f.) | *lahspeereen* |
| assault | l'agression (f.) | *lahgrehsyawn* |
| at home | à la maison | *ah lah mehzawn* |
| at night | la nuit | *lah nwee* |
| at the back | à l'arrière | *ah lahryehr* |
| at the front | à l'avant | *ah lahvohn* |
| at the latest | au plus tard | *oa plew tahr* |
| August | août | *oot* |
| automatic | automatique | *loatoamahteek* |
| automatically | automatiquement | *oatoamahteekmohn* |
| autumn | l'automne (m.) | *loatonn* |
| avalanche | l'avalanche (f.) | *lahvahlohnsh* |
| awake | réveillé | *rayvay-yay* |
| awning | le parasol | *luh pahrahsol* |

**B**

| baby | le bébé | *luh baybay* |
|---|---|---|
| baby food | la nourriture pour | *lah nooreetewr poor* |
| | bébé | *baybay* |
| babysitter | le/la baby-sitter | *luh/lah behbee seetehr* |
| back | le dos | *luh doa* |
| backpack | le sac à dos | *luh sahk ah doa* |
| bacon | le lard | *luh lahr* |

| bad | mauvais | moaveh |
|---|---|---|
| bag | le sac | luh sahk |
| baker (cakes) | le pâtissier | luh pahteesyay |
| baker | le boulanger | luh boolohnjhay |
| balcony (theatre) | le balcon | luh bahlkawn |
| balcony (to building) | le balcon | luh bahlkawn |
| ball | la balle | lah bahl |
| ballet | le ballet; la danse | luh bahleh; la dohns |
| ballpoint pen | le stylo à bille | luh steeloa ah beey |
| banana | la banane | lah bahnahn |
| bandage | le pansement | luh pohnsmohn |
| Bandaids | le sparadrap | luh spahrahdrah |
| bangs | la frange | lah frohnjh |
| bank (river) | la rive | lah reev |
| bank | la banque | lah bohnk |
| bank card | la carte bancaire | lah kahrt bohnkehr |
| bar (café) | le bar | luh bahr |
| bar (in one's room) | le bar | luh bahr |
| barbecue | le barbecue | luh bahrbuhkew |
| bath | le bain | luh bahn |
| bath attendant | le maître nageur | luh mehtr nahjhuhr |
| bath foam | la mousse de bain | lah moos duh bahn |
| bath towel | la serviette de bain | lah sehrvyeht duh bahn |
| bathing cap | le bonnet de bain | luh boneh duh bahn |
| bathing suit | le maillot de bain | luh mahyoa duh bahn |
| bathroom | la salle de bain | lah sahl duh bahn |
| battery (car) | l'accumulateur (m.) | lahkewmewlahtuhr |
| battery | la pile | lah peel |
| beach | la plage | lah plahjh |
| beans | les haricots | lay ahreekoa |
| beautiful | beau/belle | boa/behl |
| beautiful | magnifique | mahnyeefeek |
| beauty parlor | le salon de beauté | luh sahlawn duh boatay |
| bed | le lit | luh lee |
| bee | l'abeille (f.) | lahbehy |
| beef | la viande de boeuf | lah vyohnd duh buhf |
| beer | la bière | lah byehr |
| beet | la betterave | lah behtrahv |
| begin | commencer | komohnsay |
| beginner | le débutant | luh daybewtohn |
| behind | derrière | dehryehr |
| Belgian (f) | la belge | lah behljh |
| Belgian (m) | le belge | luh behljh |
| Belgium | la Belgique | lah behljheek |
| belt | la ceinture | lah sahntewr |
| berth | la couchette | lah koosheht |
| better | mieux | myuh |
| bicarbonate of soda | le bicarbonate de soude | luh beekahrbonaht duh sood |
| bicycle | la bicyclette/le vélo | lah beeseekleht/luh vayloa |
| bicycle pump | la pompe à bicyclette | lah pawnp ah beeseekleht |
| bicycle repairman | le réparateur de vélos | luh raypahrahtuhr duh vayloa |
| bikini | le bikini | luh beekeenee |
| bill | l'addition | lahdeesyawn |

117

| birthday | l'anniversaire (m.) | lahneevehrsehr |
| bite | mordre | mordr |
| bitter | amer | ahmehr |
| black | noir | nwahr |
| bland | fade | fahd |
| blanket | la couverture | lah koovehrtewr |
| bleach | blondir | blawndeer |
| blister | la cloque | lah klok |
| blond | blond | blawn |
| blood | le sang | luh sohn |
| blood pressure | la tension | lah tohnsyawn |
| blouse | le chemisier | luh shuhmeezyay |
| blow dry | sécher | sayshay |
| blue | bleu | bluh |
| blunt | épointé/émoussé | aypwahntay/aymoosay |
| boat | le bateau | luh bahtoa |
| bobbypins | les barrettes | lay bahreht |
| body | le corps | luh kor |
| body milk | le lait corporel | luh leh korporehl |
| boil | bouillir | boo-yeer |
| boiled | cuit | kwee |
| boiled ham | jambon cuit | jhohnbawn kwee |
| bone | l'os (m.) | los |
| book | le livre | luh leevr |
| bookshop | la librairie | lah leebrehree |
| border | la frontière | lah frawntyehr |
| bored (to be) | s'ennuyer | sonweeyay |
| boring | ennuyeux | onweeyuh |
| born | né | nay |
| botanical gardens | le jardin botanique | luh jhahrdahn botahneek |
| both | tous/toutes les deux | too/toot lay duh |
| bottle-warmer | le chauffe-biberon | luh shoaf beebrawn |
| bottle (baby's) | le biberon | luh beebrawn |
| bottle | la bouteille | lah bootehy |
| box | la boîte | lah bwaht |
| box office | le bureau de réservation | luh bewroa duh rayzehrvahsyawn |
| box (theater) | la loge | lah lojh |
| boy | le garçon | luh gahrsawn |
| bra | le soutien-gorge | luh sootyahn gorjh |
| bracelet | le bracelet | luh brahsleh |
| braised | braisé | brehzay |
| brake | le frein | luh frahn |
| brake fluid | le liquide de freins | luh leekeed duh frahn |
| brake oil | l'huile à frein (f.) | lweel ah frahn |
| bread | le pain | luh pahn |
| break | casser | kahssay |
| breakfast | le petit déjeuner | luh puhtee dayjhuhnay |
| breast | la poitrine | lah pwahtreen |
| bridge | le pont | luh pawn |
| briefs | la culotte | lah kewlot |
| brochure | la brochure | lah broshewr |
| broken | cassé | kahssay |
| broth | le consommé | luh kawnsomay |
| brother | le frère | luh frehr |
| brown | brun | bruhn |

| brush | la brosse | *lah bros* |
| Brussels sprouts | les choux de Bruxelles | *lay shoo duh brewxehl* |
| bucket | le seau | *luh soa* |
| bugs | les insectes nuisibles | *lay zahnsehkt nweezeebl* |
| building | le bâtiment | *luh bahteemohn* |
| buoy | la bouée | *lah booway* |
| burglary | le cambriolage | *luh kohnbryolajh* |
| burn (verb) | brûler | *brewlay* |
| burn | la brûlure | *lah brewlewr* |
| burnt | brûlé | *brewlay* |
| bus | l'autobus (m.) | *loatoabews* |
| bus station | la station d'autobus | *lah stahsyawn doatoabews* |
| bus stop | l'arrêt d'autobus (m.) | *lahreh doatoabews* |
| business class | la classe affaire (f.) | *lah klahs ahfehr* |
| business trip | le voyage d'affaires | *luh vwahyahjh dahfehr* |
| busy | animé | *ahneemay* |
| butane gas | le gaz butane | *luh gahz bewtahnn* |
| butcher | le boucher | *luh booshay* |
| butter | le beurre | *luh buhr* |
| button | le bouton | *luh bootawn* |
| buy | acheter | *ahshtay* |
| by airmail | la poste aérienne/ par avion | *lah post ahayryehn/ pahr ahvyawn* |

# C

| cabaña | la cabine de bain | *lah kahbeen duh ban* |
| cabbage | le chou | *luh shoo* |
| cabin | la cabine | *lah kahbeen* |
| cake | le gâteau | *luh gahtoa* |
| call | appeler | *ahpuhlay* |
| called (name) | s'appeler | *sahpuhlay* |
| camera | l'appareil-photo (m.) | *lahpahrehy foatoa* |
| camp | faire du camping | *fehr dew kohnpeeng* |
| camp shop | le magasin du camping | *luh mahgahzahn dew kohnpeeng* |
| camp site | le camping | *luh kohnpeeng* |
| camper | le camping-car | *luh kohnpeeng kahr* |
| campfire | le feu de camp | *luh fuh duh kohn* |
| camping guide | le guide de camping | *luh gueed duh kohnpeeng* |
| camping permit | le permis de camping | *luh pehrmee duh kohnpeeng* |
| canal boat | la péniche | *lah payneesh* |
| cancel | annuler | *ahnewlay* |
| candies | les bonbons | *lay bawnbawn* |
| candle | la bougie | *lah boojhee* |
| canoe (verb) | faire du canoë | *fehr dew kahnoaeh* |
| canoe | le canoë | *luh kahnoaeh* |
| car (train) | le wagon | *luh vahgawn* |
| car | la voiture | *lah vwahtewr* |
| car deck | le pont à voitures | *luh pawn ah vwahtewr* |
| car documents | les papiers de voiture | *lay pahpyay duh vwahtewr* |
| car trouble | la panne | *lah pahnn* |

| carafe | la carafe | *lah kahrah* |
| cardigan | le cardigan/le gilet | *luh kahrdeegahn/ luh jheeleh* |
| careful | prudent | *prewdohn* |
| carrot | la carotte | *lah kahrot* |
| cartridge (gun) | la cartouche | *lah kahrtoosh* |
| cascade | la cascade | *lah kahskahd* |
| cash desk | la caisse | *lah kehss* |
| casino | le casino | *luh kahzeenoa* |
| cassette | la cassette | *lah kahseht* |
| castle | le château | *luh shahtoa* |
| cat | le chat | *luh shah* |
| catalogue | le catalogue | *luh kahtahlog* |
| cathedral | la cathédrale | *lah kahtaydrahl* |
| cauliflower | le chou-fleur | *luh shoo fluhr* |
| cave | la grotte | *lah grot* |
| CD | le compact disc | *luh kawnpahkt deesk* |
| celebrate | célébrer | *saylaybray* |
| cemetery | le cimetière | *luh seemtyehr* |
| center (in the) | au milieu | *oa meelyuh* |
| center (of town) | le centre | *luh sohntr* |
| centimeter | le centimètre | *luh sohnteemehtr* |
| central heating | le chauffage central | *luh shoafahjh sohntrahl* |
| cereal | la céréale | *lah sayrayahl* |
| chair | la chaise | *lah shehz* |
| chambermaid | la femme de chambre | *lah fahm duh shohnbr* |
| chamois | la peau de chamois | *lah poa duh shahmwah* |
| champagne | le champagne | *luh shohnpany* |
| change (verb) | modifier | *modeefyay* |
| | changer | *shohnjhay* |
| change | la monnaie | *lah moneh* |
| change the baby's diaper | changer la couche du bébé | *shohnjhay lah koosh dew baybay* |
| change the oil | changer l'huile | *shohnjhay lweel* |
| chapel | la chapelle | *lah shahpehl* |
| charcoal tablets | les pastilles de charbon | *lay pahsteey duh shahrbawn* |
| charter flight | le vol charter | *luh vol shahrtehr* |
| chat | causer | *kohzay* |
| check | le chèque | *luh shehk* |
| check (verb) | contrôler | *kawntroalay* |
| checked luggage | consigné | *kawnseenyay* |
| check in | enregistrer | *ohnruhjheestray* |
| cheers | à votre santé | *ah votr sohntay* |
| cheese | le fromage | *luh fromahjh* |
| chef | le chef | *luh shehf* |
| cherries | les cerises | *lay suhreez* |
| chess (play) | jouer aux échecs | *jhooay oa zayshehk* |
| chewing gum | le chewing-gum | *luh shweenguhm* |
| chicken | le poulet | *luh pooleh* |
| chicory | les endives | *lay zohndeev* |
| child | l'enfant (m./f.) | *lohnfohn* |
| child seat | le siège-enfant | *luh seeyehjh ohnfohn* |
| chilled | rafraîchi | *rahfrehshee* |
| chin | le menton | *luh montawn* |
| chocolate | le chocolat | *luh shoakoalah* |

| | | |
|---|---|---|
| choose | choisir | shwahzeer |
| chop (meat) | la côtelette | lah koatuhleht |
| christian/given name | le prénom | luh praynawn |
| church | l'église (f.) | laygleez |
| church service | le service religieux | luh sehrvees ruhleejhyuh |
| cigar | le cigare | luh seegahr |
| cigar shop | le tabac | luh tahbah |
| cigarette | la cigarette | lah seegahreht |
| cigarette paper | le papier à cigarettes | luh pahpay ah seegahreht |
| circle | le cercle | luh sehrkl |
| circus | le cirque | luh seerk |
| city | la ville | lah veel |
| city map | le plan | luh plohn |
| classical concert | le concert classique | luh kawnsehr klahsseek |
| clean (verb) | nettoyer | nehtwahyay |
| clean | propre | propr |
| clear | clair | klehr |
| clearance | les soldes | lay sold |
| closed | fermé | fehrmay |
| closed off | bloqué | blokay |
| clothes | les habits | lay zahbee |
| clothes hanger | le cintre | luh sahntr |
| clothes pin | la pince à linge | lah pahns ah lahnjh |
| clothing | vêtements | vehtmohn |
| coat | le manteau | luh mohntoa |
| cockroach | le cafard | luh kahfahr |
| cocoa | le cacao | luh kahkahoa |
| cocoa (drink) | le chocolat au lait | luh shohkohlah oh lay |
| cod | le cabillaud | luh kahbeeyoa |
| coffee | le café | luh kahfay |
| coffee filter | le filtre de cafetière | luh feeltr duh kahftyehr |
| cognac | le cognac | luh konyahk |
| cold | froid | frwah |
| cold (illness) | le rhume | luh rewm |
| cold cuts | la charcuterie | lah shahrkewtree |
| collarbone | la clavicule | lah klahveekewl |
| colleague | le collègue | luh kolehg |
| collision | la collision | lah koleezyawn |
| cologne | l'eau de toilette (f.) | loa duh twahleht |
| color | la couleur | lah kooluhr |
| color pencils | les crayons de couleur | lay krayawn duh kooluhr |
| color TV | la télévision en couleurs | lah taylayveezyawn ohn kooluhr |
| coloring book | l'album de coloriage (m.) | lahlbuhm duh koloryajh |
| comb | le peigne | luh pehnyuh |
| come | venir | vuhneer |
| come back | revenir | ruhvuhneer |
| compartment | le compartiment | luh kawnpahrteemohn |
| complaint | la plainte | lah plahnt |
| complaints book | le cahier de réclamations | luh kahyay duh rayklahmahsyawn |
| completely | entièrement | ohntyehrmohn |

| | | |
|---|---|---|
| compliment | le compliment | luh kawnpleemohn |
| compulsory | obligatoire | obleegahtwahr |
| concert | le concert | luh kawnsehr |
| concert hall | la salle de concert | lah sahl duh kawnsehr |
| concussion | la commotion cérébrale | lah koamoasyawn sayraybrahl |
| condensed milk | le lait condensé | luh leh kawndohnsay |
| condom | le préservatif | luh prayzehrvahteef |
| congratulate | féliciter | fayleeseetay |
| connection | la liaison | lah lyehzawn |
| constipation | la constipation | lah kawnsteepahsyawn |
| consulate | le consulat | luh kownsewlah |
| consultation | la consultation | lah kawnsewltahsyawn |
| contact lens | la lentille de contact | lah lohnteey duh kawntahkt |
| contact lens solution | le liquide pour lentille de contact | luh leekeed poor lohnteey duh kawntahkt |
| contagious | contagieux | kawntahjhyuh |
| contraceptive | le contraceptif | luh kawntrahsehpteef |
| contraceptive pill | la pilule anticonceptionnelle | lah peelewl ohnteekawnseh-psyonehl |
| convent | le couvent | luh koovohn |
| cook (verb) | cuisiner | kweezeenay |
| cook | le cuisinier | luh kweezeenyay |
| copper | le cuivre | luh kweevr |
| copy | la copie | lah kopee |
| corkscrew | le tire-bouchon | luh teerbooshawn |
| cornflour | la maïzena | lah maheezaynah |
| corner | le coin | luh kwahn |
| correct | correct | korehkt |
| correspond | correspondre | korehspawndr |
| corridor | le couloir | luh koolwahr |
| costume | le costume | luh kostewm |
| cot | le lit d'enfant | luh lee dohnfohn |
| cotton | le coton | luh koatawn |
| cotton (antiseptic) | le coton | luh koatawn |
| cough | la toux | lah too |
| cough syrup | le sirop pectoral | luh seeroa pehktoaral |
| counter | la réception | lah raysehpsyawn |
| country | le pays | luh pehy |
| country code | l'indicatif du pays (m.) | lahndeekahteef dew pehy |
| country side | la campagne | lah kohnpahnyuh |
| cousin (f) | la cousine | lah koozeen |
| cousin (m) | le cousin | luh koozahn |
| crab | le crabe | luh krahb |
| cracker | le biscuit | luh beeskwee |
| cream | la crème | lah krehm |
| credit card | la carte de crédit | lah kahrt duh kraydee |
| croissant | le croissant | luh krwahssohn |
| cross-country run | la piste de ski de fond | lah peest duh skee duh fawn |
| cross-country skiing | faire du ski de fond | fehr dew skee duh fawn |

| cross-country skis | les skis de fond | *lay skee duh fawn* |
| cross the road | traverser | *trahvehrsay* |
| crossing | la traversée | *lah trahvehrsay* |
| cross roads | le croisement | *luh krwahzmohn* |
| cry | pleurer | *pluhray* |
| cubic meter | le mètre cube | *luh mehtr kewb* |
| cucumber | le concombre | *luh kawnkawnbr* |
| cuddly toy | l'animal en | *lahneemahl* |
| | peluche (m.) | *ohn plewsh* |
| cuff links | les boutons de | *lay bootawn* |
| | manchette | *duh mohnsheht* |
| cup | la tasse | *lah tahs* |
| curly | frisé | *freezay* |
| current | la circulation | *lah seerkewlahsyawn* |
| cushion | le coussin | *luh koossahn* |
| customary | habituel | *ahbeetewehl* |
| customs | la douane | *lah dwahnn* |
| customs | le contrôle douanier | *luh kawntrol* |
| | | *dwahnnyay* |
| cut (verb) | couper | *koopay* |
| cutlery | couverts | *koovehr* |
| cycling | faire de la bicyclette/ | *fehr duh lah* |
| | du vélo | *beeseekleht/dew* |
| | | *vayloa* |

# D

| dairy produce | les produits laitiers | *lay prodwee laytyay* |
| damaged | abîmé | *ahbeemay* |
| dance | danser | *dohnsay* |
| dandruff | les pellicules | *lay payleekewl* |
| danger | le danger | *luh dohnjhay* |
| dangerous | dangereux | *dohnjhuhruh* |
| dark | sombre | *sawnbr* |
| date | le rendez-vous | *luh rohndayvoo* |
| daughter | la fille | *lah feey* |
| day | le jour | *luh jhoor* |
| day after tomorrow | après-demain | *ahpreh duhmahn* |
| day before yesterday | avant-hier | *ahvohn tyehr* |
| death | la mort | *lah mor* |
| decaffeinated | le décaféiné | *luh daykahfayeenay* |
| December | décembre | *daysohnbr* |
| deck chair | la chaise longue | *lah shehz lawng* |
| declare (customs) | déclarer | *dayklahray* |
| deep | profond | *profawn* |
| deep sea diving | la plongée | *lah plawnjhay* |
| | sous-marine | *soo mahreen* |
| deep freeze | le congélateur | *luh kawnjhaylahtuhr* |
| degrees | les degrés | *lay duhgray* |
| delay | le retard | *luh ruhtahr* |
| delicious | délicieux | *dayleesyuh* |
| dentist | le dentiste | *luh dohnteest* |
| dentures | le dentier | *luh dohntyay* |
| deodorant | le déodorant | *luh dayodorohn* |
| department (in store) | le rayon | *luh rayawn* |
| department store | le grand magasin | *luh grohn* |
| | | *mahgahzahn* |
| departure | le départ | *luh daypahr* |

| | | |
|---|---|---|
| departure time | l'heure de départ (f.) | ler duh daypahr |
| depilatory cream | la crème épilatoire | lah krehm aypeelahtwahr |
| deposit | arrhes, acompte | ahr, ahkawnt |
| dessert | le dessert | luh dehssehr |
| destination | la destination | lah dehsteenahsyawn |
| detergent | le détergent | luh daytehrjhohn |
| develop | développer | dayvlopay |
| diabetes | le diabète | luh deeahbeht |
| diabetic | le diabétique | luh dyahbayteek |
| dial | composer | kawnpoazay |
| diamond | le diamant | luh deeahmohn |
| diaper | la couche | lah koosh |
| diarrhea | la diarrhée | lah deeahray |
| dictionary | le dictionnaire | luh deeksyonehr |
| diesel | le diesel | luh dyayzehl |
| diesel oil | le gas-oil | luh gahzwahl |
| diet | le régime | luh rayjheem |
| difficulty | la difficulté | lah deefeekewltay |
| dining room | la salle à manger | lah sahl ah mohnjhay |
| dining/buffet car | le wagon-restaurant | luh vahgawn rehstoaron |
| dinner (to have) | dîner | deenay |
| dinner | le dîner | luh deenay |
| dinner jacket | le smoking | luh smokeeng |
| direction | la direction | lah deerehksyawn |
| directly | directement | deerehktuhmohn |
| dirty | sale | sahl |
| disabled | l'invalide (m./f.) | lahnvahleed |
| disco | la discothèque | lah deeskotehk |
| discount | la réduction | lah raydewksyawn |
| disgusting | dégoûtant | daygootohn |
| dish | le plat | luh plah |
| dish of the day | le plat du jour | luh plah dew jhoor |
| disinfectant | le désinfectant | luh dayzahnfehktohn |
| distance | la distance | lah deestohns |
| distilled water | l'eau distillée (f.) | loa deesteelay |
| disturb | déranger | dayrohnjhay |
| disturbance | troubles, tapage | troobl, tapahjh |
| dive | plonger | plawnjhay |
| diving | la plongée | lah plawnjhay |
| diving board | le plongeoir | luh plawnjhwahr |
| diving gear | l'équipement de plongeur (m.) | laykeepmohn duh plawnjhuhr |
| dizzy | pris de vertige | pree duh vehrteejh |
| do (verb) | faire | fehr |
| Do-it-yourself-shop | le magasin de bricolage | luh mahgahzahn duh breekolajh |
| doctor | le médecin | luh maydsahn |
| dog | le chien | luh shyahn |
| doll | la poupée | lah poopay |
| domestic | l'intérieur (m.) du pays | lahntayryuhr dew pehy |
| door | la porte | lah port |
| down | en bas | ohn bah |
| draft | le courant d'air | luh koorohn dehr |
| dream | rêver | rehvay |

| dress | la robe | *lah rob* |
|---|---|---|
| dressing gown | le peignoir | *luh paynywahr* |
| drink (verb) | boire | *bwahr* |
| drink | le verre | *luh vehr* |
| drinking water | l'eau potable (f.) | *loa potabl* |
| drive | conduire | *kawndweer* |
| driver | le chauffeur | *luh shoafuhr* |
| driving license | le permis de | *luh pehrmee duh* |
| | conduire | *kawndweer* |
| drought | la sécheresse | *lah sayshrehs* |
| drugstore | la droguerie | *lah drohgree* |
| dry (verb) | sécher | *sayshay* |
| dry | sec | *sehk* |
| dry clean | nettoyer à sec | *nehtwahyay ah sehk* |
| dry cleaner's | la teinturerie | *lah tahntewruhree* |
| dry shampoo | le shampooing sec | *luh shohnpwahn sehk* |
| during | pendant | *pohndohn* |
| during the day | de jour | *duh jhoor* |

# E

| each time | chaque fois | *shahk fwah* |
|---|---|---|
| ear | l'oreille (f.) | *lorehy* |
| ear, nose and throat (ENT) specialist | l'oto-rhino (m.) | *loatoa reenoa* |
| earache | le mal d'oreille | *luh mahl dorehy* |
| eardrops | les gouttes pour | *lay goot poor* |
| | les oreilles | *lay zorehy* |
| early | tôt | *toa* |
| earrings | les boucles d'oreilles | *lay bookl dorehy* |
| earth | la terre | *lah tehr* |
| earthenware | la poterie | *lah potree* |
| east | l'est (m.) | *lehst* |
| easy | facile | *fahseel* |
| eat | manger | *mohnjhay* |
| eczema | l'eczéma (m.) | *lehgzaymah* |
| eel | l'anguille (f.) | *lohngeey* |
| egg | l'oeuf (m.) | *luhf* |
| eggplant | l'aubergine (f.) | *lohbehrjeen* |
| electric | électrique | *aylehktreek* |
| electric current | le courant | *luh koorohn* |
| electricity | l'électricité (f.) | *laylehktreeseeetay* |
| elevator | l'ascenseur | *lahsohnsuhr* |
| embassy | l'ambassade (f.) | *lohnbahsahd* |
| emergency brake | le frein de secours | *luh frahn duh suhkoor* |
| emergency cone (car) | le triangle de | *luh treeohngl duh* |
| | signalisation | *seenyahleezahsyawn* |
| emergency exit | la sortie de secours | *lah sortee duh suhkoor* |
| emergency number | le numéro | *luh newmayroa* |
| | d'urgence (m.) | *dewrzhohns* |
| emergency phone | le téléphone | *luh taylayfon* |
| | d'urgence (m.) | *dewrjhohns* |
| emery board | la lime à ongles | *lah leem ah awngl* |
| empty | vide | *veed* |
| engaged | occupé | *okewpay* |
| England | Angleterre | *ohngluhtehr* |
| English | anglais | *ohngleh* |

Word list

| | | |
|---|---|---|
| entertainment guide | le journal des spectacles | *luh jhoornal day spehktahkl* |
| envelope | l'enveloppe (f.) | *lohnvlop* |
| escort | l'hôtesse | *loatehs* |
| evening | le soir | *luh swahr* |
| evening wear | la tenue de soirée | *lah tuhnew duh swahray* |
| event | l'évènement (m.) | *layvehnmohn* |
| everything | tout | *too* |
| everywhere | partout | *pahrtoo* |
| examine | examiner | *ehgzahmeenay* |
| excavation | les fouilles | *lay fooeey* |
| excellent | excellent | *ehxaylohn* |
| exchange | échanger | *ayshohnjhay* |
| exchange office | le bureau de change | *luh bewroa duh shohnjh* |
| exchange rate | le cours du change | *luh koor dew shohnjh* |
| excursion | l'excursion (f.) | *lehxkewrsyawn* |
| exhibition | l'exposition (f.) | *lehxpoazeesyawn* |
| exit | la sortie | *lah sortee* |
| expenses | les frais | *lay freh* |
| expensive | cher | *shehr* |
| explain | expliquer | *ehxpleekay* |
| express | l'express (m.) | *lehxprehs* |
| external | extérieur | *ehxtayryuhr* |
| eye | l'oeil (m.) | *luhy* |
| eye drops | les gouttes pour les yeux | *lay goot poor lay zyuh* |
| eye shadow | le fard à paupières | *luh fahr ah poapyehr* |
| eye specialist | l'ophtalmologue (m.) | *loftahmolog* |
| eyeliner | l'eye-liner (m.) | *lahy leehnehr* |

## F

| | | |
|---|---|---|
| face | le visage | *luh veezajh* |
| factory | l'usine (f.) | *lewzeen* |
| fair | la foire | *lah fwahr* |
| fall | tomber | *tawnbay* |
| family | la famille | *lah fahmeey* |
| famous | célèbre | *saylehbr* |
| far away | éloigné | *aylwahnyay* |
| farm | la ferme | *lah fehrm* |
| farmer | le fermier | *luh fehrmyay* |
| fashion | la mode | *lah mod* |
| fast | rapidement | *rahpeedmohn* |
| father | le père | *luh pehr* |
| fault | la faute | *lah foat* |
| fax | faxer | *fahxay* |
| fear | la peur | *lah puhr* |
| February | février | *fayvryay* |
| feel | sentir | *sohnteer* |
| feel like | avoir envie (de) | *ahvwahr ohnvee (duh)* |
| fence | la clôture | *lah kloatewr* |
| fever | la fièvre | *lah feeyehvr* |
| filling (tooth) | plomber | *plawnbay* |
| fill out | remplir | *rohnpleer* |
| filling | le plombage | *luh plawnbahjh* |
| film | la pellicule | *lah payleekewl* |

| filter | le filtre | *luh feeltr* |
|---|---|---|
| filthy | crasseux | *krahssuh* |
| find | trouver | *troovay* |
| fine | la caution | *lah koasyawn* |
| fine (parking) | la contravention | *lah kawntrahvohn-syawn* |
| finger | le doigt | *luh dwah* |
| fire | le feu | *luh fuh* |
| fire department | les sapeurs-pompiers | *lay sahpuhr pawnpyay* |
| fire escape | l'escalier de secours (m.) | *lehskahlyay duh suhkoor* |
| fire extinguisher | l'extincteur (m.) | *lehxtahntuhr* |
| first | le premier | *luh pruhmyay* |
| first aid | les premiers soins | *lay pruhmyay swahn* |
| first class | la première classe | *lah pruhmyehr klahs* |
| fish (verb) | pêcher | *payshay* |
| fish | le poisson | *luh pwahssawn* |
| fishing rod | la canne à pêche | *lah kahnn ah pehsh* |
| fitness club | le centre de mise en forme | *luh sohntr duh meez ohn form* |
| fitness training | l'entraînement de mise en forme (m.) | *lohntrehnmohn duh meez ohn form* |
| fitting room | la cabine d'essayage | *lah kahbeen dehsayahjh* |
| fix | réparer | *raypahray* |
| flag | le drapeau | *luh drahpoa* |
| flash bulb | l'ampoule de flash (f.) | *lohnpool duh flahsh* |
| flash cube | le cube-flash | *luh kewb flahsh* |
| flash gun | le flash | *luh flahsh* |
| flat | l'appartement (m.) | *lahpahrtuhmohn* |
| flea market | le marché aux puces | *luh mahrshay oa pews* |
| flight | le vol | *luh vol* |
| flight number | le numéro de vol | *luh newmayroa duh vol* |
| flood | l'inondation (f.) | *leenawndahsyawn* |
| floor | l'étage (m.) | *laytahjh* |
| flour | la farine | *lah fahreen* |
| flu | la grippe | *lah greep* |
| fly (insect) | la mouche | *lah moosh* |
| fly (verb) | voler | *volay* |
| fog | le brouillard | *luh brooy-yahr* |
| foggy (to be) | faire du brouillard | *fehr dew brooy-yahr* |
| folkloristic | folklorique | *folkloreek* |
| follow | suivre | *sweevr* |
| food | la nourriture | *lah nooreetewr* |
| food poisoning | l'intoxication alimentaire (f.) | *lahntoxeekahsyawn ahleemohntehr* |
| foodstuffs | les produits alimentaires | *lay prohdwee zahleemohntehr* |
| foot | le pied | *luh pyay* |
| for hire | à louer | *ah looay* |
| forbidden | interdit | *ahntehrdee* |
| forehead | le front | *luh frawn* |
| foreign | étranger | *aytrohnjhay* |
| forget | oublier | *oobleeay* |
| fork | la fourchette | *lah foorsheht* |
| form | le questionnaire | *luh kehstyonehr* |
| fort | le fort | *luh for* |

| fountain | la fontaine | *lah fawntehn* |
|---|---|---|
| four star gasoline | le super | *luh sewpehr* |
| frame | la monture | *lah mawntewr* |
| franc | le franc | *luh frohn* |
| free | libre | *leebr* |
| free of charge | gratuit | *grahtwee* |
| free time | les loisirs | *lay lwahzeer* |
| freeze | geler | *jhuhlay* |
| French | français | *frohnseh* |
| French (language) | le français | *luh frohnseh* |
| French bread | la baguette | *lah bahgeht* |
| French fries | les pommes frites | *lay pom freet* |
| fresh | frais | *freh* |
| Friday | vendredi | *vohndruhdee* |
| fried | frit | *free* |
| fried egg | l'oeuf sur le plat (m.) | *luhf sewr luh plah* |
| friend | l'ami(e) (m./f.) | *lahmee* |
| friendly | amical | *ahmeekahl* |
| fruit | le fruit | *luh frwee* |
| fruit juice | le jus de fruits | *luh jhew duh frwee* |
| frying pan | la poêle à frire | *lah pwahl ah freer* |
| full | plein | *plahn* |
| fun | le plaisir | *luh playzeer* |
| funny | drôle | *droal* |

# G

| gallery | la galerie | *lah gahlree* |
|---|---|---|
| game | le jeu | *luh jhuh* |
| garage | le garage | *luh gahrahjh* |
| garbage bag | le sac poubelle | *luh sahk poobehl* |
| garden | le jardin | *luh jhahrdahn* |
| gasoline | l'essence (f.) | *lehssohns* |
| gas station/service station | la station service | *lah stahsyawn sehrvees* |
| gastroenteritis | la gastro-entérite | *gahstroa ohntayreet* |
| gauze | la compresse de gaze | *lah kawnprehs duh gahz* |
| gel (hair) | le gel | *luh jhehl* |
| German | allemand | *ahlmohn* |
| get married | (se) marier | *(suh) mahryay* |
| get off | descendre | *daysohndr* |
| gift | le cadeau | *luh kahdoa* |
| gilt | doré | *doray* |
| ginger | le gingembre | *luh jhahnjhohnbr* |
| girl | la fille | *lah feey* |
| girlfriend | l'amie | *lahmee* |
| giro card | la carte de chèque postal | *lah kahrt duh shehk postahl* |
| giro check | le chèque postal | *luh shehk postahl* |
| glacier | le glacier | *luh glahsyay* |
| glass (wine -) | le verre | *luh vehr* |
| glasses (sun -) | les lunettes | *lay lewneht* |
| glide | faire du vol à voile | *fehr dew vol ah vwahl* |
| glove | le gant | *luh gohn* |
| glue | la colle | *lah kol* |
| go | aller | *ahlay* |

| | | |
|---|---|---|
| go back | reculer, retourner | *ruhkewlay, ruhtoornay* |
| go out | sortir | *sorteer* |
| goat's cheese | le fromage de chèvre | *luh fromajh duh shehvr* |
| gold | l'or (m.) | *lor* |
| golf course | le terrain de golf | *luh tehrahn duh golf* |
| good afternoon | bonjour | *bawnjhoor* |
| good evening | bonsoir | *bawnswahr* |
| good morning | bonjour | *bawnjhoor* |
| good night | bonne nuit | *bon nwee* |
| good-bye | au revoir | *oa ruhvvahr* |
| grade crossing | le passage à niveau | *luh pahssahj ah neevoh* |
| graduation (high school) | le bac | *luh bahk* |
| gram | le gramme | *luh grahm* |
| grandchild | le petit enfant | *luh puhtee tohnfohn* |
| grandfather | le grand-père | *luh grohn pehr* |
| grandmother | la grand-mère | *lah grohn mehr* |
| grape juice | le jus de raisin | *luh jhew duh rayzahn* |
| grapefruit | le pamplemousse | *luh pohnpluhmoos* |
| grapes | les raisins | *lay rayzahn* |
| grass | l'herbe (f.) | *lehrb* |
| grave | la tombe | *lah townb* |
| gray | gris | *gree* |
| greasy | gras | *grah* |
| green | vert | *vehr* |
| green card | la carte verte | *lah kahrt vehrt* |
| greet | saluer | *sahleway* |
| grill | griller | *greeyay* |
| grilled | grillé | *greeyay* |
| grocer | l'épicier (m) | *laypeesyay* |
| ground | le sol | *luh sol* |
| group | le groupe | *luh groop* |
| guest house | la pension | *lah pohnsyawn* |
| guide (book) | le guide | *luh gueed* |
| guide (person) | le/la guide | *luh/lah gueed* |
| guided tour | la visite guidée | *lah veezeet gueeday* |
| gynecologist | le gynécologue | *luh jheenaykolog* |

## H

| | | |
|---|---|---|
| hair | les cheveux | *lay shuhvuh* |
| hairbrush | la brosse à cheveux | *lah bros ah shuhvuh* |
| hairdresser | le coiffeur | *luh kwahfuhr* |
| hairspray | la laque | *lah lahk* |
| half (adj.) | demi | *duhmee* |
| half | la moitié | *lah mwahtyay* |
| half full | à moitié plein | *ah mwahtyay plahn* |
| hammer | le marteau | *luh mahrtoa* |
| hand | la main | *lah mahn* |
| hand brake | le frein à main | *luh frahn ah mahn* |
| handbag | le sac à main | *luh sahk ah mahn* |
| handkerchief | le mouchoir | *luh mooshwahr* |
| handmade | fait-main | *feh mahn* |
| happy | heureux | *uhruh* |
| harbor | le port | *luh por* |
| hard | dur | *dewr* |
| hat | le chapeau | *luh shahpoa* |
| hay fever | le rhume des foins | *luh rewm day fwahn* |
| hazelnut | la noisette | *lah nwahzeht* |

| | | |
|---|---|---|
| head | la tête | *lah teht* |
| headache | le mal de tête | *luh mahl duh teht* |
| headscarf | le foulard | *luh foolahr* |
| health | la santé | *lah sohntay* |
| health food shop | le magasin diététique | *luh mahgahzahn dyaytayteek* |
| hear | entendre | *ohntohndr* |
| hearing aid | la correction auditive | *lah korehksyawn oadeeteev* |
| heart | le coeur | *luh kuhr* |
| heater | le chauffage | *luh shoafahjh* |
| heavy | lourd | *loor* |
| heel | le talon | *luh tahlawn* |
| hello | bonjour, salut | *bawnjhoor, sahlew* |
| helmet | le casque | *luh kahsk* |
| help (verb) | aider | *ayday* |
| help | l'aide (f.) | *lehd* |
| herbal tea | l'infusion (f.) | *lahnfewzyawn* |
| here | ici | *eesee* |
| herring | le hareng | *luh ahrohn* |
| high | haut | *oa* |
| high tide | le flux | *luh flew* |
| highchair | la chaise d'enfant | *lah shehz dohnfohn* |
| highway | l'autoroute (f.) | *lohtohroot* |
| hiking | la marche à pied | *lah mahrsh ah pyay* |
| hiking trip | la randonnée | *lah rohndonay* |
| hip | la hanche | *lah ohnsh* |
| hire | louer | *looay* |
| hitchhike | faire de l'auto-stop | *fehr duh loatoastop* |
| hobby | le passe-temps | *luh pahstohn* |
| hold-up | l'attaque (f.) | *lahtahk* |
| holiday rental | la maison de vacances | *lah mehzawn duh vahkohns* |
| holidays | les vacances | *lay vahkohns* |
| homesickness | le mal du pays | *luh mahl dew pehy* |
| honest | honnête | *oneht* |
| honey | le miel | *luh myehl* |
| hood (car) | le capot | *luh cahpoh* |
| horizontal | horizontal | *oareezawntahl* |
| horrible | horrible | *oareebl* |
| horse | le cheval | *luh shuhvahl* |
| hospital | l'hôpital (m.) | *loapeetahl* |
| hospitality | l'hospitalité (f.) | *lospeetahleetay* |
| hot | chaud | *shoa* |
| hot-water bottle | la bouillotte | *lah booy-yot* |
| hot (spicy) | pimenté | *peemohntay* |
| hotel | l'hôtel (m.) | *loatehl* |
| hour | l'heure (f.) | *luhr* |
| house | la maison | *lah mehzawn* |
| household appliances | les appareils | *lay zahpahrehy* |
| houses of parliament | le parlement | *luh pahrluhmohn* |
| housewife | la femme au foyer | *lah fahm oa fwahyay* |
| how? | comment? | *komohn?* |
| how far? | c'est loin? | *seh lwahn?* |
| how long? | combien de temps? | *kawnbyahn duh tohn?* |
| how much? | combien? | *kawnbyahn?* |

Word list

15

| | | |
|---|---|---|
| hungry (to be) | avoir faim | *ahvwahr fahn* |
| hurricane | l'ouragan (m.) | *loorahgohn* |
| hurry | la hâte | *lah aht* |
| husband | le mari | *luh mahree* |
| hut | la cabane | *lah kahbahnn* |
| hyperventilation | l'hyperventilation (f.) | *leepehrvohnteelah-syawn* |

## I

| | | |
|---|---|---|
| ice cream | la glace | *lah glahs* |
| ice cubes | les glaçons | *lay glahsawn* |
| ice skate | patiner | *pahteenay* |
| idea | l'idée (f.) | *leeday* |
| identification | la pièce d'identité | *lah pyehs deedohnteetay* |
| identify | identifier | *eedohnteefyay* |
| ignition key | la clef de contact | *lah klay duh kawntahkt* |
| ill | malade | *mahlahd* |
| illness | la maladie | *lah mahlahdee* |
| imagine | imaginer | *eemahjheenay* |
| immediately | immédiatement | *eemaydyahtmohn* |
| import duty | les droits de douane | *lay drwah duh dwahnn* |
| impossible | impossible | *ahnposeebl* |
| in | dans | *dohn* |
| in the evening | le soir | *luh swahr* |
| in the morning | le matin | *luh mahtahn* |
| included | compris | *kawnpree* |
| indicate | indiquer | *ahndeekay* |
| indicator | le clignotant | *luh kleenyotohn* |
| inexpensive | bon marché | *bawn mahrshay* |
| infection (viral/bacterial) | l'infection (virale/bactérielle) (f.) | *lahnfehksyawn (veerahl, bahktayryehl)* |
| inflammation | l'inflammation (f.) | *lahnflahmahsyawn* |
| information | l'information (f.) | *lahnformahsyawn* |
| information | le renseignement | *luh rohnsehnymohn* |
| information office | le bureau de renseignements | *luh bewroa duh rohnsehnymohn* |
| injection | la piqûre | *lah peekewr* |
| injured | blessé | *blehssay* |
| inner ear | l'oreille interne (f.) | *lorehy ahntehrn* |
| inner tube | la chambre à air | *lah shohnbr ah ehr* |
| innocent | innocent | *eenosohn* |
| insect | l'insecte (m.) | *lahnsehkt* |
| insect bite | la piqûre d'insecte | *lah peekewr dahnsehkt* |
| insect repellent | l'huile contre les moustiques | *lweel kawntr lay moosteek* |
| inside | à l'intérieur | *ah lahntayryuhr* |
| instructions | le mode d'emploi | *luh mod dohnplwah* |
| insurance | l'assurance (f.) | *lahsewrohns* |
| intermission | la pause | *lah poaz* |
| international | international | *ahntehrnahsyonahl* |
| interpreter | l'interprète (m./f.) | *lahntehrpreht* |
| intersection | le carrefour | *luh kahrfoor* |
| introduce oneself | se présenter | *suh prayzohntay* |
| invite | inviter | *ahnveetay* |
| invoice | la facture | *lah fahktewr* |

**Word list**

**15**

| iodine | l'iode (m.) | *Iyod* |
| Ireland | l'Irlande (f.) | *leerlohnd* |
| Irish | irlandais | *leerlohndeh* |
| iron (verb) | repasser | *ruhpahsay* |
| iron | le fer à repasser | *luh fehr ah ruhpahsay* |
| ironing board | la table à repasser | *lah tahbl ah ruhpahsay* |
| island | l'île (f.) | *leel* |
| it's a pleasure | je vous en prie | *jhuh voo zohn pree* |
| Italian | italien | *eetahlyahn* |
| itch | la démangeaison | *lah daymohnjhehzawn* |

## J

| jack | le cric | *luh kreek* |
| jacket | la veste | *lah vehst* |
| jam | la confiture | *lah kawnfeetewr* |
| January | janvier | *jhohnvyay* |
| jaw | la mâchoire | *lah mahshwahr* |
| jellyfish | la méduse | *lah maydewz* |
| jeweller | le bijoutier | *luh beejhootyay* |
| jewellery | les bijoux | *lay beejhoo* |
| jog | faire du jogging | *fehr dew jogeeng* |
| joke | la blague | *lah blahg* |
| juice | le jus | *luh jhew* |
| July | juillet | *jhweeyeh* |
| jumper cables | le câble de | *luh kahbl duh* |
| | démarrage | *daymahrahjh* |
| June | juin | *jhwahn* |

## K

| key | la clef/clé | *lah klay* |
| kilo | le kilo | *luh keeloa* |
| kilometer | le kilomètre | *luh keeloamehtr* |
| king | le roi | *luh rwah* |
| kiss (verb) | embrasser | *ohnbrahssay* |
| kiss | le baiser | *luh bayzay* |
| kitchen | la cuisine | *lah kweezeen* |
| knee | le genou | *luh jhuhnoo* |
| knee socks | les mi-bas | *lay mee bah* |
| knife | le couteau | *luh kootoa* |
| knit | tricoter | *treekotay* |
| know | savoir | *sahvwahr* |

## L

| lace | la dentelle | *lah dohntehl* |
| ladies' rooms | les toilettes pour | *lay twahleht* |
| | dames | *poor dahm* |
| lake | le lac | *luh lahk* |
| lamp | la lampe | *lah lohnp* |
| land | atterrir | *ahtayreer* |
| lane | la voie | *lah vwah* |
| language | la langue | *lah lohng* |
| large | grand | *grohn* |
| last | dernier, passé | *dehrnyay, pahssay* |
| last night | la nuit passée | *lah nwee pahssay* |
| late | tard | *tahr* |
| later | tout à l'heure | *too tah luhr* |
| laugh | rire | *reer* |

| launderette | la laverie | lah lahvree |
| | automatique | oatoamahteek |
| laundry soap | le détergent | luh dayterjhohn |
| law | la loi | lah lwah |
| lawyer | l'avocat | lahvohkah |
| laxative | le laxatif | luh lahxahteef |
| leaky | crevé | kruhvay |
| leather | le cuir | luh kweer |
| leather goods | les articles | lay zahrteekl |
| | de maroquinerie | duh mahrokeenree |
| leave | partir | pahrteer |
| leek | le poireau | luh pwahroa |
| left | gauche | goash |
| left, on the | à gauche | ah goash |
| leg | la jambe | lah jhohnb |
| lemon | le citron | luh seetrawn |
| lemonade | la limonade | lah leemonahd |
| lend | prêter (à) | prehtay (ah) |
| lens | la lentille | lah lohnteey |
| lentils | les lentilles | lay lohnteey |
| less | moins | mwahn |
| lesson | la leçon | lah luhsawn |
| letter | la lettre | lah lehtr |
| lettuce | la laitue | lah laytew |
| library | la bibliothèque | lah beebleeotehk |
| lie (down) | s'étendre | saytohndr |
| lie (verb) | mentir | mohnteer |
| lift (chair) | le télésiège | luh taylaysyehjh |
| light (not dark) | clair | klehr |
| light (not heavy) | léger | layjhay |
| light | la lumière | lah lewmyehr |
| lighter | le briquet | luh breekeh |
| lighthouse | le phare | luh fahr |
| lightning | la foudre | lah foodr |
| like | aimer | aymay |
| line | la ligne | lah leenyuh |
| linen | le lin | luh lahn |
| lipstick | le rouge à lèvres | luh roojh ah lehvr |
| liquor/wine store | magasin de spiritueux | mahgahsan duh |
| | et vins | speereetooewr/ |
| | | duh van |
| liquorice | le réglisse | luh rayglees |
| listen | écouter | aykootay |
| liter | le litre | luh leetr |
| literature | la littérature | lah leetayrahtewr |
| little | peu | puh |
| live (place) | habiter | ahbeetay |
| live | vivre | veevr |
| live together | habiter ensemble | ahbeetay ohnsohnbl |
| lobster | le homard | luh omahr |
| locally | localement | lokahlmohn |
| lock | la serrure | lah sehrewr |
| long | long | lawn |
| long distance | interurbain | anntehrewrban |
| look | regarder | ruhgahrday |
| look for | chercher | shehrshay |
| look up | rechercher | ruhshehrshay |

| | | |
|---|---|---|
| lose | perdre | *pehrdr* |
| loss | la perte | *lah pehrt* |
| lost | introuvable, perdu | *ahntroovahbl, pehrdew* |
| lost item | l'objet perdu (m.) | *lohbjeh pehrdew* |
| lost and found office | les objets trouvés | *lay zobjheh troovay* |
| lotion | la lotion | *lah loasyawn* |
| loud | fort | *for* |
| love (to be in) | être amoureux | *ehtr ahmooruh* |
| love (verb) | aimer | *aymay* |
| love | l'amour (m.) | *lahmoor* |
| low | bas | *bah* |
| low tide | le reflux | *luh ruhflew* |
| luck | la chance | *lah shohns* |
| luggage | le bagage | *luh bahgahjh* |
| luggage locker | la consigne | *lah kawnseenyuh* |
| | automatique | *oatoamahteek* |
| lunch | le déjeuner | *luh dayjhuhnay* |
| lunchroom | le café | *luh kahfay* |
| lungs | les poumons | *lay poomawn* |

## M

| | | |
|---|---|---|
| macaroni | les macaronis | *lay mahkahroanee* |
| madam | madame | *mahdahm* |
| magazine | la revue | *lah ruhvew* |
| mail | le courrier | *luh kooryay* |
| mailman | le facteur | *luh fahktuhr* |
| main post office | le bureau de | *luh bewroa duh* |
| | poste central | *post sohntral* |
| main road | la grande route | *lah grohnd root* |
| make an appointment | prendre un | *prohndr uhn* |
| | rendez-vous | *rohndayvoo* |
| make love | faire l'amour | *fehr lahmoor* |
| makeshift | provisoirement | *proveezwahrmohn* |
| man | l'homme (m.) | *lom* |
| manager | le directeur | *luh deerehktuhr* |
| mandarin (fruit) | la mandarine | *lah mohndahreen* |
| manicure | la manucure | *lah mahnewkewr* |
| map | la carte | *lah kahrt* |
| | géographique | *jhayoagrahfeek* |
| marble | le marbre | *luh mahrbruh* |
| March | mars | *mahrs* |
| margarine | la margarine | *lah mahrgahreen* |
| marina | le port de plaisance | *luh por duh playzohns* |
| market | le marché | *luh mahrshay* |
| marriage | le mariage | *luh mahryajh* |
| married | marié | *mahreeay* |
| Mass | la messe | *lah mehs* |
| massage | le massage | *luh mahsahjh* |
| matte | mat | *maht* |
| match | le match | *luh mahch* |
| matches | les allumettes | *lay zahlewmeht* |
| May | mai | *meh* |
| maybe | peut-être | *puh tehtr* |
| mayonnaise | la mayonnaise | *lah mahyonehz* |
| mayor | le maire | *luh mehr* |
| meal | le repas | *luh ruhpah* |
| mean | signifier | *seenyeefyay* |

| meat | la viande | *lah vyohnd* |
| medical insurance | l'assurance | *lahsewrohns* |
| | maladie (f.) | *mahlahdee* |
| medication | le médicament | *luh maydeekahmohn* |
| medicine | le médicament | *luh maydeekahmohn* |
| meet | rencontrer | *rohnkohntray* |
| melon | le melon | *luh muhlawn* |
| membership | l'adhésion (f.) | *lahdayzyawn* |
| menstruate | avoir ses règles | *ahvwahr say rehgl* |
| menstruation | les règles | *lay rehgl* |
| menu | la carte | *lah kahrt* |
| menu of the day | le menu du jour | *luh muhnew dew jhoor* |
| message | le message | *luh mehsahjh* |
| metal | le métal | *luh maytahl* |
| meter | le compteur | *luh kawntuhr* |
| meter | le mètre | *luh mehtr* |
| migraine | la migraine | *lah meegrehn* |
| mild (tobacco) | léger | *layjhay* |
| milk | le lait | *luh leh* |
| millimeter | le millimètre | *luh meeleemehtr* |
| mineral water | l'eau minérale (f.) | *loa meenayral* |
| minute | la minute | *lah meenewt* |
| mirror | le miroir | *luh meerwahr* |
| miss | manquer | *mohnkay* |
| missing (to be) | manquer | *mohnkay* |
| mistake | l'erreur (f.) | *lehruhr* |
| misunderstanding | le malentendu | *luh mahlohntohndew* |
| mocha | le moka | *luh mokah* |
| modern art | l'art moderne (m.) | *lahr modehrn* |
| molar | la molaire | *lah molehr* |
| molasses | la mélasse | *lah maylahs* |
| moment | le moment | *luh momohn* |
| Monday | lundi | *luhndee* |
| money | l'argent (m.) | *lahrjhohn* |
| month | le mois | *luh mwah* |
| moped | le cyclomoteur | *luh seekloamotuhr* |
| morning-after pill | la pilule du | *lah peelewl dew* |
| | lendemain | *lohnduhmahn* |
| mosque | la mosquée | *lah moskay* |
| motel | le motel | *luh moatehl* |
| mother | la mère | *lah mehr* |
| moto-cross | le moto-cross | *luh moatoakros* |
| motorbike | la motocyclette | *lah moatoaseekleht* |
| motorboat | le bateau à moteur | *luh bahtoa ah motuhr* |
| mountain | la montagne | *lah mawntanyuh* |
| mountain hut | le refuge | *luh ruhfewjh* |
| mountaineering | l'alpinisme (m.) | *lahlpeeneesm* |
| mountaineering shoes | les chaussures | *lay shoasewr duh* |
| | de montagne | *mawntanyuh* |
| mouse | la souris | *lah sooree* |
| mouth | la bouche | *lah boosh* |
| movie camera | la caméra | *lah kahmayrah* |
| much/many | beaucoup | *boakoo* |
| multi-storey car park | le parking | *luh pahrkeeng* |
| muscle | le muscle | *luh mewskl* |
| muscle spasms | les crampes | *lay krohnp* |
| | musculaires | *mewskewlehr* |

| museum | le musée | *luh mewzay* |
| mushrooms | les champignons | *lay shohnpeenyawn* |
| music | la musique | *lah mewzeek* |
| musical | la comédie musicale | *lah komaydee mewzeekahl* |
| mussels | les moules | *lay mool* |
| mustard | la moutarde | *lah mootahrd* |

## N

| nail (on hand) | l'ongle (m.) | *lawngl* |
| nail | le clou | *luh kloo* |
| nail polish | le vernis à ongles | *luh vehrnee ah awngl* |
| nail polish remover | le dissolvant | *luh deesolvohn* |
| nail scissors | le coupe-ongles | *luh koop awngl* |
| naked | nu | *new* |
| nationality | la nationalité | *lah nahsyonahleetay* |
| natural | naturel | *nahtewrehl* |
| nature | la nature | *lah nahtewr* |
| naturism | le naturisme (m.) | *luh nahtewreesm* |
| nauseous | (avoir) mal de coeur | *(ahvwahr) mahl duh kuhr* |
| near | près | *preh* |
| nearby | tout près | *too preh* |
| necessary | nécessaire | *naysehsehr* |
| neck | le cou | *luh kooh* |
| necklace | la chaîne | *lah shehn* |
| nectarine | la nectarine | *lah nehktahreen* |
| needle | l'aiguille (f.) | *laygweey* |
| negative | le négatif | *luh naygahteef* |
| neighbors | les voisins | *lay vwahzahn* |
| nephew | le neveu | *luh nuhvuh* |
| Netherlands | les Pays-Bas | *lay pehy bah* |
| never | jamais | *jhahmeh* |
| new | nouveau | *noovoa* |
| news | les informations | *lay zahnformahsyawn* |
| news stand | le kiosque | *luh kyosk* |
| newspaper | le journal | *luh jhoornahl* |
| next | le prochain | *luh proshahn* |
| next to | à côté de | *ah koatay duh* |
| nice (friendly) | gentil | *jhohntee* |
| nice | agréable, bon | *ahgrayahbl, bawn* |
| niece | la nièce | *lah nyehs* |
| night | la nuit | *lah nwee* |
| night duty | le service de nuit | *luh sehrvees duh nwee* |
| nightclub | la boîte de nuit/ le night-club | *lah bwaht duh nwee/ luh naheet kluhb* |
| nightlife | la vie nocturne | *lah vee noktewrn* |
| nipple | la tétine | *lah tayteen* |
| no one | personne | *pehrson* |
| no | non | *nawn* |
| no passing | l'interdiction de dépasser (f.) | *lahntehrdeeksyawn duh daypahsay* |
| noise | le bruit | *luh brwee* |
| nonstop | continu | *kawnteenew* |
| normal | normal, ordinaire | *normahl, ordeenehr* |
| north | le nord | *luh nor* |
| nose | le nez | *luh nay* |

| | | |
|---|---|---|
| nose bleed | le saignement de nez | *luh sehnyuhmohn dew nay* |
| nose drops | les gouttes pour le nez | *lay goot poor luh nay* |
| notepaper | le papier postal | *luh pahpyay postahl* |
| nothing | rien | *ryahn* |
| November | novembre | *novohnbr* |
| nowhere | nulle part | *newl pahr* |
| nudist beach | la plage de nudistes | *lah plahjh duh newdeest* |
| number | le numéro | *luh newmayroa* |
| number plate | la plaque d'immatriculation | *lah plahk deemahtree-kewlahsyawn* |
| nurse | l'infirmière (f.) | *lahnfeermyehr* |
| nutmeg | la noix de muscade | *lah nwah duh mewskahd* |
| nuts | les noix | *lay nwah* |

# O

| | | |
|---|---|---|
| October | octobre | *oktobr* |
| odometer | le compteur kilométrique | *luh kawntuhr keelohmaytreek* |
| offer | offrir | *ofreer* |
| office | le bureau | *luh bewroa* |
| oil | l'huile (f.) | *lweel* |
| oil level | le niveau d'huile | *luh neevoa dweel* |
| ointment | le baume | *luh boam* |
| ointment for burns | la pommade contre les brûlures | *lah pomahd kawntr lay brewlewr* |
| okay | d'accord | *dahkor* |
| old | vieux | *vyuh* |
| old town | la vieille ville | *lah vyehy veel* |
| olive oil | l'huile d'olive | *lweel doleev* |
| olives | les olives | *lay zoleev* |
| omelette | l'omelette (f.) | *lomleht* |
| on | sur | *sewr* |
| on board | à bord | *ah bor* |
| on the way | en cours de route | *ohn koor duh root* |
| oncoming car | le véhicule en sens inverse | *luh vayeekewl ohn sohns ahnvehr* |
| one-way traffic | la circulation à sens unique | *lah seerkewlahsyawn ah sohns ewneek* |
| one hundred grams | cent grammes | *sohn grahm* |
| onion | l'oignon (m.) | *lonyawn* |
| open (verb) | ouvrir | *oovreer* |
| open | ouvert | *oovehr* |
| opera | l'opéra (m.) | *loapayrah* |
| operate | opérer | *oapayray* |
| operator (telephone) | la téléphoniste | *lah taylayfoneest* |
| operetta | l'opérette (f.) | *loapayreht* |
| opposite | en face | *ohn fahs* |
| optician | l'opticien (m.) | *lopteesyahn* |
| or | ou | *oo* |
| orange | l'orange (f.) | *lorohnjh* |
| orange (adj.) | orange | *orohnjh* |
| orange juice | le jus d'orange | *luh jhew dorohnjh* |
| orchestra (theater) | la salle | *lah sahl* |

| | | |
|---|---|---|
| order (verb) | commander | komohnday |
| order | la commande | lah kohmohnd |
| other | l'autre | loatr |
| other side | l'autre côté | loatr koatay |
| outside | dehors | duh-or |
| overpass | le viaduc | luh vyadewk |
| overtake | doubler | dooblay |
| oysters | les huîtres | lay zweetr |

## P

| | | |
|---|---|---|
| package (mail) | le paquet postal | luh pahkeh postahl |
| packed lunch | le casse-croûte | luh kahs kroot |
| page | la page | lah pahjh |
| pain | la douleur | lah dooluhr |
| painkiller | le calmant | luh kahlmohn |
| paint | la peinture | lah pahntewr |
| painting (art) | le tableau | luh tahbloa |
| pajamas | le pyjama | luh peejhahmah |
| palace | le palais | luh pahleh |
| pan | la casserole | lah kahsrol |
| pancake | la crèpe | lah krehp |
| pane | la vitre | lah veetr |
| pants | la culotte | lah kewlot |
| panty liner | le protège-slip | luh protehjh sleep |
| paper | le papier | luh pahpyay |
| paraffin oil | le pétrole | luh paytrol |
| parasol | le parasol | luh pahrahsol |
| parcel | le colis | luh kolee |
| pardon | pardon | pahrdawn |
| parents | les parents | lay pahrohn |
| park | le parc | luh pahrk |
| park (verb) | garer | gahray |
| parking space | la place de parking | lah plahs duh pahrkeeng |
| parsley | le persil | luh pehrsee |
| part | la pièce | lah pyehs |
| partition | la séparation | lah saypahrahsyawn |
| partner | le/la partenaire | luh/lah pahrtuhnehr |
| party | la fête | lah feht |
| passable (of roads) | praticable | prahteekahbl |
| passenger | le passager | luh pahsahjhay |
| passport | le passeport | luh pahspor |
| passport photo | la photo d'identité | lah foatoa deedohnteetay |
| patient | le patient | luh pahsyohn |
| pavement | le trottoir | luh trotwahr |
| pay | payer | payay |
| peach | la pêche | lah pehsh |
| peanuts | les cacahuètes | lay kahkahweht |
| pear | la poire | lah pwahr |
| peas | les petits pois | lay puhtee pwah |
| pedal | la pédale | lah paydahl |
| pedestrian crossing | le passage clouté | luh pahsahjh klootay |
| pedicure | le/la pédicure | luh/lah paydeekewr |
| pen | le stylo | luh steeloa |
| pencil | le crayon | luh krayawn |
| penis | le pénis | luh paynees |

| | | |
|---|---|---|
| pepper (capsicum) | le poivron | *luh pwahvrawn* |
| pepper | le poivre | *luh pwahvr* |
| performance | la représentation de théâtre | *lah ruhprayzohntahsyawn duh tayahtr* |
| perfume | le parfum | *luh pahrfuhn* |
| perm (verb) (hair) | faire une permanente à | *fehr ewn pehrmahnohnt ah* |
| perm (hair) | la permanente | *lah pehrmahnohnt* |
| permit | le permis | *luh pehrmee* |
| person | la personne | *lah pehrson* |
| personal | personnel | *pehrsonehl* |
| pets | les animaux domestiques | *lay zahneemoa domehsteek* |
| pharmacy | la pharmacie | *lah fahrmahsee* |
| phone (by) | par téléphone | *pahr taylayfon* |
| phone (tele-) | le téléphone | *luh taylayfon* |
| phone (verb) | téléphoner | *taylayfonay* |
| phone box | la cabine téléphonique | *lah kahbeen taylayfoneek* |
| phone directory | l'annuaire | *lahnnewehr* |
| phone number | le numéro de téléphone | *luh newmayroa duh taylayfon* |
| photo | la photo | *la foatoa* |
| photocopier | le photocopieur | *luh foatoakopyuhr* |
| photocopy (verb) | photocopier | *foatoakopyay* |
| photocopy | la photocopie | *lah foatoakopee* |
| pick up | aller chercher | *ahlay shehrshay* |
| picnic | le pique-nique | *luh peek neek* |
| pier | la jetée | *lah jhuhtay* |
| pigeon | le pigeon | *luh peejhyawn* |
| pill (contraceptive) | la pilule | *lah peelewl* |
| pillow | le coussin | *luh koossahn* |
| pillowcase | la taie d'oreiller | *lah tay dorehyay* |
| pin | l'épingle (f.) | *laypahngl* |
| pineapple | l'ananas (m.) | *lahnahnahs* |
| pipe | la pipe | *lah peep* |
| pipe tobacco | le tabac à pipe | *luh tahbah ah peep* |
| pity | dommage | *domahjh* |
| places of entertainment | les possibilités de sortie | *lay poseebeeleetay duh sortee* |
| places of interest | les curiosités | *lay kewryozeetay* |
| plan | l'intention (f.) | *lahntohnsyawn* |
| plant | la plante | *lah plohnt* |
| plastic | plastique | *plahsteek* |
| plastic bag | le sac en plastique | *luh sahk ohn plahsteek* |
| plate | l'assiette (f.) | *lahsyeht* |
| platform | la voie, le quai | *lah vwah, luh kay* |
| play (theater) | la pièce de théâtre | *lah pyehs duh tayahtr* |
| play (verb) | jouer | *jhooay* |
| play basketball | jouer au basket | *jhooay oa bahskeht* |
| play billiards | jouer au billiard | *jhooay oa biy-yahr* |
| play checkers | jouer aux dames | *jhooay oa dahm* |
| play chess | jouer aux échecs | *jhooay oa zayshehk* |
| play golf | jouer au golf | *jhooay oa golf* |
| playing cards | les cartes à jouer | *lay kahrt ah jhooay* |
| pleasant | agréable | *ahgrayahbl* |

| please | s'il vous plaît | *seel voo pleh* |
| pleasure | la satisfaction | *lah sahteesfahksyawn* |
| plum | la prune | *lah prewn* |
| pocketknife | le canif | *luh kahneef* |
| point | indiquer | *ahndeekay* |
| poison | le poison | *luh pwahzawn* |
| police | la police | *lah polees* |
| police station | le poste de police | *luh post duh polees* |
| policeman | l'agent de police (m.) | *lahjhohn duh polees* |
| pond | le bassin | *luh bahsahn* |
| pony | le poney | *luh poaneh* |
| pop concert | le concert pop | *luh kawnsehr pop* |
| population | la population | *lah popewlahsyawn* |
| pork | la viande de porc | *lah vyohnd duh por* |
| port | le porto | *luh portoa* |
| porter | le porteur | *luh portuhr* |
| post (zip) code | le code postal | *luh kod postahl* |
| post office | la poste | *lah post* |
| postage | le port | *luh por* |
| postbox | la boîte aux lettres | *lah bwaht oa lehtr* |
| postcard | la carte postale | *lah kahrt postahl* |
| postman | le facteur | *luh fahktuhr* |
| potato | la pomme de terre | *lah pom duh tehr* |
| potato chips | les chips | *lay sheeps* |
| poultry | la volaille | *lah vohlahy* |
| pound | la livre | *lah leevr* |
| powdered milk | le lait en poudre | *luh leh ohn poodr* |
| prawns | les crevettes roses | *lay kruhveht roaz* |
| precious | précieux | *praysyuh* |
| prefer | préférer | *prayfayray* |
| preference | la préférence | *lah prayfayrohns* |
| pregnant | enceinte | *ohnsahnt* |
| present (adj.) | présent | *prayzohn* |
| present (gift) | le cadeau | *luh kahdoa* |
| press | appuyer | *ahpweeyay* |
| pressure | la pression | *lah prehsyawn* |
| price | le prix | *luh pree* |
| price list | la liste de prix | *lah leest duh pree* |
| print (verb) | faire tirer | *fehr teeray* |
| print | l'épreuve (f.) | *laypruhv* |
| probably | probablement | *probahbluhmohn* |
| problem | le problème | *luh problehm* |
| profession | la profession | *lah profehsyawn* |
| program | le programme | *luh prograhm* |
| pronounce | prononcer | *proanawnsay* |
| propane gas | le gaz propane | *luh gahz propahn* |
| pull | arracher | *ahrahshay* |
| pull a muscle | froisser un muscle | *frwahsay uhn mewskl* |
| pure | pur | *pewr* |
| purple | violet | *veeoleh* |
| purse | le porte-monnaie | *luh port moneh* |
| push | pousser | *poossay* |
| pushcart (shopping) | la poussette | *lah poosseht* |
| puzzle | le puzzle | *luh puhzl* |

**Q**

| quarter | le quart | *luh kahr* |

| | | |
|---|---|---|
| quarter of an hour | le quart d'heure | *luh kahr duhr* |
| queen | la reine | *lah rehn* |
| question | la question | *lah kehstyawn* |
| quick | rapide | *rahpeed* |
| quiet | tranquille | *trohnkeey* |

# R

| | | |
|---|---|---|
| radio | la radio | *lah rahdyoa* |
| railways | les chemins de fer (m.) | *lay shuhmahn duh fehr* |
| rain (verb) | pleuvoir | *pluhvwahr* |
| rain | la pluie | *lah plwee* |
| raincoat | l'imperméable (m.) | *lahnpehrmayahbl* |
| raisins | les raisins secs | *lay rehzahn sehk* |
| rape | le viol | *luh vyol* |
| rapids | le courant rapide | *luh koorohn rahpeed* |
| raspberries | les framboises | *lay frohnbwahz* |
| raw | cru | *krew* |
| raw ham | le jambon cru | *luh jhohnbawn krew* |
| raw vegetables | les crudités | *lay krewdeetay* |
| razor blades | les lames de rasoir | *lay lahm duh rahzwahr* |
| read (verb) | lire | *leer* |
| ready | prêt | *preh* |
| really | vraiment | *vrehmohn* |
| receipt (cash register) | le ticket de caisse | *luh teekeh duh kehs* |
| receipt | le reçu, la quittance | *luh ruhsew, lah keetohns* |
| recipe | la recette | *lah ruhseht* |
| reclining chair | la chaise longue | *lah shehz lawng* |
| recommend | recommander | *ruhkomohnday* |
| recovery service (towing) | l'assistance routière (f.) | *lahseestohns rootyehr* |
| rectangle | le rectangle | *luh rehktohngl* |
| red | rouge | *roojh* |
| red wine | le vin rouge | *luh vahn roojh* |
| reduction | la réduction | *lah raydewksyawn* |
| refrigerator | le réfrigérateur | *luh rayfreejhayrahtuhr* |
| regards | les amitiés | *lay zahmeetyay* |
| region | la région | *lah rayjhyawn* |
| registration | la carte grise | *lah kahrt greez* |
| relatives | la famille | *lah fahmeey* |
| reliable | sûr | *sewr* |
| religion | la religion | *lah ruhleejhyawn* |
| rent out | louer | *looay* |
| repair (verb) | réparer | *raypahray* |
| repairs | la réparation | *lah raypahrahsyawn* |
| repeat | répéter | *raypaytay* |
| report | le procès-verbal | *luh proseh vehrbahl* |
| resent | prendre mal | *prohndr mahl* |
| reserve | réserver | *raysehrvay* |
| reserved | réservé | *raysehrveh* |
| responsible | responsable | *rehspawnsahbl* |
| rest | se reposer | *suh ruhpoazay* |
| restaurant | le restaurant | *luh rehstoarohn* |
| result | le résultat | *luh rayzewltah* |
| retired | à la retraite | *ah lah ruhtreht* |
| retirement | la retraite | *lah ruhtreht* |

| | | |
|---|---|---|
| return (ticket) | l'aller-retour (m.) | *lahlay ruhtoor* |
| reverse (vehicle) | faire marche arrière | *fehr mahrsh ahryehr* |
| rheumatism | le rhumatisme | *luh rewmahteesm* |
| rice | le riz | *luh ree* |
| ridiculous | ridicule | *reedeekewl* |
| riding (horseback) | faire du cheval | *fehr dew shuhvahl* |
| riding school | le manège | *luh mahnehjh* |
| right | la droite | *lah drwaht* |
| right of way | la priorité | *lah preeoreetay* |
| right, on the | à droite | *ah drwaht* |
| ripe | mûr | *mewr* |
| risk | le risque | *luh reesk* |
| river | la rivière | *reevyehr* |
| road | la route | *lah root* |
| roasted | rôti | *roatee* |
| rock | le rocher | *luh roshay* |
| roll (bread) | le petit pain | *luh puhtee pahn* |
| rolling tobacco | le tabac à rouler | *luh tahbah ah roolay* |
| roof rack | la galerie | *lah gahlree* |
| room | la pièce | *lah pyehs* |
| room number | le numéro de chambre | *luh newmayroa duh shohnbr* |
| room service | le service de chambre | *luh sehrvees duh shohnbr* |
| rope | la corde | *lah kord* |
| rose | la rose | *lah roaz* |
| rosé | le rosé | *luh roazay* |
| rotary | le rond-point | *luh rawn pwahn* |
| route | l'itinéraire (m.) | *leeteenayrehr* |
| rowing boat | la barque | *la bahrk* |
| rubber | le caoutchouc | *luh kah-oochoo* |
| rubber band | l'élastique | *lay lahsteek* |
| rubbish | les détritus | *luh daytreetews* |
| rude | mal élevé | *mahl aylvay* |
| ruins | les ruines (f.) | *lay rween* |
| run into | rencontrer | *rohnkawntray* |
| running shoes | les chaussures de sport | *lay shoasewr duh spor* |

## S

| | | |
|---|---|---|
| sad | triste | *treest* |
| safari | le safari | *luh sahfahree* |
| safe (adj.) | en sécurité | *ohn saykewreetay* |
| safe | le coffre-fort | *luh kofr for* |
| safety pin | l'épingle de nourrice (f.) | *laypahngl duh noorees* |
| sail | faire de la voile | *fehr duh lah vwahl* |
| sailing boat | le voilier | *luh vwahlyay* |
| salad | la salade | *lah sahlahd* |
| salad oil | l'huile de table (f.) | *lweel duh tahbl* |
| salami | le salami | *luh sahlahmee* |
| sale | les soldes | *lay sold* |
| salt | le sel | *luh sehl* |
| same | le même | *luh mehm* |
| sandwich | le sandwich | *luh sohndweech* |
| sandy beach | la plage de sable | *lah plahjh duh sahbl* |

| sanitary napkin | la serviette hygiénique | lah sehrvyeht eejhyayneek |
| sardines | les sardines | lay sahrdeen |
| satisfied | content (de) | kawntohn (duh) |
| Saturday | samedi | sahmdee |
| sauce | la sauce | lah soas |
| sauna | le sauna | luh soanah |
| sausage | la saucisse | lah soasees |
| savory | salé | sahlay |
| say | dire | deer |
| scarf | l'écharpe (f.) | layshahrp |
| scenic walk | le circuit pédestre | luh seerkwee paydehstr |
| school | l'école (f.) | laykol |
| scissors | les ciseaux | lay seezoa |
| scooter | le scooter | luh skootehr |
| scorpion | le scorpion | luh skorpyawn |
| scotch tape | le scotch | luh scahch |
| Scotland | l'Ecosse (f.) | laykos |
| Scottish | écossais | aykosseh |
| scrambled eggs | l'oeuf brouillé (m.) | lef brooy-yay |
| screw | la vis | lah vees |
| screwdriver | le tournevis | luh toornuhvees |
| sculpture | la sculpture | lah skewltewr |
| sea | la mer | lah mehr |
| seasick (to be) | avoir le mal de mer | ahvwahr luh mahl duh mehr |
| seat | la place | lah plahs |
| second-hand | d'occasion | dokahzyawn |
| second (adj.) | deuxième | duhzyehm |
| second | la seconde | lah suhgawnd |
| sedative | le tranquillisant | luh trohnkeeleezohn |
| self-timer | le déclencheur automatique | luh dayklohnshuhr oatoamahteek |
| semi-skimmed | demi-écrémé | duhmee aykraymay |
| send | expédier | ehxpaydyay |
| sentence | la phrase | lah frahz |
| separated | séparé | saypahray |
| September | septembre | sehptohnbr |
| serious | sérieux | sayryuh |
| service | le service | luh sehrvees |
| serviette | la serviette | lah sehrvyeht |
| set (hair) | faire une mise en plis | fehr ewn meez ohn plee |
| sewing thread | le fil à coudre | luh feel ah koodr |
| shade | l'ombre (f.) | lawnbr |
| shallow | peu profond | puh profawn |
| shampoo | le shampooing | luh shohnpwahn |
| shark | le requin | luh ruhkahn |
| shave (verb) | se raser | suh rahzay |
| shaver | le rasoir électrique | luh rahzwahr aylehktreek |
| shaving brush | le blaireau | luh blayroa |
| shaving cream | la crème à raser | lah krehm ah rahzay |
| shaving soap | le savon à raser | luh sahvawn ah rahzay |
| sheet | le drap | luh drah |
| sherry | le xérès | luh ksayrehz |

**Word list**

**15**

143

| | | |
|---|---|---|
| shirt | la chemise | *lah shuhmeez* |
| shoe | la chaussure | *lah shoasewr* |
| shoe polish | le cirage | *luh seerajh* |
| shoe shop | le magasin de chaussures | *luh mahgahzahn duh shoasewr* |
| shoelace | le lacet | *luh lahseh* |
| shoemaker | le cordonnier | *luh kordonyay* |
| shop (verb) | faire les courses | *fehr lay koors* |
| shop | le magasin | *luh mahgahzahn* |
| shop assistant | la vendeuse | *lah vohnduhz* |
| shop window | la vitrine | *lah veetreen* |
| shopping bag | le cabas | *luh kahbah* |
| shopping center | le centre commercial | *luh sohntr komehrsyahl* |
| short | court | *koor* |
| short circuit | le court-circuit | *luh koor seerkwee* |
| shorts | le bermuda | *luh behrmewdah* |
| shoulder | l'épaule (f.) | *laypoal* |
| show | le spectacle | *luh spehktahkl* |
| shower | la douche | *lah doosh* |
| shutter | l'obturateur (m.) | *lobtewrahtuhr* |
| sieve | la passoire | *lah pahswahr* |
| sign (verb) | signer | *seenyay* |
| sign | le panneau | *luh pahnoa* |
| signature | la signature | *lah seenyahtewr* |
| silence | le silence | *luh seelohns* |
| silver | l'argent (m.) | *lahrjhohn* |
| silver-plated | argenté | *ahrjhohntay* |
| simple | simple | *sahnpl* |
| single (ticket) | l'aller simple (m. ) | *lahlay sahnpl* |
| single (unmarried) | célibataire | *sayleebahtehr* |
| single | le célibataire | *luh sayleebahtehr* |
| sir | monsieur | *muhsyuh* |
| sister | la soeur | *lah suhr* |
| sit (verb) | s'asseoir | *sahswahr* |
| size | la pointure, la taille | *lah pwahntewr, lah tahy* |
| ski (verb) | skier, faire du ski | *skeeay, fehr dew skee* |
| ski boots | les chaussures de ski | *lay shoasewr duh skee* |
| ski goggles | les lunettes de ski | *lay lewneht duh skee* |
| ski instructor | le moniteur de ski | *luh moneetuhr duh skee* |
| ski lessons/class | le cours de ski, la classe de ski | *luh koor duh skee, lah klahs duh skee* |
| ski lift | le remonte-pente | *luh ruhmawnt pohntski* |
| pants | le pantalon de ski | *luh pohntahlawn duh skee* |
| ski pass | le forfait de ski | *luh forfeh duh skee* |
| ski slope | la piste de ski | *lah peest duh skee* |
| ski stick | le bâton de ski | *luh bahtawn duh skee* |
| ski suit | la combinaison de ski | *lah kawnbeenehzawn duh skee* |
| ski wax | le fart à ski | *luh fahr ah skee* |
| skimmed | écrémé | *aykraymay* |
| skin | la peau | *lah poa* |
| skirt | la jupe | *lah jhewp* |
| skis | les skis | *lay skee* |
| sledge | la luge | *lah lewjh* |
| sleep (verb) | dormir | *dormeer* |

| sleep well | dormez-bien | *dormay byahn* |
|---|---|---|
| sleeping car | le wagon-lit | *luh vahgawn lee* |
| sleeping pills | les somnifères | *lay somneefehr* |
| slide | la diapositive | *lah deeahpozeeteev* |
| slim | mince | *mahns* |
| slip | la combinaison | *lah kawnbeenehzawn* |
| slow | lentement | *lohntuhmohn* |
| small | petit | *puhtee* |
| small change | la monnaie | *lah moneh* |
| smell (verb) | puer | *peway* |
| smoke | la fumée | *lah fewmay* |
| smoke (verb) | fumer | *fewmay* |
| smoked | fumé | *fewmay* |
| smoking compartment | le compartiment fumeurs | *luh kawnpahrteemohn fewmuhr* |
| snake | le serpent | *luh sehrpohn* |
| snorkel | le tuba | *luh tewbah* |
| snow (verb) | neiger | *nehjhay* |
| snow | la neige | *lah nehjh* |
| snow chains | les chaînes | *lay shehn* |
| soap | le savon | *luh sahvawn* |
| soap box | la boîte à savon | *lah bwaht ah sahvawn* |
| soccer (play) | jouer au football, le football | *jhooay oa footbol, luh footbol* |
| soccer match | le match de football | *luh mahch duh footbol* |
| socket | la prise | *lah preez* |
| socks | les chaussettes | *lay shoasseht* |
| soft drink | la boisson fraîche | *lah bwahssawn frehsh* |
| sole (fish) | la sole | *lah sol* |
| sole (shoe) | la semelle | *lah suhmehl* |
| someone | quelqu'un | *kehlkuhn* |
| something | quelque chose | *kehlkuhshoaz* |
| sometimes | parfois | *pahrfwah* |
| somewhere | quelque part | *kehlkuhpahr* |
| son | le fils | *luh fees* |
| soon | bientôt | *byahntoa* |
| sorbet | le sorbet | *luh sorbeh* |
| sore (be) | faire mal | *fehr mal* |
| sore throat | le mal de gorge | *luh mahl duh gorjh* |
| sorry | pardon | *pahrdawn* |
| sort | la sorte | *lah sort* |
| soup | la soupe | *lah soop* |
| sour | acide | *ahseed* |
| sour cream | la crème fraîche | *lah krehm frehsh* |
| source | la source | *lah soors* |
| south | le sud | *luh sewd* |
| souvenir | le souvenir | *luh soovneer* |
| spaghetti | les spaghetti | *lay spahgehtee* |
| spare parts | les pièces détachées | *lay pyehs daytashay* |
| spare tire | le pneu de rechange | *luh pnuh duh ruhshohnjh* |
| spare wheel | la roue de secours | *lah roo duh suhkoor* |
| speak (verb) | parler | *pahrlay* |
| special | spécial | *spaysyahl* |
| specialist | le spécialiste | *luh spaysyahleest* |

| | | |
|---|---|---|
| specialty | la spécialité | lah spaysyahleetay |
| speed limit | la vitesse maximum | lah veetehs mahxeemuhm |
| spell (verb) | épeler | aypuhlay |
| spices | les épices | lay zaypees |
| spicy | épicé | aypeesay |
| splinter | l'écharde (f.) | layshahrd |
| spoon | la cuillère | lah kweeyehr |
| spoonful | la cuillerée | lah kweeyuhray |
| sport | le sport | luh spor |
| sports center | la salle de sport | lah sahl duh spohr |
| spot | l'endroit (m.) | lohndrwah |
| sprain | fouler | foolay |
| spring | le printemps | luh prahntohn |
| square | le carré | luh kahray |
| square (town) | la place | lah plahs |
| square meter | le mètre carré | luh mehtr kahray |
| squash (veg.) | la courgette | lah koorjheht |
| stadium | le stade | luh stahd |
| stain | la tache | lah tahsh |
| stain remover | le détachant | luh daytahshohn |
| stairs | l'escalier (m.) | lehskahlyay |
| stamp | le timbre | luh tahnbr |
| start (verb) | démarrer | daymahray |
| station | la gare | lah gahr |
| statue | la statue | lah stahtew |
| stay (lodge) | loger | lohjhay |
| stay (remain) | rester | rehstay |
| stay | le séjour | luh sayjhoor |
| steal | voler | volay |
| steel | acier | ahsyay |
| stench | la mauvaise odeur | lah moavehz oduhr |
| sting | piquer | peekay |
| stitch (med.) | la suture | lah sewtewr |
| stitch (verb) | suturer | sewtewray |
| stock | le consommé | luh kawnsomay |
| stockings | les bas | lay bah |
| stomach | l'estomac (m.) | lehstomah |
| stomach | le ventre | luh vohntr |
| stomach ache | mal au ventre | mahl oa vohntr |
| stomach ache | le mal d'estomac | luh mahl dehstomah |
| stomach cramps | les spasmes abdominaux | lay spahzm zahbdomeenoa |
| stools | les selles | lay sehl |
| stop (verb) | arrêter | ahrehtay |
| stop | l'arrêt (m.) | lahreh |
| stopover | l'escale (f.) | lehskahl |
| storm | la tempête | lah tohnpeht |
| straight | raide | rehd |
| straight ahead | tout droit | too drwah |
| straw | la paille | lah pahy |
| street | la rue | lah rew |
| street (side) | côté rue | koatay rew |
| strike | la grève | lah grehv |
| study | faire des études | fehr day zaytewd |
| subscriber's number | le numéro d'abonné | luh newmayroa dahbonay |

| | | |
|---|---|---|
| subtitled | sous-titré | *soo teetray* |
| subway | le métro | *luh maytroh* |
| subway station | la station de métro | *lah stahsawn duh maytroh* |
| succeed | réussir | *rayewsseer* |
| sugar | le sucre | *luh sewkr* |
| sugar lumps | les morceaux de sucre | *lay morsoa duh sewkr* |
| suit | le costume | *luh kostewm* |
| suitcase | la valise | *lah vahleez* |
| summer | l'été (m.) | *laytay* |
| summertime | l'heure d'été (f.) | *luhr daytay* |
| sun | le soleil | *luh solehy* |
| sun hat | le chapeau de soleil | *luh shahpoa duh solehy* |
| sun hat | le bonnet | *luh boneh* |
| sunbathe | prendre un bain de soleil | *prohndr uhn bahn duh solehy* |
| sunburn | le coup de soleil | *luh koo duh solehy* |
| Sunday | dimanche | *deemohnsh* |
| sunglasses | les lunettes de soleil | *lay lewneht duh solehy* |
| sunrise | le lever du soleil | *luh luhvay duh solehy* |
| sunset | le coucher du soleil | *luh kooshay duh solehy* |
| suntan lotion | la crème solaire | *lah krehm solehr* |
| suntan oil | l'huile solaire (f.) | *lweel sohlehr* |
| supermarket | le supermarché | *luh sewpehrmahrshay* |
| surcharge | le supplément | *luh sewplaymohn* |
| surf board | la planche à voile | *lah plohnsh ah vwahl* |
| surgery | la consultation | *lah kawnsewltahsyawn* |
| surname | le nom | *luh nawn* |
| surprise | la surprise | *lah sewrpreez* |
| swallow | avaler | *ahvahlay* |
| swamp | le marais | *luh mahreh* |
| sweat | la transpiration | *lah trohnspeerahsyawn* |
| sweater | le pullover | *luh poolovehr* |
| sweet (kind) | gentil | *jhohntee* |
| sweet (adj.) | sucré | *sewkray* |
| sweet corn | le maïs | *luh mahees* |
| swim | nager | *nahjhay* |
| swimming pool | la piscine | *lah peeseen* |
| swimming trunks | le maillot de bain | *luh mahyoa duh bahn* |
| swindle | l'escroquerie (f.) | *lehskrokree* |
| switch | l'interrupteur (m.) | *lahntayrewptuhr* |
| synagogue | la synagogue | *lah seenahgog* |

# T

| | | |
|---|---|---|
| table | la table | *lah tahbl* |
| table tennis | jouer au ping-pong | *jhooay oa peeng pawng* |
| tablet | le comprimé | *luh kawnpreemay* |
| take | prendre | *prohndr* |
| take (to last) | durer | *dewray* |
| take pictures | photographier | *foatoagrahffay* |
| taken | occupé | *okewpay* |
| talcum powder | le talc | *luh tahlk* |
| talk | parler | *pahrlay* |
| tall | grand | *grohn* |
| tampons | les tampons | *lay tohnpawn* |
| tanned | brun | *bruhn* |

| tap | le robinet | *luh robeeneh* |
|---|---|---|
| tap water | l'eau du robinet (f.) | *loa dew robeeneh* |
| tartlet | la tartelette | *lah tahrtuhleht* |
| taste | goûter | *gootay* |
| tax free shop | le magasin | *luh mahgahzahn* |
| | hors-taxes | *or tahx* |
| taxi | le taxi | *luh tahxee* |
| taxi stand | la station de taxis | *lah stahsyawn duh tahxee* |
| tea | le thé | *luh tay* |
| teapot | la théière | *lah tay-yehr* |
| teaspoon | la petite cuillère | *lah puhteet kweeyehr* |
| telegram | le télégramme | *luh taylaygrahm* |
| telephoto lens | le téléobjectif | *luh taylayobjhehkteef* |
| television | la télévision | *lah taylayveezyawn* |
| telex | le télex | *luh taylehx* |
| temperature | la température | *lah tohnpayrahtewr* |
| temporary filling | le plombage | *luh plawnbahjh* |
| | provisoire | *proveezwahr* |
| tender | tendre | *tohndr* |
| tennis (play) | jouer au tennis | *jhooay oa taynees* |
| tennis ball | la balle de tennis | *lah bahl duh taynees* |
| tennis court | le court de tennis | *luh koor duh taynees* |
| tennis racket | la raquette de tennis | *lah rahkeht duh taynees* |
| tent | la tente | *lah tohnt* |
| tent peg | le piquet | *luh peekay* |
| terrace | la terrasse | *lah tehrahs* |
| terrible | épouvantable | *aypoovohntahbl* |
| thank | remercier | *ruhmehrsyay* |
| thank you | merci bien | *mehrsee byahn* |
| thanks | merci | *mehrsee* |
| thaw | dégeler | *dayjhuhlay* |
| theatre | le théâtre | *luh tayahtr* |
| theft | le vol | *luh vol* |
| there | là | *lah* |
| thermal bath | le bain thermal | *luh bahn tehrmahl* |
| thermometer | le thermomètre | *luh tehrmomehtr* |
| thick | gros | *groa* |
| thief | le voleur | *luh voluhr* |
| thigh | la cuisse | *lah kwees* |
| thin | maigre | *mehgr* |
| think | penser | *pohnsay* |
| third | le tiers | *luh tyehr* |
| thirsty, to be | la soif | *lah swahf* |
| this afternoon | cet après-midi | *seht ahpreh meedee* |
| this evening | ce soir | *suh swahr* |
| this morning | ce matin | *suh mahtahn* |
| thread | le fil | *luh feel* |
| throat | la gorge | *lah gorjh* |
| throat lozenges | les pastilles | *lay pahsteey* |
| | pour la gorge | *poor lah gorjh* |
| throw up | vomir | *vomeer* |
| thunderstorm | l'orage (m.) | *lorajh* |
| Thursday | jeudi | *jhuhdee* |
| ticket (admission) | le billet | *luh beeyeh* |
| ticket (travel) | le ticket | *luh teekeh* |

| ticket office | le bureau de réservation | *luh bewroh duh raysehrvahsyawn* |
| tickets | les billets | *lay beeyeh* |
| tidy | ranger | *rohnjhay* |
| tie | la cravate | *lah krahvaht* |
| tights | le collant | *luh kolohn* |
| time (clock) | l'heure (f.) | *luhr* |
| time (occasion) | la fois | *lah fwah* |
| timetable | l'horaire des arrivées et des départs | *lorehr day zahreevay ay day daypahr* |
| tin can | la boîte de conserve | *lah bwaht duh kawnsehrv* |
| tip | le pourboire | *luh poorbwahr* |
| tire | le pneu | *luh pnuh* |
| tire lever | le démonte-pneu | *luh daymawnt pnuh* |
| tire pressure | la pression des pneus | *lah prehsyawn day pnuh* |
| tissues | les mouchoirs en papier | *lay mooshwahr ohn pahpyay* |
| toast | le toast | *luh toast* |
| tobacco | le tabac | *luh tahbah* |
| toboggan | la luge | *lah lewjh* |
| today | aujourd'hui | *oajhoordwee* |
| toe | l'orteil (m.) | *lortehy* |
| together | ensemble | *ohnsohnbl* |
| toilet | les toilettes | *lay twahleht* |
| toilet paper | le papier hygiénique | *luh pahpyay eejhyayneek* |
| toiletries | les articles de toilette | *lay zahrteekl duh twahleht* |
| tomato | la tomate | *lah tomaht* |
| tomato purée | le concentré de tomates | *luh kawnsohntray duh tomaht* |
| tomato sauce | le ketchup | *luh kehtchuhp* |
| tomorrow | demain | *duhmahn* |
| tongue | la langue | *lah lohng* |
| tonic water | le tonic | *luh toneek* |
| tonight | ce soir | *suh swahr* |
| tonight | cette nuit | *seht nwee* |
| too much | trop | *troa* |
| tools | les outils | *lay zootee* |
| tooth | la dent | *lah dohn* |
| toothache | le mal de dents | *luh mahl duh dohn* |
| toothbrush | la brosse à dents | *lah bros ah dohn* |
| toothpaste | le dentifrice | *luh dohnteefrees* |
| toothpick | le cure-dent | *luh kewrdohn* |
| top up | remplir | *rohnpleer* |
| total | le total | *luh totahl* |
| tough | dur | *dewr* |
| tour | le tour | *luh toor* |
| tour guide | le guide | *luh geed* |
| tourist card | la carte touristique | *lah kahrt tooreesteek* |
| tourist class | la classe touriste | *lah klahs tooreest* |
| Tourist Information office | l'office de tourisme | *lofees duh tooreesm* |
| tow | remorquer | *ruhmorkay* |
| tow cable | le câble | *luh kahbl* |
| towel | la serviette de toilette | *lah sehrvyeht duh twahleht* |

**Word list**

**15**

| tower | la tour | *lah toor* |
| town | la ville | *lah veel* |
| town hall | la mairie | *lah mayree* |
| toy | le jouet | *luh jhooeh* |
| traffic | la circulation | *lah seerkewlahsyawn* |
| traffic light | le feu de signalisation | *luh fuh duh seenyahleezahsyawn* |
| trailer | la caravane | *lah karahvahn* |
| train | le train | *luh trahn* |
| train ticket | le billet de train | *luh beeyeh duh trahn* |
| train timetable | l'indicateur des chemins de fer | *lahndeekahtuhr day shuhmahn duh fehr* |
| translate | traduire | *trahdweer* |
| travel | voyager | *vvahyahjhay* |
| travel agent | l'agence de voyages (f.) | *lahjhohns duh vvahyahjh* |
| travel guide | le guide touristique | *luh geed tooreesteek* |
| traveler | le voyageur | *luh vvahyahjhuhr* |
| traveler's check | le chèque de voyage | *luh shehk duh vvahyahjh* |
| treatment | le traitement | *luh trehtmohn* |
| triangle | le triangle | *luh treeohngl* |
| trim | tailler | *tahy-yay* |
| trip | l'excursion (f.) | *lehxkewrsyawn* |
| trip | le voyage | *luh vvahyahjh* |
| trout | la truite | *lah trweet* |
| truck | le camion | *luh kahmyawn* |
| trustworthy | de confiance | *duh kawnfyohns* |
| try on | essayer | *ehsay-yay* |
| tube | le tube | *luh tewb* |
| Tuesday | mardi | *mahrdee* |
| tumble drier | le sèche-linge | *luh sahsh lahnjh* |
| tuna | le thon | *luh tawn* |
| tunnel | le tunnel | *luh tewnehl* |
| TV | la télé | *lah taylay* |
| tweezers | la pince | *lah pahns* |

## U

| ugly | laid | *leh* |
| umbrella | le parapluie | *luh pahrahplwee* |
| under | sous | *soo* |
| underground railway system | le réseau métropolitain | *luh rayzoa maytroapoleetahn* |
| underpants | le slip | *luh sleep* |
| understand | comprendre | *kawnprohndr* |
| underwear | les sous-vêtements | *lay soovehtmohn* |
| undress | (se) déshabiller | *suh dayzahbeeyay* |
| unemployed | au chômage | *oa shoamahjh* |
| uneven | irrégulier | *eeraygewlyay* |
| university | l'université (f.) | *lewneevehrseetay* |
| unleaded | sans plomb | *sohn plawn* |
| up | en haut | *ohn oa* |
| urgent | urgent | *ewrjhohn* |
| urine | l'urine (f.) | *lewreen* |
| use | utiliser | *ewteeleezay* |
| usually | généralement | *jhaynayrahlmohn* |

# V

| | | |
|---|---|---|
| vacate | évacuer | *ayvahkeway* |
| vaccinate | vacciner | *vahkseenay* |
| vagina | le vagin | *luh vahjhahn* |
| vaginal infection | l'infection | *lahnfehksyawn* |
| | vaginale | *vahjheenahl* |
| valid | valable | *vahlahbl* |
| valley | la vallée | *lah vahlay* |
| van | la camionnette | *lah kahmyoneht* |
| vanilla | la vanille | *lah vahneey* |
| vase | le vase | *luh vahz* |
| vaseline | la vaseline | *lah vahzleen* |
| veal | la viande de veau | *lah vyohnd duh voa* |
| vegetable soup | la soupe de légumes | *lah soop duh laygewm* |
| vegetables | le légume | *luh laygewm* |
| vegetarian | le végétarien | *luh vayjhaytahryahn* |
| vein | la veine | *lah vehn* |
| vending machine | le distributeur | *luh deestreebewtuhr* |
| venereal disease | la maladie | *lah mahlahdee* |
| | vénérienne | *vaynayryehn* |
| via | par | *pahr* |
| video recorder | le magnétoscope | *luh manyehtoskop* |
| video tape | la bande vidéo | *lah bohnd veedaoya* |
| view | la vue | *lah vew* |
| village | le village | *luh veelahjh* |
| visa | le visa | *luh veezah* |
| visit (verb) | rendre visite à | *rohndr veezeet ah* |
| visit | la visite | *lah veezeet* |
| vitamin tablet | le comprimé de | *luh kawnpreemay* |
| | vitamines | *duh veetahmeen* |
| vitamin | la vitamine | *lah veetahmeen* |
| volcano | le volcan | *luh volkohn* |
| volleyball | jouer au volley | *jhooay oa volay* |
| vomit | vomir | *vomeer* |

# W

| | | |
|---|---|---|
| wait | attendre | *ahtohndr* |
| waiter | le serveur | *luh sehrvuhr* |
| waiting room | la salle d'attente | *lah sahl dahtohnt* |
| waitress | la serveuse | *lah sehrvuhz* |
| wake up | réveiller | *rayvay-yay* |
| walk | la promenade | *lah promnahd* |
| walk (verb) | se promener | *suh promnay* |
| | marcher | *mahrshay* |
| wallet | le portefeuille | *luh portuhfuhy* |
| wardrobe | la garde-robe | *lah gahrd rob* |
| warm | chaud | *shoa* |
| warn | prévenir | *prayvuhneer* |
| warning | l'avertissement (m.) | *lahvehrteesmohn* |
| wash | laver | *lahvay* |
| washing | le linge | *luh lahnjh* |
| washing line | la corde à linge | *lah kord ah lahnjh* |
| washing machine | la machine à laver | *lah mahsheen ah* |
| | | *lahvay* |
| wasp | la guêpe | *lah gehp* |
| water | l'eau (f.) | *loa* |
| water ski | faire du ski nautique | *fehr dew skee noateek* |

| waterproof | imperméable | *ahnpehrmayahbl* |
| wave-pool | la piscine à vagues artificielles | *lah peeseen ah vahg zahrteefeesyehl* |
| way (method) | le moyen | *luh mwahyahn* |
| way | la direction | *lah deerehksyawn* |
| we | nous | *noo* |
| weak | faible | *fehbl* |
| weather | le temps | *luh tohn* |
| weather forecast | le bulletin météorologique | *luh bewltahn maytayoarolojheek* |
| wedding | les noces | *lay nos* |
| wedding | le mariage | *luh mahryajh* |
| Wednesday | mercredi | *mehrkruhdee* |
| week | la semaine | *lah suhmehn* |
| weekend | le week-end | *luh week-ehnd* |
| weekend duty | le service de garde | *luh sehrvees duh gahrd* |
| weekly ticket | l'abonnement hebdomadaire (m.) | *lahbonmohn ehbdomahdehr* |
| welcome | bienvenu | *byahnvuhnew* |
| well | bien | *byahn* |
| west | l'ouest (m.) | *lwehst* |
| wet | humide | *ewmeed* |
| wetsuit | la combinaison de planche à voile | *lah kawnbeenehzawn duh plohnsh ah vwahl* |
| what? | quoi? | *kwah?* |
| wheel | la roue | *lah roo* |
| wheelchair | la chaise roulante | *lah shehz roolohnt* |
| when? | quand? | *kohn?* |
| where? | où? | *oo?* |
| which? | quel? | *kehl?* |
| whipped cream | la crème Chantilly | *lah krehm shohnteeyee* |
| white | blanc | *blohn* |
| who? | qui? | *kee?* |
| whole wheat bread | le pain complet | *luh pahn kawnpleh* |
| why? | pourquoi? | *poorkwah?* |
| wide-angle lens | le grand-angle | *luh grohn tohngl* |
| widow | la veuve | *lah vuhv* |
| widower | le veuf | *luh vuhf* |
| wife | l'épouse (f.) | *laypooz* |
| wind | le vent | *luh vohn* |
| windbreak | le pare-vent | *luh pahrvohn* |
| windmill | le moulin | *luh moolahn* |
| window (desk) | le guichet | *luh gueesheh* |
| window | la fenêtre | *lah fuhnehtr* |
| windshield wiper | l'essuie-glace (m.) | *lehswee glahs* |
| windsurf | faire de la planche à voile | *fehr duh lah plohnsh ah vwahl* |
| wine | le vin | *luh vahn* |
| wine list | la carte des vins | *lah kahrt day vahn* |
| winter | l'hiver (m.) | *leevehr* |
| witness | le témoin | *luh taymwahn* |
| woman | la femme | *lah fahm* |
| wood | le bois | *luh bwah* |
| wool | la laine | *lah lehn* |
| word | le mot | *luh moa* |
| work | le travail | *luh trahvahy* |

**W** Word list

*15*

| | | |
|---|---|---|
| working day | le jour ouvrable | *jhoor oovrahbl* |
| worn | usé | *ewzay* |
| worried | inquiet | *ahnkyeh* |
| wound | la blessure | *lah blehsewr* |
| wrap | emballer | *ohnbahlay* |
| wrench (tool) | la clef à molette | *lah clay ah moleht* |
| wrist | le poignet | *luh pwahnnyeh* |
| write | écrire | *aykreer* |
| write down | noter | *notay* |
| writing pad | le bloc-notes | *luh blok not* |
| writing paper | le papier à lettres | *luh pahpyay ah lehtr*written |
| écrit | *aykree* | |
| wrong | mauvais | *moaveh* |

## Y

| | | |
|---|---|---|
| yacht | le yacht | *luh yot* |
| year | l'année (f.) | *lahnay* |
| yellow | jaune | *jhoan* |
| yes | oui | *wee* |
| yes, please | volontiers | *volawntyay* |
| yesterday | hier | *yehr* |
| yogurt | le yaourt | *luh yahoort* |
| you | vous | *voo* |
| you too | de même | *duh mehm* |
| youth hostel | l'auberge de jeunesse (f.) | *loabehrjh duh jhuhnehs* |

## Z

| | | |
|---|---|---|
| zip | la fermeture éclair | *lah fehrmuhtewr ayklehr* |
| zip code | le code postal | *luh kod postahl* |
| zoo | le parc zoologique | *luh pahrk zoaolojheek* |

**Word list**

15

# Basic grammar

## 1 The article

French nouns are divided into 2 categories: masculine and feminine. The definite article (the) is **le,la** or **l'**:

**le** is used before masculine words starting with a consonant, **le magasin** (the shop)

**la** is used with feminine words starting with a consonant, **la plage** (the beach)

**l'** is used before masculine and feminine words starting with a vowel, **l'argent** (the money), **l'assiette** (the plate).

Other examples are:

| | |
|---|---|
| **le toit** | the roof |
| **la maison** | the house |
| **l'hôtel** (m.) | the hotel |
| **l'entrée** (f.) | the entrance |

in the case of the indefinite article (**a**, **an**):

**un** is used before masculine words, **un livre** (a book)

**une** is used before feminine words, **une pomme** (an apple)

**des** is used before plural words, both masculine and feminine, **des camions** (trucks), **des voitures** (cars).

Other examples are:

| | | | |
|---|---|---|---|
| **un père** | a father | **une mère** | a mother |
| **un homme** | a man | **une femme** | a woman |
| **des hommes** | men | **des femmes** | women |

## 2 The plural

The plural of **le**, **la** and **l'** is **les**.

The plural of most French nouns ends in **s**, but this **s** is not pronounced. However when the noun begins with a vowel or a silent **h**, then the **s** of **les** or **des** is pronounced **z**, **les affaires** (*layzahfehr*), **des enfants** (*dayzohngfohn*).

Other examples are:

| | | | |
|---|---|---|---|
| **le lit** | *luh lee* | **les lits** | *lay lee* |
| **la table** | *lah tahbl* | **les tables** | *lay tahbl* |
| **l'avion** (m.) | *lahveeawn* | **les avions** | *layzahvyeeawn* |
| **l'heure** (f.) | *luhr* | **les heures** | *layzuhr* |

Certain plurals end in **aux** (mainly words ending in **"al"**)

| | |
|---|---|
| **le cheval** | **les chevaux** |
| **le canal** | **les canaux** |

## 3 Personal pronouns

| I | je |
| You | tu |
| He/she/it | il/elle |
| We | nous |
| You | vous |
| They | ils/elles |

In general "tu" is used to translate "you" only when speaking to close friends, relatives and children. **Vous** is used in all other cases. "It" becomes **il** or **elle** according to whether the noun referred to is masculine or feminine.

## 4 Possessive pronouns

| | masculine | feminine | plural |
|---|---|---|---|
| my | mon | ma | mes |
| your | ton | ta | tes |
| his/her/its | son | sa | ses |
| our | notre | notre | nos |
| your | votre | votre | vos |
| their | leur | leur | leurs |

They agree with the object they refer to, e.g. her hat = **son chapeau**.

## 5 Verbs

| **parler** | | to speak |
|---|---|---|
| **je parle** | root + -e | I speak |
| **tu parles** | root + -es | you speak |
| **il/elle parle** | root + -e | he/she/it speaks |
| **nous parlons** | root + -ons | we speak |
| **vous parlez** | root + -ez | you speak |
| **ils/elles parlent** | root + -ent | they speak |
| **parlé** (past participle) | | spoken |

Here are some useful verbs.

| **être** | to be |
|---|---|
| **je suis** | I am |
| **tu es** | you are |
| **il/elle est** | he/she/it is |
| **nous sommes** | we are |
| **vous êtes** | you are |
| **ils/elles sont** | they are |
| **été** (past participle) | been |

| **avoir** | to have |
|---|---|
| **j'ai** | I have |
| **tu as** | you have |
| **il/elle a** | he/she/it has |
| **nous avons** | we have |
| **vous avez** | you have |
| **ils/elles ont** | they have |
| **eu** (past participle) | had |

| | |
|---|---|
| **faire** | to do/make |
| **je fais** | I do |
| **tu fais** | you do |
| **il/elle fait** | he/she does |
| **nous faisons** | we do |
| **vous faites** | you do |
| **ils/elles font** | they do |
| **fait** (past participle) | done/made |

## 6 Countries and prepositions

Names of countries take the article:

| | |
|---|---|
| **L'Angleterre** | England |
| **Le Canada** | Canada |
| **Les États Unis** | The United States |
| **La France** | France |

| | |
|---|---|
| in Paris | **à Paris** |
| in France | **en France** |
| in Canada | **au Canada** |

## 7 Negatives

Negatives are formed by using:

| | |
|---|---|
| **ne** (verb) **pas** | not |
| **ne** (verb) **jamais** | never |

| | |
|---|---|
| **Je ne parle pas français.** | I don't speak French. |
| **Je ne fume jamais.** | I never smoke. |